MUSICAL FESTIVAL FLOATS
OF JAPAN

LUND
UNIVERSITY
PRESS

LUND
UNIVERSITY

Musical festival floats of Japan

Festival ensembles in the Chita Peninsula and Aichi

HÅKAN LUNDSTRÖM

Lund University Press

Lund University Press
The Joint Faculties of Humanities and Theology

**LUND
UNIVERSITY
PRESS**

LUND
UNIVERSITY

P.O. Box 192
SE-221 00 LUND
Sweden
https://lunduniversitypress.lu.se

Lund University Press books are published in collaboration with Manchester University Press.

British Library Cataloguing-in-Publication Data
A catalogue record for this book is available from the British Library

Lund University Press gratefully acknowledges publication assistance from the Einar Hansen Allhem Foundation and the Hilda and Håkan Theodor Ohlsson Foundation.

ISBN   978-91-985578-6-2   hardback

First published 2025

EU authorised representative for GPSR:
Easy Access System Europe, Mustamäe tee 50, 10621 Tallinn, Estonia
gpsr.requests@easproject.com

Typeset
by Cheshire Typesetting Ltd, Cuddington, Cheshire

Contents

Illustrations

Where not otherwise noted in the caption, all photographs are by Håkan Lundström.

Figures

Maps

Examples

Tables

Recordings

These recordings are available on Manchester Open Hive, www. manchesteropenhive.com/

The recordings are 'audiovisual field-notes' made by handycams with the intention of documenting actual situations. They may contain shaky pictures and irrelevant noise. They were made over a long time-period, with internal microphone and without light, using the technology available at the time.

- 1 Nagao spring festival, *Nagao no harumatsuri* 1992. Taketoyo 11–12 April 1992.
  - a) Starting on the eve of the festival: *Shagiri*, Tamanuki ward.
  - b) Parading on the day of the festival, *Michiyuki*: *Komenari*, Tamanuki ward.
  - c) On the slope to the shrine, Takeo jinja, on the festival day: *Shinguruma*, Tamanuki ward.
  - d) Entering the shrine Takeo jinja on the festival eve: *Shagiri*, Tamanuki ward.
  - e) Entering the shrine Takeo jinja on the festival eve: *Shagiri*, Ichiba ward.
  - f) Entering Takeo jinja and raising the roofs and *bonden* spires of the festival floats: *Shagiri*, Age, entering the ward and all floats backing.

- 2 The *Kanemaki tune-complex*
  - a) *Orei isami* at the shrine Toyoishi jinja in Ôashi: *Kanemaki*. Taketoyo 23 July 1997.
  - b) *Ochazuke*, Tamanuki ward, Taketoyo 10 April 2004. Main flute player: Mr Ôtomo Tadahiro.
  - c) *Kanemaki* while going downhill backwards. Futto Kanemaki (2 April 2018).

- 3 *Sanbasō* puppet performance.
  - a) *Sanbasō* indoors performance because of rain. Hon-Itayamagumi ward, Itayama, Handa 15 April 2000.

   b) *Sanbasō* float performance at the Itayama jinja shrine. Hon-Itayamagumi ward, Itayama, Handa, 16 April 2017.

- 4 The *Shagiri* tune.
   a) *Shagiri* at practice: beginning and middle section. Tamanuki ward, Taketoyo 25 March 2016.
   b) *Shagiri* when entering the shrine Takeo jinja: final part. Age ward, Taketoyo 1 May 2019.

A note on Japanese names and transliteration

A modified version of the Hepburn system is used for the romanization of Japanese words. Compound words are normally written as one word, but in some cases with a hyphen in order to facilitate the reading. Japanese personal names are given with the family name first. Often geographical names as well as names of festivals, musical instruments, and tunes are not standardized in oral tradition and have no standardized transliteration. As far as possible, readings found in official sources, for instance community information or local publications, have been used in those cases.

Prologue

Seasonal festivals take place all over Japan. In many of them, large festival floats – or *dashi* – are paraded in the communities and to a shrine, or *jinja*. These floats also produce music, for inside them there are musical ensembles, *dashibayashi*, generally consisting of flutes and drums. Pleasing the gods, *kami*, is a focal point of the festivals; and all activities and objects at a festival, including the music, serve this aim. This also goes for the music that accompanies the other activities, forming an indispensable part of the ritual and the soundscape of the festival.

The festival floats are objects of historical and cultural value. They are decorated in various ways, particularly with wooden sculptures; they are greatly admired, and are also studied as objects of art. Therefore, most people prefer to take photographs and videos of a float's front part, the exception being people who – like me – are interested in the music: we walk behind the *dashi* to record the music and to catch glimpses of the musicians as they play their instruments – that is, of those musicians that can be seen, if there is an opening in the draperies with which the floats are covered. There are not many of us, but I have met a few during my fieldwork.

This book started out as a study of the music of one local festival or *matsuri* in Japan. In Chitahantō, the Chita Peninsula south of Nagoya in central Japan, lies the town Taketoyo. Here a yearly spring festival, *harumatsuri*, takes place in the area formerly called Nagaomura, 'Nagao village'. I became particularly interested in its music, and this became the start of a journey that has now lasted for more than a quarter of a century. It has taken me all over the peninsula and to many other places in the surrounding Aichi prefecture in order to learn about the festivals, and particularly about their music. I have been lucky to receive assistance from many kind people, who have been greatly committed to sharing their knowledge.

It was in July 1990 that my wife Kazuyo, who grew up in Japan, and I were invited to a restaurant in Taketoyo for dinner with some of her old classmates from junior high school. The men were all active in the festival, and that evening they listened to a copy of an old tape-recording that had been made in 1959 in the Komukae neighbourhood, only a few months before the Isewan typhoon, a natural disaster that spread death and destruction in the area. It was followed by a break in the festival tradition, a break which in some cases lasted for more than a decade. This dinner party was my first contact with the music of that festival.

In April two years later, I was in Taketoyo to see the spring festival, *Nagao no harumatsuri*, for the first time. My guide was Mr Saitō Kiyotaka. That year he was *sairei iinchō*, 'festival general', in the Tamanuki neighbourhood. He gave me a thorough introduction to the festival. We visited each of the six neighbourhoods that would take part, we went to sessions of music practice, and we visited Takeo jinja, the local *Shintō* shrine. This gave me a good overview of the town and of the music, so when the festival began, I could see the most essential activities around the town while also having an idea about the totality of it. Mr Saitō has continued to be a source of knowledge for me over the years. So has Mr Maeda Toshio who, after retiring, moved from the Tokyo area to Taketoyo and therefore has both an inside and an outside perspective on the festival.

After a few visits, I presented this festival in lectures and at conferences. On one occasion it was included in an exhibition at the Swedish Museum of Performing Arts in Stockholm, as one of seven international festivals. For that exhibition, a copy of the back of a float was built with three dolls holding hourglass-shaped *kotsuzumi* drums, and there was a large map of the festival. Music recordings and a slideshow were also included, and a *happi*, a short jacket used at festivals, was displayed.

The visit to *Nagao no harumatsuri* had given rise to several questions. Consequently, the next time I came to Japan I decided to see other festivals in order to learn more about their music, thereby gaining a better understanding of the context of *Nagao no harumatsuri*.

As a foreigner with a limited knowledge of the Japanese language, I am aware of my limitations in coming to grips with the large and in many respects intricate life of the festivals and their music, particularly concerning literary sources. It is my hope that this will to some degree be compensated for by the outside perspective that I am able to contribute as an ethnomusicologist with experience of music and its social contexts in other cultures.

Except where otherwise stated, all the illustrations in this book are photographs taken by me. Translations ascribed to 'KL' were made by Kazuyo Lundström.

Acknowledgements

The present volume is the outcome of many years of fieldwork in Japan. Information has been gathered through observation and through contacts with many individuals, most of whom are anonymous to me. In the hectic context of festival activities, they have shown me things they thought I should know, explained their traditions, and taken pride in doing so. I am immensely grateful to all these festival people. I especially extend my thanks to those with whom I have communicated in several meetings and by e-mail. Their support has been invaluable, and they will be mentioned and referred to in the text.

I particularly wish to thank long-time friends Saitō Kiyotaka and Setoko, who introduced me to the festivals, and Maeda Toshio and Hiroko. Together they have supported my work for three decades. I am also grateful to Chief Priest Iwata Takao and Secretary General Tsuchihira Akihiro, who have given me unique insights into festival content and organization and to Fukumoto Takahisa, member of the Taketoyo town council, for assistance with matters concerning repertoire and instruments. I am greatly obliged to researchers and musicians Kanō Yoshio and Hayakawa Makoto for sharing their knowledge about ritual and festival music. Without the committed assistance of my wife Kazuyo Suzumura Lundström, the research and its publication would not have been possible. The constructive reports at two stages during the project by two anonymous peer reviewers for Lund University Press have also been enormously helpful.

The research, translation, and publication have been made possible by contributions from the Åke Wiberg Foundation, the Scandinavia–Japan Sasakawa Foundation, the Krapperup Foundation, Charles H. Burkhalter and family, Ms Mizuno Michiko, and by support from friends and relatives. A generous grant from the Allhem (Einar Hansen) Foundation paid for language editing. Special thanks to Mr Enya Shigeki for permission to use the cover photo.

1
Introduction

The locality

Aichi prefecture is in the central part of the main island of Japan, with Tokyo some 340 kilometres to the east and Kyoto about 130 kilometres to the southwest (Map 1). In the western part of Aichi, which is called Owari, lies Nagoya, the major city in the prefecture. The Chita Peninsula south of Nagoya is a part of Owari. For practical reasons, I will treat Owari as consisting of three parts: Nagoya, the Chita Peninsula, and the remainder of Owari.[1] The eastern part of Aichi prefecture, Mikawa, is subdivided into West Mikawa and East Mikawa.

The distance from the southern tip of the Chita Peninsula to central Nagoya is about 60 kilometres, and in its central part the peninsula is about 8 kilometres across. In this rather limited area, there are a very large number of festivals with well over a hundred festival floats. There are several types of floats as well as carried palanquins called *mikoshi* which are employed in offerings at shrines; but there are also many religious festivals that do not include any of these.

During the *Edo period* (also called the *Tokugawa period*, 1603–1868), travel was severely limited, and this is usually taken as the reason why so many distinct local practices have evolved. Many influences travelled along the Tōkaidō road which connected Nagoya with Tokyo and Kyoto. There were close contacts between Nagoya and the towns in the Chita Peninsula, and much of the festival music there is believed to have spread from Nagoya. Shipping has been an important means of communication for the

---

1 This is in accordance with *Aichi no dashimatsuri: Aichi-ken no dashimatsuri pōtarusaito* [Float-festivals in Aichi, portal website for float-festivals in Aichi prefecture] (Internet reference).

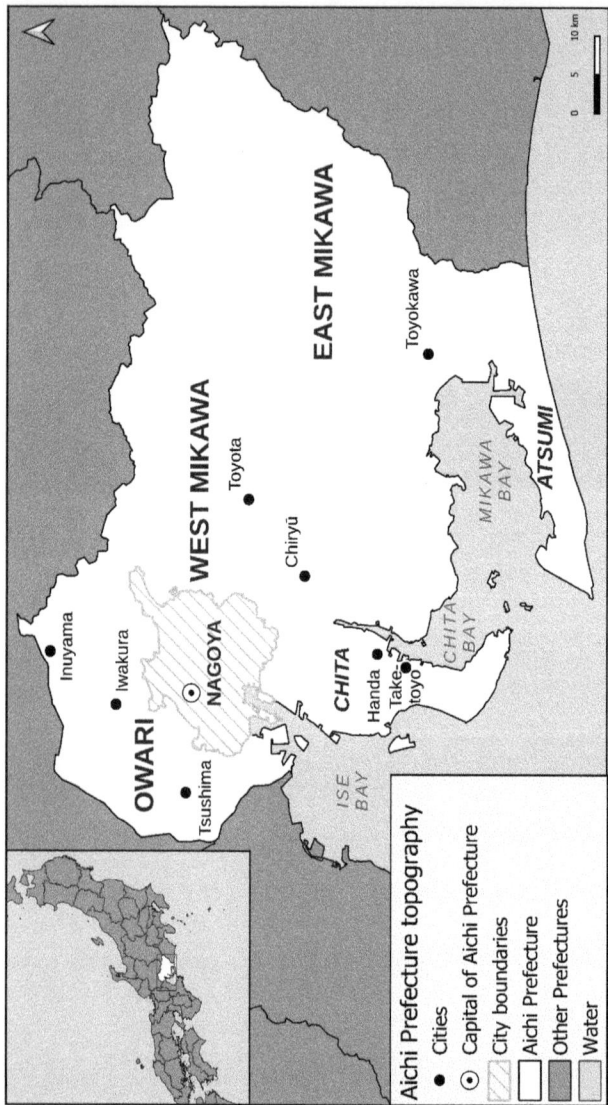

Map 1 Aichi prefecture with its major parts and approximate locations of places frequently mentioned in the text. The western part, including Chitahantō – the Chita Peninsula – is called Owari and the eastern part is called Mikawa. Mikawa is further subdivided into West and East Mikawa. Courtesy of Jakob Cederblad.

Chita Peninsula for centuries, and it made close trading connections
with Mikawa possible.

In the Chita Peninsula, names of towns like Taketoyo, Handa,
or Tokoname may refer both to the city centres and to the
municipalities – or 'local public entities' – that are formally called
Taketoyo-chō, Handa-shi, Tokoname-shi etc. *Chō* will be translated as 'town' and *shi* as 'city'. These include the administrative
units called wards, *ku*. The neighbourhoods, called *kumi*, are
sometimes smaller units within a ward; but in some cases ward and
neighbourhood are identical.

This is the case in Nagao where six of the wards, *ku*, each have a
float. In the festival context, these *ku* are often called *kumi*. On the
other hand, in Handa city there are more than 40 *ku*, and several
of these include more than one *kumi*. In connection with festivals,
the city of Handa uses the unit *chiku*, district, and there are ten
districts[2] with a total of 31 *kumi*,[3] each of which possesses one
float. Since the terminology may differ from one place to another,
I will for practical reasons use the term *neighbourhood* for those
areas that have a float.

Many villages have been merged with cities or towns. Usually,
older and newer names are used simultaneously. Consequently,
there are numerous place names in this text. Ward or neighbourhood names will only be included when necessary to identify a
specific place or when specifically referred to. Areas in Taketoyo
that occur very often in the text – like Nagao, Ōashi, Higashi-
Ōdaka, and Fuki – will be used without indicating the town's name.
Maps are included in the text to simplify the recognition of place
names.

Names of festivals often vary over time. As a rule, Japanese
names of festivals are only used in this text for those festivals that
are particularly well-known or often mentioned. Since the full
names may be of interest to researchers, they are provided in the
field-work list (Appendix 2). For the same reason, names of floats
are included only if there is a need to specify a certain float; but for
the benefit of readers who may need to identify specific floats, their
names are included in the captions of figures.

---

2 *Handa-shi shi: sairei minzoku hen* [Handbook of Handa city: festival and
   folklore] 1984, Foreword.

3 *Handa Dashimatsuri Hozonkai* [Handa Float-festival Preservation
   Society] → *Handa Dashimatsuri Hozonkai towa* [About the Float-festival
   Preservation Society] (Internet reference).

Aims

The festival music in Taketoyo differed from any Japanese music I had encountered before. What stood out as the most characteristic trait was a dominant, rather loud, and repetitive drum pattern. The hourglass drums called *kotsuzumi* and *ōtsuzumi* that are also used in the ensembles of *nō* and *kabuki* had leading roles in this pattern (Figure 1). My aims were to find out *why the festival music in Taketoyo is constructed the way it is*, and *why the hourglass drums are so prominent*. Finding answers to these questions requires information on different aspects of the festival music of Taketoyo as a starting point:

- How does the festival-float music of Taketoyo relate to other festivals in the vicinity (the Chita Peninsula) and in the larger surrounding area (Nagoya, Owari, and Mikawa), particularly regarding the combination of instruments in the festival-float ensembles?
- What roles do the *kotsuzumi* and *ōtsuzumi* drums have in other music that occurs at festivals, such as dances and puppet performances?

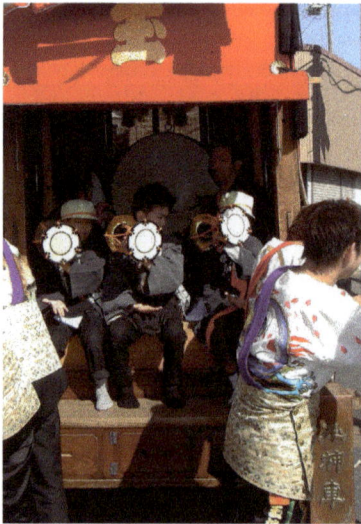

Figure 1 The three *tsuzumi* drums. Behind them the flutes. In the background the suspended *hangiri* drum. The other instruments are also inside the float. The float *Gyokushinsha* of Tamanuki in Nagao (10 April 2004).

- The festival-float music is a complex repertoire of orally transmitted tunes, and an analysis is needed to gather knowledge of functional and stylistic aspects that say something about how tunes or local variants may be related.
- While it is often assumed that the festival-float music spread from Nagoya, it is not generally known *how* this happened, which makes it necessary to consider historical sources.
- The way in which festivals and their music are carried out today must be understood in relation to social and political changes which have been quite extensive since around 1900.
- The recent processes of modernization and globalization make it interesting to see how the festival-float music relates to music in similar contexts in other cultures.

Terms and concepts

Most Japanese-language terms will be explained as they appear in the text. There are certain nationally accepted terms and a multitude of local ones. Often one object or activity has several synonymous names. A list of Japanese words and their meanings used in this text is given in Appendix 3. Some terms that are used often will be introduced here.

Originally, the term *matsuri* carries the meaning 'to worship' or 'to show reverence',[4] and according to the pioneering folklorist Yanagita Kunio, the verb *matsuru* means the attitude of 'being around to serve'.[5] Andō Reiji explains *matsuri* as follows in a comment in one edition of Yanagita's *Nihon no matsuri*:

> The bonds between people are renewed by *matsuri*. These are not only bonds between people but also bonds with gods, animals, plants, and minerals. In other words, it includes relationships with all things in the universe.[6]

Matsuri is the main form of worship within *Shintō*, whether carried out by priests or by common people. *Shintō* is considered as an indigenous and ancient Japanese religion; but it has a more recent background, as summarized by Herbert Plutschow:

> [I]t was only in the eighteenth and nineteenth centuries that scholars tried to establish a Shinto religion and a state ideology by isolating

---

4 Havens 1988, p. 148, quoted in Schnell 1999, p. 14.
5 Yanagita 2022, p. 48.
6 Andō 2022, p. 261. English translation by KL.

what they believed to be unspoiled native elements from the combined Shinto-Buddhist religion that had, until then, pervaded the religious life of most Japanese.[7]

Nevertheless, the beliefs and rituals of today are based on old traditions. The *Shintō* deities are called *kami*, and the shrines are called *jingū* or *jinja*. 'Shrines are the concrete sites of worship of kami', whereas *Shintō* refers to structures 'that aim to integrate individual shrine cults into a larger, national or even universal system'.[8]

Yanagita used the term *matsuri* for the intimate kind of worship and the term *sairei* for those large festivals or spectacles with many onlookers that can be traced back to Kyoto's *Gion matsuri* and had become established around the eleventh to twelfth centuries.[9] In general modern usage, both the words *matsuri* and *sairei* mean 'festival'. *Matsuri* is a Japanese word (*wago* or *Yamato kotoba*), whereas *sairei* is a Sino-Japanese word.[10] The term *dashi* is the generally accepted name of the festival floats, but there are many local names as well. A festival with *dashi* is called a *dashimatsuri*, 'float-festival'. In most cases, a festival may be referred to by a town name and one of the words *matsuri*, *harumatsuri* (spring festival), *natsumatsuri* (summer festival), or *akimatsuri* (autumn festival), for instance *Inuyama matsuri* and *Tsushima akimatsuri*. However, there are also other forms of naming, and one and the same festival may have more than one name.

In intercultural studies, local words – in this case words of the English language – are often used as universals in a general sense and with an extended meaning, even though categories like these are often not equivalent between cultures. This is the case with words like 'music' or 'ensemble'.[11] Thus, the Japanese word *hayashi* (*-bayashi* in compounds) may, depending on the context, mean music, musical ensemble, or musicians.[12] In this case, it is therefore

---

7 Plutschow 1996, p. 4.

8 Teeuwen and Breen 2003, p. x.

9 Yanagita 1993, pp. 179–182 (Japanese original 1942). This view is based on the assumption that foreign influences were not representative of Japanese religiosity. See Dale 1990/1986, pp. 208–209, and Kawahashi 2008/2005, p. 453, for critiques of this view.

10 *Matsuri* is written 「マツリ」 in the Japanese alphabet *katakana*, 「まつり」 in *hiragana*, 「祭」 with *kanji*, i.e. Chinese character and 「祭り」 with *kanji* and a *hiragana* syllable. *Sairei* is written 「祭礼」 with *kanji*.

11 Nettl 1983, pp. 19–21, 24–25.

12 Okuyama 2002, p. 683.

necessary to be more specific. Music, a musical ensemble, or musicians at festivals are covered by the term *matsuribayashi*, which is a compound made up of the words *matsuri* and *hayashi*. Music, a musical ensemble, or musicians inside a *dashi* will be referred to as *dashibayashi*. To avoid confusion, the terms *matsuribayashi music* and *matsuribayashi ensemble* as well as *dashibayashi music* and *dashibayashi ensemble* will be used here.[13] The Japanese word *kagura* refers to dance and music directed at the deities, *kami*, that are often performed at festivals apart from the *dashibayashi music*. Since *kagura* is mainly associated with dance, the term *kagura music* will be used when speaking specifically of the music of *kagura* performances. Similarly, the music for *michiyuki*, 'walking along the road' and in this case meaning parading at walking speed, will be referred to as *michiyuki music*. The individual pieces or melodies within a category of music will be called *tunes*.

Similarly, the words 'religion' or 'religious' are often used as universals; but this practice is debated, not least in the case of Japan.[14] Religious practice and entertainment are closely connected, which makes words such as 'sacred' or 'secular' problematic as well.[15] Michael Ashkenazi regards '[a]ll actions addressed to the moot entities' as religious actions.[16] Some ritual actions in *Shintō*, for instance bowing or clapping your hands at a shrine, are commonly practised, while some are performed by priests. Satsuki Kawano calls the latter 'key ritual actions'.[17] When I use words like 'religion', it will be in a very general sense, while 'religious ritual' will refer to observable key ritual actions. As will be evident from the text, particularly in Chapters 3 and 4, religious rituals are central to the traditional float-festivals in the Chita Peninsula. Therefore, I will use the term 'religious festival' for this kind of festival. Festivals relating to a *Shintō* shrine will be referred to as 'shrine festivals', whereas other float-festivals will be called 'city float-festivals'.

Festival research

The concept *festival* includes a wide variety of events. An inclusive definition, developed with the aim of covering as many such

---

13 This is in line with the English terminology used by Fujie 1986a, p. 44.
14 Hardacre 1989, p. 10; Fitzgerald 1997; Reader 2016.
15 Horii 2021, 43–45.
16 Ashkenazi 1993, p. 36.
17 Kawano 2005, pp. 40–47.

activities as possible, is supplied in *The Routledge handbook of festivals*:

> [S]hort term, recurring, publicly accessible events that usually celebrate and/or perform particular elements of culture that are important to the place in which they are held or the communities which hold them; that provide opportunities for recreation and entertainment; and that give rise to feelings of belonging.[18]

This broad definition works for a whole spectrum of festivals, spanning from historical or old traditional festivals to the most modern events, like rock festivals or pride parades. It has come out of the needs of the rather young field of festival and events studies, which deals especially with festival production, organization, and economy. As Nicola Frost has noted, researchers in disciplines that use ethnographic methods are more apt to focus on one type of festival:

> Anthropological studies of festivals have also tended to make use of ethnographic research methods, which inevitably locate the anthropologist within the event, and tend to lay emphasis on phenomenological, or at least experiential forms of analysis.[19]

Many attempts have been made to define 'festival' in this more narrow sense, in ways suitable for the individual researcher.[20] Waldemar Cudny has listed the main criteria of a festival typology compiled from such definitions: attitude to religion; location; social-class structure, power distribution and social roles; important moments in life; season; scale and status, rank; theme.[21] In his discussion of festival types, Alessandro Falassi comments on the common distinction between the sacred and the secular:

> Scholars have defined various types of festival, relying mainly on the sacred/secular dichotomy first discussed by Durkheim. This is more a theoretical than a practical distinction, since each type usually includes elements of the other.[22]

The type of Japanese festivals studied here are a good example of the difficulty inherent in making clear-cut distinctions between typology criteria. The festivals investigated in this book are

---

18 Mair 2018, p. 5.
19 Frost 2016, p. 570.
20 Mair 2018, p. 5.
21 Cudny 2014, 649–650.
22 Falassi 1987, p. 2.

normally thought of as traditional religious festivals; but they are also seasonal and related to the farming cycle, as well as defined by locality. Social roles and status are important, and so are crucial moments in people's lives.

The larger festivals, in particular, such as *Gion matsuri* in Kyoto and *Kanda matsuri* in Tokyo, have been subjected to major studies in the Japanese language, and some local festivals have also been studied in detail. From the local perspective of the Chita Peninsula, an extensive report on festivals in the Nagoya castle area and a description of the festivals of Tsushima are particularly relevant.[23] Two major studies of Japanese festivals in the English language are useful in a comparative perspective, dealing respectively with Yuzawa in Akita prefecture and Furukawa, close to Takayama in Gifu prefecture.[24]

Information about float-festivals in the Chita Peninsula is available in various kinds of publications. A useful overview of festival floats that also includes articles on their history is provided in *Chita no dashimatsuri* [Float-festivals in Chita].[25] Two documentations of festival puppets include an overview of the Chita Peninsula.[26] At present, the most extensive and updated overviews of festivals and festival floats are found on the Internet, particularly *Aichi dashimatsuri zukan* [Picture book of the float-festivals in Aichi], *Aichi dashi zukan* [Picture book of the festival floats in Aichi], *Aichi no dashimatsuri: Aichi-ken no dashimatsuri pōtarusaito* [Float-festivals in Aichi, a portal website for float-festivals in Aichi prefecture], and *Owari no dashimatsuri* [Float-festivals of the Owari province].[27] An English-language dissertation in the field of architecture deals with the history of float-festivals in Chita with a particular focus on one float in the city of Handa.[28]

---

23 Kuroda and Yokoi 2013 and *Nagoya jōka no dashi gyōji chōsa hōkokusho: Nagoya no dashi gyōji sōgō chōsa* [Survey report of festival float events in the castle town Nagoya: a comprehensive survey of Nagoya festival float events] 2018.
24 Ashkenazi 1993; Schnell 1999.
25 Iga 1994.
26 Senda 1997, 2006. The 2006 publication covers float-festivals with puppets representing all the eight municipalities (cities and towns) in the Chita Peninsula that have float-festivals.
27 See References: B. Internet references.
28 McPherson 2007.

Chronicles from individual cities in the Chita Peninsula are quite numerous, and several of them contain information on local festival traditions. Some neighbourhoods have published their festival's history in local publications, and there are also locally produced audio or audiovisual documentations. In recent years, some cities have introduced official websites with special sections on festivals in the respective city.[29] Only a few neighbourhood groups have their own websites as yet, but their number is gradually increasing.

In Japan as well as globally, recent research on festivals is not limited to historical or ethnographic studies. As most of the research referred to in this study shows, it is affected by new views within the different disciplines that deal with various social aspects, gender issues, and ethnic questions. An early Japanese example is Yoneyama Toshinao's overview from 1986, called (in translation) 'Anthropology of cities and festivals'.[30]

Music and dance are normally important parts of festivals. The music varies with local traditions and with the focus of the respective festival, and it may be both vocal and instrumental. In this study, the focus is on music belonging to parades or processions during seasonal religious festivals. Though such music is often mentioned in descriptions of various festivals, there is comparatively little research on the music *per se*, or about its functions within the festivals. Such studies are mainly found in book chapters and journal articles. They cover the music of festivals in South Asia, where carts or palanquins are often used in the parades;[31] of Catholic pilgrimages in Europe and elsewhere;[32] of multicultural or diaspora carnivals in the West Indies and Latin America;[33] and of festivals in China,[34] insular southeast Asia,[35] and Africa.[36]

An American dissertation in ethnomusicology by Linda Fujie focuses on festival music traditions in Tokyo.[37] In that case the festival music is not performed in floats but by ensembles that

---

29 An example with quite detailed information is *Tokoname dashi zukan* [Encyclopedia of float-festivals, Tokoname city] (Internet reference).
30 Yoneyama 1986.
31 Tingey 1994, 1995; Wolf 2000, 2006; Halperin 2016.
32 Davis 1972; Reily 1994; Lameiro 1997; Brucher 2013.
33 Averill 1994; Pinto 1994; Bilby 2010.
34 Jones 1995, 2002, and 2007.
35 Harnish 1997; Downing 2010.
36 Nketia 1974; Fahm 2015; Omigbule 2017.
37 Fujie 1986a.

accompany palanquins, *mikoshi*, which are carried along. The dissertation includes definitions, description of the music, and the history of major ensemble groups, and it devotes special attention to the supporting organizations. Though the festival music of Tokyo differs from that of the Nagoya area in many respects, there are similarities on a principal level. Fujie's dissertation and other articles on the subject are therefore useful material.

Hayakawa Masao, a former music educator in Yokosuka in the northwest Chita Peninsula, has produced a large compilation of festival music, mainly festival-float music, *dashibayashi*. Over a period of twenty years or more, he made tape recordings at festival music rehearsals in Aichi prefecture. These recordings were then transcribed into Western notation, which is a complicated process, and the handwritten notations were then published in three volumes: one with the festival music of Tōkai in Hayakawa's home area, one covering the Chita Peninsula, and one covering the Chubu area, which basically includes all of Aichi prefecture.[38] Each book has a text section and a notation section. In principle, the text consists of a list of festivals with information about where and when they take place; but it also includes information on instruments and tunes for each place, as well as comments on history and on local variations. Completeness is impossible in this orally transmitted and constantly changing repertoire, so even though these books contain hundreds of tunes the information is in no way complete. Nevertheless, it includes most of the common tunes used in festivals in Aichi prefecture and is perhaps the most extensive documentation of Japanese festival music in existence. Hayakawa has also been most helpful in sharing his knowledge with me.

A major project in Nagoya focuses on *kagura*, which is dance and music also performed at festivals, normally on a separate stage in a shrine area. This music is called *Atsuta kagura* or *Miyaryū kagura* and is based on the tradition at the large shrine Atsuta jingū. The project was started by Kanō Yoshio, a clinic director and flute player, with the intention of reconstructing thirteen *kagura* tunes that had been recorded on tape in 1959, but not been used since then. In this process, *Atsuta kagura* tunes and their variations in several locations in the surroundings of Nagoya were also documented by him and co-workers in the project. One of them, the flute player Hayakawa Makoto from Nagoya, has also recorded

38 Hayakawa 1984, 2003a, and 2003b.

tunes from the Chita Peninsula, where we have sometimes met and
had the opportunity to exchange information.[39]

The above-mentioned project's material is available on a website
including lists of variants of tunes with their local names and
comments about them.[40] There are also historical comments,
Japanese notations, and pedagogically intended recordings. In
practice, there is some overlapping between *kagura music* and
dashibayashi music, and this material is hence important for the
festival-float music.

Apart from these rather broad documentations, the sources used
in this book contain descriptions of the music at individual festivals
in the area. Thus, a book on the *Nagoya matsuri* has one chapter
on the music.[41] Some local historical chronicles contain information on the festival music, in the Chita Peninsula particularly those
of Agui, Handa, Sakai, Taketoyo, and Tokoname.[42] Music is often
mentioned in publications by local neighbourhoods, and booklets
or brochures about specific festivals may occasionally contain
information on the music. In addition, there are several locally
produced audio or audiovisual documentations issued on CDs or
DVDs and on YouTube.

Method

Since there is no written history or any comparative studies of
float-festival music in this part of Japan, I chose to use the ethnographic method of fieldwork combined with interviews while
conducting further searches for published documentation. Festival
music appears as a rather disparate continuum of local practices
in living oral tradition and may be designated as multiform.[43] This
means that there is a multitude of variations that do not have *one*

39 *Kagura ga musubu chiiki ya sedai* [Areas and generations connected by
kagura].
40 *Atsuta kagura to Miyaryū kagura* [Atsuta kagura and Miyaryū kagura]
(Internet reference).
41 *Nagoya jōka no dashi gyōji chōsa.*
42 *Tokoname-shi shi: bunkazai hen* [Handbook of Tokoname city: cultural
assets] 1983; *Handa-shi shi* 1984; *Taketoyo-chō shi: honbun-hen*
[Handbook of Taketoyo town: main text] 1984; *Agui-chō shi: shiryō hen 8,
Minzoku* [Handbook of Agui town: reference material 8, Folklore] 1995;
Sakai no ayumi to matsuri [History and festival of Sakai] 2005.
43 The term 'multiform' was introduced in Lord 1960, p. 100.

obvious origin or norm. To establish some order in this material, a research strategy that I had previously used in another context was employed, which is to treat one of the moving variables as a stable point of reference.[44] I chose the float-festival music that I knew best, namely that of the *Nagao no harumatsuri* of Taketoyo town, against which all other material could be reflected.

During my fieldwork, I went to numerous festivals in Chita Peninsula and adjacent parts of Aichi, and some of them I visited several times.[45] Most of these visits have been video-documented. Initially, my intention was to accomplish as complete documentations as possible; but as I learnt more my questions became more specific, and it became possible to focus on certain parts of the festivals. Still, new questions that arose often made it necessary to revisit some already documented festivals in order to check things that might have been missed.

In the beginning it was a cumbersome process even to find out where and when the festivals occurred and to find relevant maps and time-plans. Though there are still cases about which information is hard to find, the growth of Internet communication has radically simplified this part of the work. As will be shown later, this increase in available information reflects an increased use of festivals for marketing a town and for attracting tourists. My usual procedure has been to locate the information and schedule; to visit the site in advance, finding important points like the shrine and – not least – parking places; to ask the people who prepare the festivals for details; to go there on festival days; and to select which activities I would need to see in order to find answers to my most important questions.

For practical reasons, the possibility of spending extended periods of time in Japan have been limited. For many years I could, owing to my commitments at home in Sweden, only be there over the New Year holiday, for a couple of weeks in April around Easter time, and in the summer. In the southern-central and southern parts of the Chita Peninsula, there are several festivals every weekend from the end of March to the beginning of May, many going on during the same weekend, and under these circumstances it took several years to cover them. This could be a nuisance, as festivals are sometimes cancelled because of heavy rain or storms; this

---

44 Lundström 2010, pp. 16–17.
45 See Appendix 2: Fieldwork list.

would spoil my fieldwork plan for a particular festival, and it would sometimes take years until the dates fitted again. From 2013 onwards my schedule became more flexible, and it also became possible to see festivals in May and above all in the autumn, when several festivals in north Chita Peninsula, Nagoya, and Mikawa take place.

In some cases, visiting festivals has also meant visiting training sessions for the musicians of the ensembles. It is easier to hear details of the music in that situation. On the other hand, even though the manner of playing is intended to imitate the real situation, the actual performance context of the festival is of course missing. Oral information from persons involved in the local festival has been another important source of knowledge – with the help of a translator, in most cases my wife Kazuyo Lundström. I have also often been given copies of various kinds of local documents and recordings.

The main part of my material stems from my own observations, which have taken place over a long period of time, from 1990 to 2019. The most important part consists of video recordings and photographs made during festivals, with the aim of documenting what people actually do. Besides my own observations, the field notes include oral information about festival activities and their local backgrounds.

Since details of festival practices often change, and variations may occur from time to time, even within an on-going festival, it must be understood that each observation relates to the specific occasion when it was made. For example, a certain drum might have been missing from an ensemble because of some incidental reason. However, since several of the festivals have been observed more than once and since stability nevertheless dominates in festival practices, the totality should be quite reliable. One advantage with studying festival music over a long period of time is that it provides insights into the actual nature of any change that occurs, as well as into the balance between stability, continuity, and change. Printed sources, audio, and audiovisual materials as well as the Internet have been important additional sources for certain detailed information, for comparisons, and for checking information.

Delimitations

It has been necessary to delimit the scope of the study. I have therefore chosen to focus on those festivals that use floats. For my purpose, I define a float as a vehicle for festivals of a sturdy construction that can carry a music ensemble of about five people or more. My focus is on music that is played inside the floats while they are paraded along. This music genre is generally referred to as *michiyuki music*.

It is not always possible to make a clear distinction between *michiyuki music* and *kagura music*. There are many cases when a tune that functions for *kagura* in one place is used for *michiyuki* in another. Consequently, it is the context of the tunes in each place that determines whether it is one or the other; both genres must hence often be considered when looking at the music in different localities.

Even though certain forms of written notation exist, the transmission of festival music is largely oral, and each neighbourhood with a festival float has its own way of performing it. While there is an increasing interest in documenting the music and making it available on audio or audiovisual media, there is also a tradition of keeping certain musical knowledge within the neighbourhood.

Among the float-festivals in the Chita Peninsula, the focus of my research has been on those of the town of Taketoyo and its immediate surroundings. Within Taketoyo my focus has been on the district of Nagao, and within Nagao on the Tamanuki neighbourhood. This is largely reflected in the structure of this text, which starts with Tamanuki, continues with Nagao and the remainder of the Chita Peninsula, then moves on to a glance at the Nagoya area and Mikawa whereupon it finally returns to Chita, Taketoyo, and Nagao, viewed from a comparative and historic perspective. This order of priorities was, to a certain extent, determined by practical reasons, but it also reflects the research strategy according to which *Nagao no harumatsuri* forms one stable point of reference.

Ethical considerations

During the research process it has been essential to fully respect rules of behaviour, people's integrity, and the fact that there are places where those involved in the festivals want to keep the traditional knowledge to themselves. Documentation pertaining to learning or practising situations is acceptable to some neighbourhoods, though, and in those cases my presence and documentation methods have been agreed to by the organizers. There are neighbourhoods that do not allow documentation of special playing techniques, and as a researcher I have respected these views.

Most of my audiovisual material stems from the public part of the festivals. As often as possible, those who represent the leaders of the festival-float organization have been informed about my research. They are often very busy people, and the public occasions are frequently so crowded or stressful that discussions are impossible. On the other hand, the active participants are proud to show what they are doing and generally encourage photographing and video recording.

Out of respect for the tradition and for the sensitive process of oral transmission, a minimum of musical notation is used, limited to some graphs or short notated examples.

Structure of the book

The text starts by providing background information on float-festivals and festival floats. Chapter 3 is devoted to a description of the festivals in the town of Taketoyo. The most common instruments in the float-music ensembles are described in Chapter 4, which also shows how the playing of the instruments is passed on to new generations.

The practices regarding the instrumentation of all other float-festivals in the Chita Peninsula are summarized in Chapter 5, leading to the definition of four ensemble types and their geographical distribution. It turns out that the simultaneous use of the hourglass drums *kotsuzumi* and *ōtsuzumi* is especially concentrated to an area in the southern-central Chita Peninsula.

One of these drums, the *kotsuzumi*, is fairly widely used in Nagoya and Owari. The comparison is extended so as to include these areas, with a focus on ensemble types and the geographical distribution of the hourglass drums (Chapter 6). This proceeding brings out the differences and similarities between the southern-central Chita Peninsula and Nagoya/Owari.

The comparison is further extended to include parts of Mikawa (Chapter 7), where both the hourglass drums *kotsuzumi* and *ōtsuzumi* are used. The construction of the floats and the seating of the instrumentalists inside them are other parameters in the comparison between the relevant localities; there are significant differences between these localities, differences to which the various parameters are seen to be relevant.

The relationship between the drum types and other performing arts at festivals is discussed in Chapter 8. At festivals, there will be dances or puppet performances with musical accompaniment.

Map 2 The Chita Peninsula with the approximate locations of float-festivals. They are listed per shrine and not per city. This means that owing to local differences in the organization of festivals, not all neighbourhoods with a float are listed on the map. Courtesy of Jakob Cederblad.

Some are performed on the floats or just in front of them, and the musicians are often seated inside the floats.

The main part of the repertoire of each festival location contains many tunes that are widely used and that have spread over time. As a result of oral transmission, parts of tunes have been combined into new tunes. Different tunes sometimes have the same name, and at times the same tunes have different names. With the intention of momentarily catching or 'freezing' the tunes of a fluid continuum, they were grouped into *tune-complexes*. The analysis in Chapter 9 shows that there are two dominating traditions in the Chita Peninsula, one closer to Nagoya and one that is centred in the southern-central part of the peninsula.

The historical perspective is developed in Chapter 10 where the results of the comparisons are combined with literary sources and accounts of oral history, the aim being to help the reader understand how the float-festival music of the Chita Peninsula spread and developed over time.

Throughout the book, social and ritual matters that are part of the float-festival music tradition and its development – such as rituals, demography, gender matters, and festivalization – are touched upon. These are summed up in Chapter 11, and Chapter 12 brings in an intercultural perspective.

2
Float-festivals

In present-day Japan, the tradition of organizing festivals, *matsuri* or *sairei* – particularly at the time of rice-planting and on other important seasonal occasions – is still upheld in many places. These festivals go back to beliefs according to which the guardian deity of the rice fields comes to dwell in the fields and protect the rice plants. The religious aspects of the festivals focus on the protective deity or deities, *kami*, connected to the local shrine, *jinja*, in *Shintō* practice.

Most festivals are conducted by an organization involving *Shintō* priests, laymen, and local neighbourhood groups. In modern times, city offices play an increasingly important role. Though shrine festivals are religious rituals in themselves, they also have other functions in society, particularly social ones.[1]

The local festivals are of many different kinds. Some are very small and only concern those who live in the closest neighbourhood of a *Shintō* shrine, while others are large shows that attract thousands of onlookers. Festivals include music and other forms of performing arts. Float-festivals have a long history, but the individual festivals have also been modified and modernized up to the present time, and they are still continually revised. Some festivals have disappeared and others have started in more recent times. Some have been discontinued for one reason or another and then been revived after a lapse of some years.

In modern times, the rapid growth of cities has on the one hand increased the population from which festival people may be recruited; but on the other hand it has partly broken the stability of the units on which festivals used to rely: the community, the neighbourhood, and the unit of five households, the *goningumi*,

---

1 See Ashkenazi 1993 and Schnell 1999 for the organization and functions of festivals.

that was established during the *Edo period*. In rural areas there are sometimes not enough people to organize a festival, while those who have moved into the cities have developed different lifestyles and not really joined the *Shintō* shrines and their activities.[2] There was a period of a certain decline with regard to festival traditions in the early twentieth century, followed by discontinuation during the Second World War, but the most recent fifty years or so have seen a revitalization. Natural disasters may cause discontinuation, too. This was the case in the Chita Peninsula south of Nagoya when it was struck by the severe Isewan typhoon in September 1959.

Early float-festivals

Festivals with various kinds of floats can be traced back to the *Gion matsuri* in the old capital city of Kyoto.[3] According to the general history, a devastating plague claimed many lives in the second half of the ninth century. Attempting to drive away the disaster, people started to appease the deity and the spirits of the dead with 66 halberds, one for each of the sixty-six provinces.[4] Ever since the 970s, prayers for protection from future epidemics have – with some intermissions – been organized annually in mid-July, including the pulling of tall, decorated floats through the city streets, many with spires that symbolize the halberds.[5]

The *Gion matsuri* of Kyoto centres around Yasaka shrine in the Gion district and its enshrined deity *Gozu Tennō*, a god of good health and guardian deity of the Jetavana monastery in India, which is called *Gion Shōja* in Japanese. The summer festivals dedicated to this deity were called *Tennō matsuri* or *Tennōsai*, but since the Meiji restoration many have been renamed *Gion Matsuri*.[6] The *Shintō* ritual was revised after the Meiji restoration in 1868. Up till then, *Shintō* and Buddhist practices had been rather mixed, but as part of the new policy a sharp line was drawn between so-called *state Shintō* and Buddhism. In this process, *Gion matsuri* became a *Shintō* affair, even though there were still some Buddhist

---

2 Arai 1996, p. 99.
3 For *Gion matsuri*, see for instance Bauer and Carlquist 1974, pp. 44–55, and Shimada 2006; Teeuwen 2023.
4 Endō 2020, p. 190.
5 Higuchi 2012, p. 124.
6 Bocking 1995, p. 202.

elements left.[7] The focal deity of the festival was shifted to *Susanoo no Mikoto*.[8] The floats (called *yamaboko*) developed in the four-teenth century and gradually acquired the form they have today. Floats have been damaged through fires or war, and many have been restored.[9]

This type of festival spread over the country, especially during the *Edo period*. In Edo (present-day Tokyo) which took over the role of capital city, the festivals *Kanda matsuri* and *Sannō matsuri* started. The *Kanda matsuri* had 36 floats. As they were so tall that they interfered with the overhead telegraph lines and streetcar system that were introduced in the first decade of the twentieth century, the floats dropped out of use in Tokyo. As a result, most festivals in Tokyo now use palanquins called *mikoshi*. The floats were sold to places outside the city. They are considered to have been of the same kind as those now used in the *Kawagoe matsuri* just outside central Tokyo, which can be traced back to Edo times and embodies many characteristics of the old Edo festivals.[10]

Nagoya was one of many growing castle towns in the early *Edo period*. Apart from early influences from Kyoto's *Gion matsuri*, it was now also influenced by the new festivals in the capital city of Edo.[11] Nagoya became a local centre for festivals in Owari, including the Chita Peninsula and Mikawa. Similarly influential was the *Tennō matsuri* of Tsushima just west of Nagoya. North of Nagoya are *Inuyama matsuri* and the *Takayama matsuri* in Gifu prefecture, which date back to approximately the same time. When considering the age of a festival, it is important to bear in mind that we are usually talking about the time when it started under its particular designation. There were frequently forerunners, and festivals would often be temporarily discontinued; their floats as well as various other activities might have been lost and recon-structed. Festivals thus include an element of traditional stability as well as an element of change.

---

7 Bocking 1995, p. 33.
8 Porcu 2020, p. 42. The romanization 'Susanoo no Mikoto' is according to Konishi 1984, p. 472.
9 Shimada 2006, pp. 150–151.
10 Bocking 1995, pp. 87, 92, 223; Lancashire 2011, p. 172; McPherson 2012, p. 9.
11 Endō 2003, p. 117.

Float-festivals in the Chita Peninsula

Nagoya is located at the tip of the Ise Bay. Down its west coast lies
the large and important shrine *Ise jingū*, where some of the essential
imperial ceremonies are conducted and where large numbers of
people have travelled on pilgrimages through the centuries. On the
eastern side of the bay stands a *torii* gate in the water of the rocky
shore, signifying the direction to Ise. This is the peninsula south of
Nagoya called Chitahantō or just Chita, which is also the name of
a city there. Here there are numerous spring festivals, *harumatsuri*,
in April, when the rice was traditionally planted and the cherry
trees are in bloom. There are a few summer festivals, *natsumatsuri*,
too, and in the northern part of Chita several festivals take place
in the autumn, *akimatsuri*. A festival usually lasts for one or two
days and is often preceded by a 'festival eve' or *yoimatsuri*. Every
weekend from late March into May and from late September to the
end of October, there are several festivals going on at the same time
in different locations.

One basic activity at this kind of festival is the transportation of
the float and the deities, *kami*, along the streets of the neighbourhood. In *Shintō* faith, it is believed that the *kami* can be attracted to
an object or a place.[12] This is summarized by Inokuchi:

> In Japan, the divine spirit resides beyond the sky and the sea. On
> the invitation of a human or by its own will, the divine spirit visits
> the villages regularly or temporarily, receives *matsuri* [worship], and
> reveals its intention.[13]

A festival starts with a ritual by which the *kami* is summoned to
the floats (Figure 2). The popular belief that is most often heard is
that the *kami* are attracted to tall objects like floats, which are in
fact also sometimes called *yama*, 'mountain'.[14] If there is more than
one float in the community, they will usually at some point during
the festival be gathered in an open space or lined up for a parade.
According to Herbert Plutschow, the parade is

> one of the means used by communities to make a deity visible, to
> allow the deity to show itself and to manifest its 'dynamic' nature.

---

12 Schnell 1999, p. 168; Williams 2000, p. 36.
13 Inokuchi 1988 (translated from the Japanese original).
14 Schnell 1999, pp. 168–169.

Figure 2 Mr Iwata Takao, Chief Priest at Takeo jinja, Taketoyo, performing the ritual of the descent of the deity to the festival float of the Age ward. The green *sakaki* leaves are waved in front of it for purification (8 April 2016).

> For the community this provides yet another occasion to identify with the visible deity and to receive its power and blessings.[15]

Those who function as leaders of a festival know the religious meaning well and normally observe rules and practices that belong to the religious ceremonial. For most of the tens of thousands who go to see the largest festivals, however, the parades of decorated floats are the main attractions, as are the puppets or other performances that go with it. To many in the audience at the smaller, local festivals, these festivals also have the character of shows rather than religious acts, but since they normally gather at a shrine, they in a sense become part of the ritual process, which is implemented by priests, laymen, and the festival participants.[16]

---

15 Plutschow 1996, p. 143.
16 For religiosity relating to *Shintō*, see Reader 1991, pp. 60–70.

The festival floats

Several forms of folk performing arts, *minzoku geinō*, occur during a festival, particularly *kagura*, which are dance and music performances directed to the deities. In the classification of Japanese *minzoku geinō*, festival floats are grouped under the heading *tsukurimono furyū*, 'ornamental constructions', which relates to their function of making parades impressive.[17]

In the whole of Aichi prefecture, there are supposedly 422 festival floats.[18] Of these, nearly 130 which are still in use may be found in the Chita Peninsula.[19] The largest festival there is that of Handa on the east coast. In fact, the spring festival in Handa consists of several festivals that take place at approximately the same time in different districts and different shrines within the city. Nowadays, Handa is perhaps best known for its modern city float-festival, the *Handa dashimatsuri*, in which 31 floats, belonging to 10 districts, participate.[20] It was held for the first time in 1979, since when it takes place in October every five years.

The most commonly used general term for a festival float is *dashi*, but there are many different appellations even in the same area.[21] For instance, various words are used within the present-day city of Handa, such as *yama* ('mountain'), *kuruma* ('wagon'), *okuruma* ('wagon' with an honorific '*o*'), and *yamaguruma* ('mountain wagon').[22] In Taketoyo town, *dashi*, *kuruma*, and *okuruma* are commonly used.[23] Other Japanese names for floats that also differ

---

17 Lancashire 2011, pp. 6–7, 73.
18 According to 'An investigation by the Aichi Prefectural Board of Education 2016' in Kaimi 2017.
19 There are variants of festival floats that are called *dashi*. Therefore, *dashi* is differently defined in different sources, and the figures are not directly comparable. In some cases, the festival floats called *hanaguruma* are counted, sometimes not. The same goes for three-wheeled *dashi*, for *dashi*-like constructions that are not equipped with wheels, and for *dashi* that are no longer in use. The number 130 given here does not include these, but floats of the *yakata type* in Higashiura are included.
20 *Handa Dashimatsuri Hozonkai* [Handa Float-festival Preservation Society] → *Handa dashimatsuri* [Handa float-festival] (Internet reference).
21 Lancashire 2011, p. 73
22 *Handa-shi shi: sairei minzoku hen* [Handbook of Handa city: festival and folklore] 1984, p. 73.
23 *Taketoyo-chō shi: shiryō-hen 2* [Handbook of Taketoyo: reference material 2] 1983, p. 226. According to Mr Iwata Takao, Chief Priest at Takeo

Figure 3 The float *Hachimansha* of Shitamo in Nagao of the *Chita type* with the top roof and the spires, *bonden*, raised (8 April 2016).

in shape are: *yatai*, which (as well as *dashi*) is generally used in East Japan, and *hoko*, *yama* ('mountain'), *danjiri*, or *hikiyama*, which are more common in West Japan.[24]

In the Chita Peninsula, these wooden vehicles are most commonly about five to seven metres high with two storeys (Figure 3). The first storey is called *dōyama*. The second storey, *uwayama*, contains the upper part with a smaller roof that can be raised or lowered. A float may weigh around 3–6 tons.[25] The wooden

---

jinja, Taketoyo, the term for float used in ritual context is *onyamaguruma* (personal communication 29 October 2023).

24 Tatematsu 1994, p. 24; Lancashire 2011, p. 73. For the relation between *dashi*, *hoko*, and *yama*, see Orikuchi 1975, p. 208.

25 The weight of the float is according to *Jingūsha sairei no ayumi: Ichiba-ku* [History of the Jingūsha float-festival: Ichiba ward] 2007, p. 1; *Bishū Nagao Komukaegumi Hōōsha: sōken hyakugojisshūnen kinenshi* [The festival float Hōōsha of the neighbourhood Komukae, Nagao district, Owari province: memorial magazine for the 150th anniversary of its construction] 2013, p. 20; *Owari no* [Float-festivals of the Owari province] → *Chita no dashikan A* [Festival float museum of Chita] (Internet reference).

structure of the float's body is covered with draperies, usually red, in the front and in the back. Most also have decorated edgings of various colours on the sides. Sometimes there are embroideries on the draperies. From the back of its top, two rods, *bonden* or *bonten*, with tassels, can be elevated higher than the raised roof. Many floats are richly adorned with wooden sculptures. In the Chita Peninsula, about half of them are equipped with different kinds of puppets. During the year(s) between festivals, each float is partly disassembled and stored in a special tall building, *sayagura* (in some places called *dashigura*), which will be located near a shrine or in a local neighbourhood, often beside the collective assembly hall, *kōminkan*.

There are different types of floats, all characteristic of the time and the area in which they were built. Just as the shrine buildings are continually renewed, so old floats contain new parts made according to traditional techniques. In the Chita Peninsula, floats have developed in their own way, both with regard to shape and in respect of the way they are pulled. This so-called *Chita type* is higher and narrower than the *Nagoya type* and hence well suited to the narrow roads of the old towns and villages in the southern-central parts of the peninsula. 'It has its centre in Handa and is also called *Handa type*'.[26] This is the dominating type of float in the towns Agui, Taketoyo, and Tokoname, as well as to the south of those towns.

The *Chita type* has four vertical poles on each side (Figure 4). In the front there is a shelf used by puppeteers, but in many cases also by musicians. This shelf is called *chūdan*, 'middle level', or *chūdan no ita*, 'middle-level board' (Figure 5). Some floats even have one higher level inside. The second storey or *uwayama* forms a balcony with a low rail around it. Usually people employ the words *ni-kai* (second floor) and *san-kai* (third floor); but depending on the construction of the float, these may refer to other parts of its construction as well. Therefore, the terms bottom level, middle level, upper level, and top level will henceforth be used with regard to *Chita-type* floats.

---

26 *Owari no dashimatsuri* [Float-festivals of the Owari province] → *Owari Chita chihō no dashimatsuri, Tokoname matsuri no tokushusei ni tsuite* [Dashimatsuri in the Chita area, Owari province, about special aspects of the Tokoname matsuri]. See also *Handa-shi shi* 1984, p. 73 and *Bishū Handa: dashi emaki* [Owari province Handa: festival-float picture scroll] (Internet reference) 2017. English translation by KL.

The upper level usually covers the rear of the float and thus becomes the roof for some of the musicians seated beneath it. Figure 6 shows the *Nishimachi dashi* of Chiryū in the process of being assembled. Though this is not a *Chita-type* float, an upper level can still be seen. Chiryū is not located in the Chita Peninsula but in West Mikawa in Aichi prefecture, not far to the southeast of Nagoya. The old *Chiryū matsuri* has influenced many others.

In the Chita Peninsula, a float is normally pulled by means of two long ropes. They are pulled by two rows of men, but recently also by women. In the very front of the float a small group, usually consisting of younger men, is pulling, too. Another small group of young men push and steer from behind by means of two shafts. Together these people handle the float, coordinating their work with loud shouts: '*wasshoi, wasshoi*'. A few of the middle-aged men who walk beside and slightly behind the float handle safety ropes (called *handozuna* or *oizuna*) tied to its top, ropes by which they are able to adjust the balance of the tall and heavy vehicle. In addition, there will be persons who signal with lanterns in front of the float and behind it.

A float is equipped with four large solid wooden wheels which cannot be turned for steering. Those who push the float from behind steer by hanging on the shafts, so that the front wheels are slightly lifted from the ground. Simultaneously they push sideways while those in front pull in the new direction. This calls for good coordination, and here the music plays a significant role.

Normally children can join the pulling at the very front of the long ropes while they are parading at a moderate pace. A group of festival participants and other neighbourhood people usually come out to watch, and some will follow behind the float. Traditionally only men have taken active part in *Shintō* rituals such as festivals, women being tabooed for ritual reasons.[27] The festivals reflect and reinforce the norms in which males dominate leadership positions and public rituals, whereas female participation is largely within domestic activities.[28] In modern times, however, females increasingly take part in the handling of floats and in the musical ensembles inside them.

---

27 Female roles in early *Shintō* practice are mentioned by Mori 2003, pp. 48–49, and after the Meiji restauration by Hardacre 1989, pp. 62–63.
28 Schnell 1999, pp. 108–113, 140–141.

Figure 4 The float *Miyamotoguruma* of Kamezaki, Handa, being assembled in the exhibition hall of the Handa City Museum. The four vertical poles along the side of the float (including the corner poles) are characteristic of the *Chita type* of float (6 November 2016). [Handbook of Handa city: festival and folklore]

Figure 5 The float *Miyamotoguruma* of Kamezaki, Handa, being assembled in the exhibition hall of the Handa City Museum. The arrow indicates the shelf that constitutes the middle level in the front of the float, a shelf on which a person is standing; only the person's legs can be seen (6 November 2016).

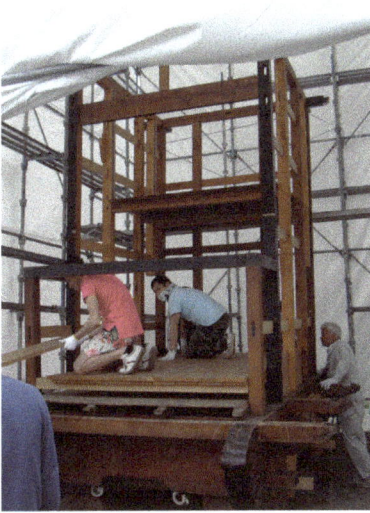

Figure 6 The *Nishimachi* float of Chiryū as it is being assembled. The last board of the bottom level is put in place by the man kneeling in the front part of the float. The upper level can be seen above the man kneeling in the back. There is no middle level in this float, but at the bottom it has the remainder of a no longer used stage floor, which could be pulled out forwards for puppet performances (29 April 2017).

3

The float-festivals in Taketoyo

Taketoyo town

Several festivals take place in the town of Taketoyo, which is located on Chita's east coast just south of Handa. This is where my research on the *dashibayashi music* of Chita started in 1992. With about 40,000 inhabitants, it is not a large town; it is only about half an hour by train from Nagoya, and it is no longer so easy to see where one city ends and the next begins. The rice fields between Taketoyo and Handa that were still there in the 1970s have now to a great extent been replaced by one-family dwellings, blocks of flats, shops, roads, and parking areas.

Taketoyo town consists of villages that have been merged. One of them was Nagao-mura (*mura* means 'village'), which is still called Nagao. The central shrine is Takeo jinja, located on a hill in the oldest part of the town (Figures 7–8). It is believed to date back to the eighth century, and the priest clan Iwata – at present the 30th generation – is said to have existed here since about the 1220s during the Kamakura period, when they founded a castle into which the shrine was moved. The main enshrined deity is *Susanoo no Mikoto*, who is considered to be the powerful storm deity who drives away evil spirits and brings favour, but who may also cause damage.[1]

Nagao merged with the village of Ōashi in 1878 and formed Taketoyo village, which later became the township of Taketoyo-chō. The name Taketoyo originates from the initial parts of the names of their respective shrines, Takeo jinja in Nagao and

---

1 The transcription of the name is according to Konishi 1984, p. 472. According to Plutschow 1996, p. 19, '[t]he mythical deity *Susanoo* also was made into a kind of scapegoat deity. As the original shape of Gozu Tennō, he caused epidemics, but also prevented them'.

Figure 7 The *torii* gate of Takeo jinja, Taketoyo (8 April 2017).

Figure 8 Takeo jinja on the morning of the eve of the festival, with designated places for the floats marked out in front of the main building (8 April 2017).

Toyoishi jinja in Ōashi. Three other villages, Fuki, Ichihara, and Higashi-Ōdaka, merged into Fuki village, which was added in 1954 to form today's Taketoyo-chō.

An important event in the growth of Taketoyo was the building of a railway fairly soon after the Meiji restoration. The Taketoyo Line was inaugurated in 1886, and ran from Taketoyo to Atsuta, close to Nagoya.[2] The reason was that building materials needed to be transported to a new inland railway, called Nakasendō, that was to connect Tokyo and Kyoto. The Nakasendō project was abandoned for economical and practical reasons, though, and a more southern railway, the present Tokaido Line, was built instead. Material was shipped to Taketoyo's harbour, which was chosen because it was especially deep, and then transported north by the new railway. Because of its natural deep harbour, Taketoyo thus became the terminus of the first railway in the prefecture. The new railway and the increased importance of the harbour were important assets in the ensuing development of the town. Its main industry has been the production of soy sauce and *miso* paste; more recent times have seen the addition of explosives, chemical production, and modern technological industry.

Nagao no harumatsuri

Nagao no harumatsuri – the spring festival of Nagao – takes place during the second weekend in April, approximately in the time span from 8/9 to 14/15 April. The festival has many names, which indicates that it is both a religious ceremony and a social festivity involving twelve neighbourhoods, *kumi*.[3] There is no formal name that covers the total festivity, but it is referred to as *Nagao-chiku sairei* ('Nagao district festival') – in external contacts – and *Takeo jinja reisai* ('Annual ritual of Takeo jinja'), which is the formal name of the festival as a *Shintō* ritual.[4] In the yearly pamphlets

---

2 *Taketoyo town: Taketoyosen no rekishi: kaitsū made no michinori* [A history of the Taketoyo line: the road to its opening] 2022 (Internet reference)

3 *Kumi* is sometimes referred to as *chōnaikai* (neighbourhood association) or *jichikai* (neighbourhood community association).

4 Personal communication: Mr Iwata Takao, Chief Priest at Takeo jinja (October 2015); Ms Kamiya Yoshimi, Director, Taketoyo Museum of History and Folklore (10 July 2021); Mr Tsuchihira Akihiro, Nagao-bu Secretary-General (19 October 2023).

and posters, the festival is at present called *Nagao no harumatsuri* (Figure 9).[5] All twelve *kumi* are included in the festival, and six of them are *dashi-gumi* with one festival float each.[6]

The current organization of this yearly event reflects the need to coordinate its different aspects. It is led by a self-governing federation of twelve neighbourhood associations represented by their respective heads called *Nagao-bu* ('The Nagao Section'). *Nagao-bu* has a Secretary-General, who is responsible for general planning, administrative work, and external and public relations.[7] The six *dashi-gumi* are responsible for the operation and management plan of their individual floats. The main priest of Takeo jinja is responsible for leading all *Shintō* rituals and all activities that relate to the shrine.[8] The festival meeting of *Nagao-bu* has the overall control of the festival. After an annual meeting, the Secretary-General meets the priest and shrine personnel in order to complete the planning.

In each ward, children or youths form ensembles made up of flutes and drums; they are seated inside the float during the festival. As will be discussed later, the instrument names are not standardized. The names and the ways in which they are written vary between different localities, sometimes even within the same neighbourhood. The commonly used names in Nagao are listed here (see further Chapter 4). The ensembles have the same basic composition and consist of:

- flutes of different kinds (*fue*),
- a suspended large drum (*hangiri*),
- a laced drum (*kozuke*),
- a large hourglass drum played with a drumstick (*ōdo*),
- small hourglass drums struck with the hand (*tsuzumi*).

---

5 That this name has been used since 2012 was confirmed by Ms Kamiya Yoshimi, Director, Taketoyo Museum of History and Folklore, personal communication 10 July 2021. From 1980 until 2011, the festival was marketed as *Nagao-bu harumatsuri*.

6 The floats of Nagao are among the eleven floats of Taketoyo that are described in *Taketoyo-chō shi: shiryō-hen 2* [Handbook of Taketoyo: reference material 2] 1983, pp. 226ff. See also Iga 1994, pp. 116–126, and Nakahashi 2011, pp. 31–36.

7 Mr Tsuchihira Akihiro, Nagao-bu Secretary-General, personal communication 19 October 2023 and 24 October 2023, concerning official names and organization.

8 Mr Iwata Takao, Chief Priest at Takeo jinja, personal communication 27 October 2023.

Figure 9 The front page of the 1992 brochure, issued by Taketoyo town, for the spring festival in Nagao, Taketoyo (courtesy of Nagao-bu Jimukyoku).

In Nagao, the neighbourhoods Age, Komukae, and Shitamo have the oldest floats and are located close to the shrine Takeo jinja; the neighbourhoods Banba, Ichiba, and Tamanuki acquired their floats later.[9] My starting point was Tamanuki.

The first pulling

In early April 1992, the spring festival is being prepared in the six different areas of the town. During the past year, the floats have been partly disassembled in their respective *sayagura*, 'float garages', but now they are already assembled and draped in red cloth. Preparations are going on in a meeting hall just beside it. Here one can find lists of all those who have donated money to the festival, and male persons of all ages from six or seven upwards have gathered.[10] Some are busy assembling and testing the puppets, while most of the youths are seated on the floor practising various musical instruments in small groups with an older player as teacher for each instrument.

The day before the festival starts, the active participants gather by their respective *sayagura*. At Tamanuki's the float is ready. As it is raining, it is being wrapped in a transparent plastic canvas. The musicians take their places inside the float, and after a simple ceremony has been performed, the long ropes by which the float will be pulled are folded out from an artful knot made at its front. The youths and the elders who are to handle the float take up their positions. The float is brought out from the *sayagura*, turned sideways, and pulled a few hundred metres down the road before it is turned around and again returned to the *sayagura*. This is the practice-pulling (*tameshibiki*) in the course of which the organization is tested, and the participants can feel how it works. Nowadays the official yearly pamphlet advertises a three-day event: first

---

9 The reading and writing of the ward names in Taketoyo adhere to the advice of Taketoyo Museum of History and Folklore (personal communication 7 September 2021); *Taketoyo-chō shi: honbun-hen* 1984: 363. The district 小迎 is sometimes read 'Komukai' (ibid. 364), but in this text the reading 'Komukae' will be used. The district Age is written in several different ways and 上ケ will be used here.

10 See Ashkenazi 1993, pp. 83–109, for a description of the principles of *matsuri* organization.

pulling (*hikizome*, Friday), festival eve (*zenyasai*, Saturday), and festival day (*honmatsuri*, Sunday).[11]

The festival eve

About 8 o'clock on the Saturday morning, all who are to take part are gathered by the *sayagura*. The adult men wear a short bluish-black jacket, *happi*, with the sign of the neighbourhood's name on its back – this one says *tama*, 'a precious stone such as jade', which is the first part of the name Tamanuki – and they wear yellow caps. The youths who are to pull and steer the float wear black trousers and white shirts and socks. They also wear a broad belt and a sash in colours that are different for the individual neighbourhoods and mark their respective functions (see Figure 10) (• 1a–f).

The doors of the *sayagura* are wide open, and the float is still standing inside. The thick ropes by which it will be pulled are tied in a knot at its front. Higher up, two papers folded in a zigzag pattern are suspended on a wooden stick. This is referred to as the *gohei*. It is a symbolic offering and indicates the presence of a deity, *kami*.[12] An altar in the shape of a narrow high table is placed in front of the float with different votive offerings on it, including fruits, green leaves, and *sake*.

The men and the boys form a semicircle in front of the float and the altar while the priest from Takeo jinja walks up and bows deeply several times in front of the float, delivers a recitation, and then claps his hands twice and bows again (Figure 10). He is calling the *kami*, and is supposed to enter the float and stay there during

---

11 In everyday language, the day before the festival day is often called *yoimat-suri*. Other names in Nagao include *yomatsuri* in Ichiba (*Jingūsha sairei no ayumi: Ichiba-ku* [History of the Jingūsha float-festival: Ichiba ward] 2007, p. 14); *yomiya* in Komukae (*Bishū Nagao Komukaegumi Hōōsha: sōken hyakugojisshūnen kinenshi* [The festival float Hōōsha of the neigh-bourhood Komukae, Nagao district, Owari province: memorial magazine for the 150th anniversary of its construction] 2013, p. 58); *yoiyama* in Tamanuki (Mr Saitō Kiyotaka, personal communication 23 September 2021); and in the Banba ward *shingaku* or *shigaku* (*Taketoyo-chō shi: shiryō-hen 2*, 1983, pp. 309 and 311). In Ōtani, Tokoname, this is also called *yomiya* but written with different characters (*Ōtani kushi: wasurenai Ōtani ima, mukashi* [The Ōtani ward: remember Ōtani now and past] 2017, p. 91).

12 Ono 1991, p. 24.

Figure 10 The front of Tamanuki's float *Gyokushinsha* partly pulled out from its storing house, *sayagura*, for the initial ceremony in the morning of the festival eve. The Chief Priest of Takeo jinja, Mr Iwata Masayoshi, dressed in a white gown and a black hat, is standing beside an altar with offerings during the ritual of the descent of the deity to the festival float of the Tamanuki ward. In the background just to the left of the priest is Mr Saitō Kiyotaka, who was festival general that year. See Figures 12–13 for the same ceremony 15 years later (11 April 1992). Photo by Kazuyo Lundström.

the festival. Through this symbolic transfer of the *kami* from the shrine to the float, it becomes a sacred object.[13]

On either side of the small triangular space are streets. The morning traffic is making a great deal of noise – motorbikes, scooters, cars, lorries, and buses. During the recitation, the rubbish lorry arrives and starts devouring the last few days' leftovers from the surrounding households. But at this moment the small space marked by the float on one side and on the other sides by the men standing there is a sacred place, where the ritual is carried out in full dignity and what is happening a few metres away is disregarded.

The priest then purifies the area and all the people present by spreading out salt. Taking a *sakaki* tree branch with evergreen leaves and swaying it in front of the float and the bowing men, he

---

13 Ono 1991, pp. 68–69.

sweeps away all that is impure. He starts reciting again and while
this goes on, music starts as if from nowhere – first a long-drawn-
out, high-pitched flute tone and then the reverberating deep sound
of the *hangiri* drum, followed by the drier sounds of the smaller
kozuke drum. It is as if the *kami* has entered it announcing its
descent, but it is the ensemble inside the float that celebrates the
kami's arrival.

A new tune starts slowly. While the altar is moved aside the long
ropes are unfolded, and the men get ready to pull the float out. The
youths take their places in front of it and behind it (Figure 11). Two
men dressed in special clothes spread salt to purify the path of the
float.

A new *sayagura* 'garage' has been built in a different place, but
as late as 2007 the initial ceremony was still carried out in the same
manner (Figures 12–13).

Gradually, the pace of the music increases. A man behind the
float lifts a lantern high into the air. This signal is followed by the
intense clatter of the wooden clappers, *hyōshigi*, which are handled
by a man in front of the float. There is an instantaneous loud cheer

Figure 11 The float of Tamanuki pulled out from its storing house.
See Figure 13 for the same occasion 12 years later. Note the change
of the edging on the top of the float's side (11 April 1992).
Photo by Kazuyo Lundström.

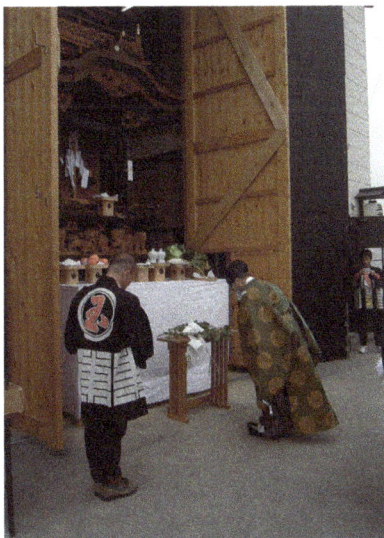

Figure 12 The Chief Priest of Takeo jinja, Mr Iwata Masayoshi, performing the ritual of the descent of the deity. Tamanuki, Nagao (13 April 2007). Photo by Kazuyo Lundström.

Figure 13 Tamanuki's float *Gyokushinsha* is pulled out of its storing house, *sayagura*, which was built in 2002, replacing the older one (10 April 2004).

Figure 14 Mr Saito Kiyotaka (left) and Mr Maeda Toshio (right) dressed for the festival. Both have been advisers, as well as good friends, to the author (13 April 2018).

from the youths, and suddenly the high and heavy vehicle is out of its garage and on its way down the street. It all happens in a few seconds. The float then stands still for a while. The ensemble cannot be seen except for three small boys with *tsuzumi* drums, who are sitting in the back of the float facing backwards. A new, high-pitched tone from a flute announces the beginning of a new musical piece. It is a calm, steady beat. This piece belongs to the *michiyuki music* category. On the same signals as before, the float is again moved forward by the youths shouting '*wasshoi, wasshoi*'. Those at the very front of the float are jumping and leading the cheering. The festival's general, *sairei iinchō*, and his closest functionaries are walking side by side behind the float.

On reaching a crossing, the float is brought to a halt, and the ensemble plays a very slow piece. This is the beginning of *Shagiri*. The tempo gradually increases until, after a few minutes, it has become quite fast. Then, within some thirty seconds, the following happens: the lantern is lifted, the clappers clatter, the youths shout, the float is pulled the last few metres to the crossing, in a powerful instant it is turned ninety degrees on the spot, and the running men quickly pull it 25–30 metres ahead. Then it stands still again until the music has reached its final crescendo. The slow *michiyuki* piece takes over and the parading continues.

On a given signal, there is a new tempo change. In a moment, the float is halted in front of a house and turned about ninety degrees, so that it stands across the road facing the building. The youths run into the house and return with its owner, whom they hoist up into the air three times. The music is fast, loud, and wild – they are playing *Ochazuke* and other joyful tunes to honour this man and bring good luck to his household. Those who receive this kind of celebration are usually people who have contributed notably to the festival, not necessarily in the form of financing.

The common explanation of the pulling of the float along the streets of the ward is the wish to purify households and give them some of the *kami*'s power, which is believed to bring good luck and prosperity. During these days, the float is believed to be empowered by the *kami*, and it is treated like a sacred object. In a sense, this also extends to the people who handle it.

The minutely scheduled route of the float goes on like this all the way to the shrine, with numerous stops to celebrate a person and to eat and drink what is being offered. Since the wheels cannot be turned sideways, every change of direction demands maximal coordination. The youths who push the float from behind lean on the shafts to lift the front wheels while pushing sideways, and those in the very front, as well as those who pull by the ropes, must turn at the right moment. The music of *Shagiri* is an important factor for coordinating this procedure.

After about five hours, Tamanuki has made the three or four kilometres to Takeo jinja, which is located on the top of a small hill in the oldest part of the town, where the narrow streets are bordered with old-style, black- and tar-coated houses. In the course of the morning, the other five neighbourhoods have gone through the same procedure: Age, Banba, Ichiba, Komukae, and Shitamo have all moved from their respective starting points to meet at Takeo jinja.

Six rectangular spaces, each big enough for a float, have been marked out with chalk on the sand space in front of Takeo jinja's main building (see Figure 8). One after the other, the floats arrive at full speed in an order decided upon in agreement with traditional rules. Each float stops in its designated space. It is pulled into this area and then immediately reversed, then pulled back into its space, reversed again, and finally pulled into the designated space for the third and last time. Entering the shrine area is a critical moment, for everybody wants to impress the spectators that have gathered – perhaps especially Tamanuki, which seems to compensate for being the youngest neighbourhood by running faster than the others and by tearing down a shower of white blossoms from a large cherry tree by the entrance. Everything goes well, and there are no incidents.

When the last of the floats comes up and gets in line, all six of them move backward on a given signal, ending up some 20 metres to the farther side of the space. There they begin to raise the roofs on the top floors as well as the two *bonden* spires (Figure 15).[14] This is accompanied by six unsynchronized musical ensembles, all playing celebrational music at full volume. It is a powerful and chaotic soundscape.

In the meantime, ceremonies have been performed inside the shrine building where the leaders of the six neighbourhoods have been given live fire which they carry outside in lanterns. After a while all floats are covered by lighted lanterns, hanging from numerous soft bamboo branches that are protruding from their fronts, sides, and backs. When fully lighted, each float is again pulled up to its place in front of the shrine building. With the others, it forms a line there, the floats standing side by side facing the building.

It is late afternoon, and it is starting to get dark. One by one the floats leave the shrine, and while the evening falls, they move back to their respective neighbourhoods. About nine o'clock it is totally dark. In the flickering pale light from some fifty lanterns, Tamanuki approaches its *sayagura* (Figure 16). A few lanterns have gone out. The drums and flutes are still sounding. Three tired little boys on the back of the float keep on beating their *tsuzumi* drums with bandaged hands. The float is put in place accompanied by cheers from strained vocal cords. Those who are old enough are going to eat and celebrate. Early next morning it will be time to start again.

The festival day

Early on Sunday morning, everybody again gathers by their respective float in the different parts of the town. The atmosphere is even more tense and expectant; this is the real festival day, and there will be more people watching along the streets. At the shrine, there will be market stalls and lots of people. Every participant wants to do

---

14 In some places '*bonden*' is called '*bonten*'.

Figure 15 The six floats of Nagao lined up facing the shrine building with the roofs and the *bonden* spires raised (11 April 2004).

Figure 16 Returning to the *sayagura* on the evening of the festival eve (Saturday). The float *Gyokushinsha*, of Tamanuki in Nagao (14 April 2007).

this as well as possible – play well and drive well. The most crucial moment is when arriving at the shrine, and they would not want anything to go wrong there.

The organization detail is minute and safety is at a maximum. The festival schedule resembles a subway map, and time is kept with great precision (Figure 17). If a float arrives early at a given point, the participants take a break, and the youths will get a chance to sing. The song heard most often at festivals in Chita Peninsula is *Ise ondo*, 'The Ise tune'. The boys take turns in being lead singers, while the others form a choir for the refrains. The only accompaniment is handclapping. There are several variants of the text.

On the festival day the float takes a slightly different route, so that after the two days it has passed through most of the area. A few hours later, the floats are again assembled at Takeo jinja with their roofs and spires up. This is the climax of the festival, and they are to entertain and please the *kami*.

A puppet on a float is generally referred to as *karakuri-ningyō*, normally translated as 'mechanical doll', though they are not strictly speaking automatic. Some are manipulated by hand as in *bunraku*, the puppet theatre that developed in the seventeenth century. This is the case with the *miko*, the shrine-maiden puppet, and the dancing trickster *Sanbasō*. Other puppets are handled by strings from inside the float, among them the puppet that cannot reach a suspended drum until it jumps on to the shoulders of another one. People enjoy watching the puppets perform, but in this case the intention behind the performance is a desire to please and entertain the *kami*. In the early 1990s there had been complaints to the effect that the audience could not really see the performances very well, and some people felt that the floats should be turned away from the shrine building and face the audience instead. Nevertheless, the performances are still aimed at the *kami*.

The float of the Ichiba neighbourhood does not have puppets; a small stage is built in front of it instead. There is an ensemble of flutes and various drums. A boy dressed in traditional clothes is carried onto the stage, sitting on a man's shoulder. As a sacred being, he must not touch the ground until he starts performing the *Sanbasō* dance as a votive offering. After these performances, the floats are returned to their *sayagura*, much like the previous day, but earlier in the afternoon. Ceremonies and celebrations remain before the festival is quite over for this year.

Figure 17 The map of *Nagao no harumatsuri* on Sunday 9 April 2017, from the brochure mentioned in Figure 9. The location of each neighbourhood's *sayagura* is marked and the names are transcribed. Blue arrows have been added, showing which float belongs to each neighbourhood. The pink area in the lower centre of the map is Takeo jinja. The time indications above it show the order and time of entrance. The list to the left shows the order and time of departure (courtesy of Nagao-bu Jimukyoku).

Ōashi Jaguruma matsuri

In Ōashi, a *Kagura hozonkai* – 'Kagura Preservation Society' – was formed in the mid-1970s. It is responsible for festival music at two shrines: Toyoishi jinja and Hotta inari jinja, located opposite each other on either side of a main road. *Hotta inari taisai*, 'Grand festival at Hotta inari jinja', takes place during the initial weekends of February (New Year), September, and December. *Kagura* dance is performed by young girls, who are recruited from the neighbourhood and are dressed in red and white as *miko*, 'shrine maidens'.

There is also a summer festival, *Ōashi Jaguruma matsuri*, at Toyoishi jinja. It takes place during a mid-July weekend with an old *Chita-type* float equipped with the head of a dragon in front on its top (Figure 18). After an interval of twenty years, the festival was resumed in 1974.[15] Back in time, a *furedaiko*, 'message drum', was

Figure 18 The float *Jaguruma* of Ōashi with its characteristic dragon's head on top (19 July 1997).

---

15 For various reasons, the festival was interrupted several times and revived from 1974. See *Network 2010: Nagoya...* [Network 2010: Nagoya...] → *Ōashi Jaguruma matsuri* (Internet reference).

used as well. This was a large and old *ōdaiko* pulled on a wagon before the float. This practice has been discontinued, but the drum still exists and is nowadays used on the above-mentioned occasions for *kagura* dance at *Hotta inari taisai* (see Figure 28).

The festival days

In 1995, the festival eve occurs on Saturday 22 July. The festival has started much in the same manner as in Tamanuki, and the float is pulled along a route through streets of the town for about four hours until it reaches Toyoishi jinja. The activity is carefully organized, and there are many instructions and rules. When starting and stopping, the signals emitted by the clappers *hyōshigi* and by the float-leader, who is the leading flute player, are adhered to. The purification leader, who purifies by means of scattering salt, must take care that no salt falls on the float or its recently purchased cloth. While moving along, the participants follow the leaders of the respective sections. Rope leaders are responsible for the children who pull in front, so that they will not get stuck between ropes and houses when the float turns. Before the float is brought into the shrine area the children's ropes will be taken off, and the children will move away. The next stage is a more dangerous part of the festival, and it must be handled by youths and adults alone.

During the festival eve, a procession pulls the float through the streets to the shrine. The float has the dragon's head on its top and dragon embroideries on the draperies at its sides. The youths in front have dyed their hair with green streaks – all kinds of colours and hairstyles were fashionable at that time. In more recent years, the youths who pull the float have also used plastic megaphones of the kind used by audiences at baseball games. They use them mainly for rhythm and for hitting one another while they sing ditties and perform a dance when the float stands still, jumping into an increasingly tightened bunch.[16]

Many children join in pulling the float by the special ropes that have been tied to the front end of the real ropes, thus lengthening them. Apart from the girls among these children and an occasional

---

16 These fashions are likely to have spread from the nearby city of Handa and occurred in other areas as well. In many places rules have been made against dyeing hair and against the use of megaphones.

mother, only men take active part in the procession. When the float is pulled along, the most common melody that is heard is *Shinguruma*, which is basically the same tune as in Nagao. When the float stops to celebrate, *Kanemaki* is generally played, a tune very similar to *Ochazuke* in Nagao. When there is a ninety-degree turn, *Shagiri* is normally played. It is built on the same basic material as in Nagao but performed slightly differently.

The final distance into Toyoishi jinja is performed at full speed while the ensemble plays *Shagiri*. The float stops in a cloud of dust in front of the shrine building while the music continues for a while. A few hundred spectators have gathered to shop at the market stalls and to watch the festival activities. There are both men and women of all ages, and for young girls this is an opportunity to wear *yukata*, 'summer *kimono*'.

Later on, the float has been adorned with lanterns, and as darkness falls it is again paraded around the block where the shrine is. Even in summer, darkness falls early, and when fireworks start around 8 p.m. it is already totally dark. A great number of different fireworks are displayed along horizontally hung ropes, and the young men run beneath them in showers of sparks. When the fireworks finish, the float is pulled up to the shrine building while the ensemble plays loudly. A man dressed in a red loincloth is standing on its top beside the dragon's head. His task is to let the dragon spew fire towards the shrine building through a nozzle connected to a gas tube. Like a gigantic sparkler, the fire is spread out while the float is moved back and forth in front of the building, until it gradually goes out as the Calor gas is used up (Figure 19). During all this time the ensemble is playing inside the float, and there is a special tune for this climax of the final stage, a tune called *Ja no kuchi kagura*, '*ja no kuchi*' meaning 'dragon's mouth'.[17] There have been accidents through the years resulting in interruptions or restrictions in the use of fireworks and gas, as well as in increased safety regulations.

About noon on the festival day, the float is pulled along a slightly different route through the town. The ensemble is playing music in the tempo used for normal parading. Then, when the float stops,

---

17 In eastern and southeastern Asia, the dragon spirit is usually associated with water – either rain, which is needed when the rice is growing, or flood disasters. According to Kawano 2005, p. 90, the dragon is thought to be the *kami* of sea and water, and dragon symbols often occur in festivals near the sea.

Figure 19 The dragon of the float *Jaguruma* of Ōashi spews fire in front of Toyoishi jinja (21 July 2001).

they play *Kanemaki* and at occasional turns *Shagiri*. The youths gather in front of the wagon and start singing *Ise ondo*, with a lead singer and choir for the refrains. When the float reaches the *sayagura* in the early afternoon, the parading is over.

Fuki-chiku sairei

Within Taketoyo town there are also spring festivals in the Fuki district. Nowadays they are called *Fuki-chiku sairei*, 'Fuki district festival[s]', and take place in April on the weekend preceding the *Nagao no harumatsuri*. Fuki itself has five wards. Of these, Fuki and Fuki-Ichiba have one float each, and both are pulled to the Hachimansha shrine. Ichihara with one float is located a little farther to the west, relating to the Agata shrine. To the north, a little closer to Nagao, lies Higashi-Ōdaka – or just Ōdaka – with one float pulled to the Chiryū jinja. The ward called Shinden has a smaller wagon and celebrates its *matsuri* at yet another shrine, the Akibasha. It carries one *ōdaiko* and one *kozuke*, and the flute players walk behind it.

Figure 20 Cheering and singing in front of the float *Tennōmaru* of Fuki-Ichiba before starting (6 April 2019).

The *sayagura* of Fuki-Ichiba is located close to the station in central Fuki. The float is characterized by having a model boat on its top (Figure 20).[18] It is paraded through the district and is pulled to Hachimansha shrine. Flute players are seated in the back of the float, and usually an *ōdo* player sits on the left shaft in its rear; but the seating varies – you will, for instance, sometimes see two *ōdo* players far to the rear of the float. A *tsuzumi* player may sit on the right shaft or inside the float. Many of the players are young children, both boys and girls.

The float of Honwakakai in Fuki ward (Figure 21) has been equipped with a puppet, *karakuri*. In the back there will be flute players, and usually one *ōdo* player will also be seated there (Figure 21). There is also a *tsuzumi* in the ensemble. When the float leaves the *sayagura*, they play the tune *Daikagura*. They have a large separate drum that is carried or moved on a wagon. A lion's head, resembling the masks used in lion dances, is brought to the

---

18 Being a peninsula, Chita is surrounded by water. Boats and fishing are important, and there are floats in boat shape as well as floats that are actually boats which float on the water.

Figure 21 *Honwakasha*, the float of Honwakakai in Fuki, with two *ōdo* players seated in the back and a flute player between them. Photograph taken during the *Taketoyo fureai dashimatsuri* (12 October 2014).

shrine as an offering, being transported in an elaborated special miniature 'house' on wheels with a double roof, called *yakata*.[19]

The float will be pulled to Hachimansha where they meet with Fuki-Ichiba. Each float enters the shrine area in turn, playing lively music, and is pulled to a stop in front of the shrine building. They will be pulled back and forth about three times until they are positioned in front of the building. When both floats have entered, they will be perfectly lined up beside each other, facing the building, and the priest and the laymen continue their ceremonies.

Ichihara is located more inland, just west of Fuki. The float of Ichihara has levels inside, and some ensemble players – notably the *ōdo* and *tsuzumi* – are placed on the third level, as is also the case in nearby Kosugaya (Tokoname) and Kaminoma (Mihama). The flute players are seated in the back. When starting out from the *sayagura* they play *Hayabune*, a tune that increases in speed and is also used in Kosugaya and Kaminoma, as well as in other

---

19 According to Kárpáti 2000, p. 116, the lion's head is a permanent incarnation of the divine spirit and is treated as a sacred object.

Figure 22 *Agatasha*, the float of Ichihara in Fuki standing at Agata jinja
(3 April 2004).

areas in Fuki. The float is paraded to Agata jinja, which is located
on a hill (Figure 22).

Higashi-Ōdaka is located slightly to the north of Fuki. When
the float is preparing to leave the *sayagura* in the morning of the
festival day, a large portable barrel drum will be played and there
will be flute players as well. This is called *Okuridaiko* (Figure 23).
Three flute players are usually seated in the back of the float,
and sometimes there will be a *tsuzumi* as well. Every second year
the float is paraded through the part of the ward that faces the
shore, and the intermediate year it will be paraded on the inland
side. The float is paraded to Chiryū jinja, where it is pulled around
the shrine area to the tune *Kanemaki* until it halts in front of the
shrine building. The portable *ōdaiko* drum has been brought here
and will also be used for music at the shrine.

During the parade, a set of tunes is played when the float is to
be turned. The tunes *Shagiri – Hayabune – Kanemaki* are played
at a high tempo. On the way back from the shrine, the parade
will halt while the portable *ōdaiko* that has been brought there is
played. By then it is already dark. Soon thereafter the float reaches
the *sayagura* to the festive and celebrational sound of the same set
of tunes.

Figure 23 The drum used for *Okuridaiko* placed in front of the *kōminkan* of Higashi-Ōdaka (2 April 2017).

Main features of the festivals in Taketoyo

The main features of the corresponding festivals in Taketoyo are basically the same. Before a float starts out from the *sayagura*, ceremonies have been performed. The float is then paraded along the streets of the town or ward to the accompaniment of slow, medium, or fast music, depending on the situation. During the parade there will be stops for pausing and eating, and music from the *hōnō* or 'offering' repertoire will be played. Along its way, the float will also stop at smaller shrines and perform *hōnō* music. The climax of the festival is when the float reaches the main shrine of the district or ward. The float will enter the shrine as fast and loud music is played, and it will ultimately stop in front of the shrine building. More *hōnō* music will then be performed with the intention of pleasing the deities. Further rituals are carried out at the shrine. After some time – a couple of hours or more – the float is again paraded along the streets and has been equipped with many lanterns. This parade leads back to the *sayagura*, and the return there is yet another climactic moment. This procedure is carried out on the festival eve, usually a Saturday; sometimes there have also been activities on the evening before, the *yoimatsuri*. The Sunday will be the festival day, *honmatsuri*, and it is characterized by the same procedure. The route of the float will be different, however, and the ceremonies at the main shrine will be more elaborate.

While the different festivals are similar on a general level, there are many differences with regard to details. Concerning the music, one obvious difference has to do with the ensemble, although the same instruments are used. The six wards of Nagao as well as Ōashi have the characteristic three *tsuzumi* drums with the players placed in the rear of the float, facing backwards. This is not the case in Fuki. Generally, there will be flutes and/or *ōdo* in the back. Although some tunes are the same, the musical repertoire differs as well. For instance, the tune *Shagiri* dominates the up-tempo tunes in Nagao and Ōashi, while the tune *Hayabune* is often heard in all parts of Fuki and Higashi-Ōdaka. These differences in the ensembles and the repertoire will be discussed later.

Taketoyo fureai dashimatsuri

The balance between religious ritual on the one hand and social and commercial needs on the other was resolved in a similar manner as in the nearby city of Handa: by means of a new float-festival, *dashimatsuri*. While the traditional yearly festivals are shrine festivals and have their spiritual meaning, the city float-festivals are not held at a shrine but at a community centre. Still, the ritual of the descent of the deity is done before the floats are taken out of their *sayagura* for the city-festival.

Both the yearly shrine festivals and the city float-festival – the latter with its own organization consisting of an Executive Committee with a chair and representatives from the *kumi* – are continued alongside each other. In this manner it has become possible to retain an essential part of the religious and social meaning while also marketing the city and attracting visitors to the show. Furthermore, Taketoyo town can be displayed as a unit, whereas the traditional festivals concern Nagao, Ōashi, and Fuki and their wards separately.

The *Taketoyo fureai dashimatsuri*, 'Taketoyo friendship float-festival', was first arranged in October 1994 and was then scheduled to occur every five years.[20] All the floats are gathered

---

20 The *Taketoyo fureai dashimastsuri* has, apart from my own observations in 2014 and 2019, been accessible to me in video recordings from 1994 and 1999. For other city float-festivals in Chita Peninsula, see Hamachiyo 2000 and Yoneyama 2000.

Figure 24 The 11 floats of Taketoyo lined up at the *Taketoyo fureai dashimatsuri* (14 October 2019).

here: 6 from Nagao, 1 from Ōashi, and 4 from Fuki. The 11 floats are pulled out from their respective *sayagura*. Those from Fuki have the longest distance to cover. About halfway they are joined by Ōashi's dragon float. All the floats eventually line up in a place chosen for this occasion, originally on a schoolyard located to the south of Chita–Taketoyo station and thereafter in a large parking lot beside the *Yumetarō Plaza*, a community centre and concert hall (Figure 24).

In the Chita Peninsula there are city float-festivals in Handa (since 1979), Taketoyo (since 1994), Tokoname (since 2004), and Mihama (so far once in 2015). Tending to be first held at a city jubilee, they generally recur in intervals of five years. All the townships' festival floats will join in, and there will be music or dance performances. The city float-festivals are one of many manifestations of modernization.

Function and meaning of the festivals

In modern times, the traditional festivals were temporarily discontinued during the Second World War and from 1959, when Chita was stricken by the great Isewan typhoon. After several years, the festivals were taken up again and have been revitalized and reorganized.[21] Their relation to the farming year is insignificant in modern industrialized society. The most active supporters now seem to be merchants or businessmen and people in general, who are mainly active in other areas than farming.

The religious meanings of the festival are still upheld, and most people are aware of this, at least on a general level. The festival serves to entertain and please the *kami* and to spread their power to the households of the city. Each year, the relation to the *kami* will be renewed at the time of year when the rice was traditionally planted. The social content is no less prominent. While girls obtain their social schooling in other situations, boys receive much of it through participation in the festival in which men of different age groups have their specific roles within a hierarchic system. The youngest boys can see most of their future roles: as teenagers, in their twenties, as middle-aged, and in old age. The festival is like a mirror of the social order of traditional Japan in a concentrated form.[22]

The young participants also learn to change between two roles – the traditional and the modern. On the Monday morning, the celebrating, cheering, singing people of the festival will return to a different world. Dressed in suits and ties, the adults will meet on the platform at the station to commute to their jobs. The younger ones will be on their way to school in school uniforms and carrying school bags. Those who played drums or a flute in the ensemble may turn up with a Walkman – nowadays an iPad or a smartphone – with earphones, listening to language exercises or perhaps to the latest pop hits.

The social essence of the festival also comprises the aspect of togetherness. Festivals bring people together in a city and in a neighbourhood, and their unity is symbolically marked by the activities of the festival. Most households contribute to the festival in one way or another, and most men will have a role in the festival at least at some point in their lives. This also concerns women, for although women were tabooed in the actual working of the

---

21 *Nagao no harumatsuri*, 'Nagao spring festival', had a period of suspension from 1960 to 1967 (*Bishū Nagao Komukaegumi Hōōsha* 2013, p. 8).

22 Compare Paden 1994, pp. 102–103, for the function of major festivals as embodiments of social relations and roles.

Figure 25 Festival floats symbolizing the united town on an advertising pillar in front of the city hall on Taketoyo's 60-year celebration (2 November 2014).

floats, they had important supporting roles in various respects. Increasingly, women may take part in the handling of the floats as well.

In Nagao, the festival has been adjusted to the needs of modern society in several ways. Thus, it always takes place on a Friday evening, Saturday, and Sunday, when people can be free from school or work. It has also been adjusted to traffic rules, and the city office plays an active part in organization and promotion.

The traditional festivals have become an important factor in marketing Taketoyo town, and they feature quite prominently in tourist brochures and on the city's website. The city float-festival has enhanced marketing opportunities still further. It was first held as part of the celebrations of Taketoyo town's forty years of existence. The float-festival is closely connected to the town which consists of villages that were merged not very long ago, and it is marketed as a symbol of a united community (Figure 25).

4

Musical instruments and learning

The musical instruments employed in most ensembles in the Chita Peninsula include flutes, a large, suspended drum, and a smaller, laced drum. There are variations, though, so in some places other instruments are used as well. In this chapter, the musical instruments will be presented, and the tune categories within the float-music repertoire – the *dashibayashi music* – and its functions will be explained, the festivals of Taketoyo serving as an example. The methods of transmitting the music to learners are then described. New children are recruited to the ensembles every year, and it will take a few years to learn all the instruments. Traditionally, the musicians were only men, often young boys. Nowadays girls are increasingly being included, too, partly because it has become more difficult to recruit boy participants owing to changes in society (see Chapter 11).

During a festival, each float contains a *dashibayashi ensemble*, and the musicians take turns. Those who are the most experienced will be chosen to perform at the most important parts of the festival, for instance when at a shrine. The leader is an experienced flute player. Occasionally an older flute player can be seen supporting the ensemble, playing while walking just behind the float, often to instruct younger players. Similarly, drum patterns may be shown by hand-movements beaten in the air.

The musical instruments

As mentioned, the names of the musical instruments are not uniform in the area, sometimes not even within the same city or district.[1] In the following list the formal name stands first, followed

---

1 The instrument names stem from my fieldwork, and the names and their Japanese writing have, as far as possible, been checked against local publications or through personal communication.

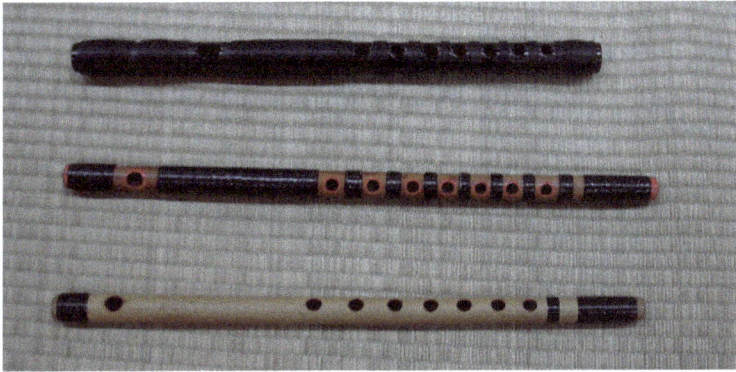

Figure 26 Flutes: *nōkan* or *shagiribue* (top), *kagurabue* or *kusabue* (middle), *shinobue* or *yokobue* (bottom). All have seven fingerholes, which is the most common variant. Nagao: Tamanuki (1 April 2016).

by the local name(s) in Taketoyo whenever it differs from the formal name. Local names used in other places in the peninsula are mentioned at the end of each instrument description.

- *Fue* is the generic term for flute. The different types of flutes are all side-blown but differ in material, length, bore, and location of the fingerholes (Figure 26). This results in different pitches and intervals or scales, but also in different overall sound. Though the different flutes normally have rather specific uses for certain categories of tunes within a repertoire, such patterns are not always followed in actual practice. One reason may be the simple fact that the neighbourhood does not possess a sufficient number of flutes. Another reason may be that one wants to have children in the ensembles, and it is easier for them if they do not need to change between different flutes. The following flute types are common:
  - *Shinobue* is an approximately 40 cm long side-blown flute, also called *utaibue, hosobue, yokobue.*
  - *Nōkan* or *shagiribue* is a side-blown flute of the kind used in *nō* drama. It is shorter than the *shinobue* and has a higher tone. In *dashibayashi music* it is often used for certain tunes of a celebratory nature, as well as for the tune *Shagiri*. In some other places, *chūkan* 'middle size' and *koshagiri* 'small shagiri' are also used.
  - *Kusabue* or *kagurabue* is a side-blown flute used for certain *kagura* pieces. It is also called *roppō, roppō no fue.*
- *Hiradaiko, hangiri*, or *tsukedaiko* is a large, double-skinned, flat drum which is suspended in a wooden frame (Figure 27). It comes

Figure 27 *Hiradaiko* (Ōashi, Taketoyo 1997).

in different sizes and is about 15–30 cm thick. It is played with thick and padded drumsticks, sometimes adorned with red or yellow ribbons. The *hiradaiko* is only struck on one of its skins. It produces a low resonant sound and is the most common type of large drum used in the ensembles. Is also called *ōdaiko, gaku, gakuko, hiratsuridaiko,* or *hirazuridaiko, ōdo, senbedaiko.*

- *Ōdaiko* or *taiko* are terms used for large drums that specifically refer to a large barrel drum with two skins (Figure 28). It comes in different sizes and may be called by different names depending on its size, for example *chūdaiko* for middle size. In some places any of these may be used inside the float, but this is not normally the case with the *Chita type* of float. Is also called *dadaiko, dōnaga.*
- *Shimedaiko, kozuke,* or *kodaiko,* 'laced drum', is a flat drum made in different sizes (Figure 29). It is normally about 35 cm in diameter and 15 cm thick. It has two skins tightened by laces and is placed on a low, leaning stand in front of the player. Thus, only one of the skins is used. It is normally struck with two short and thick drumsticks. There are several kinds of strokes. The sound that is short and moderately low varies from muffled to sharp. Basically the same type of drum as the ones used in *nō* and *kabuki,* this drum is also called *ōdo, hiradaiko.*
- *Ōtsuzumi* or *ōdo* is an hourglass drum with two thick skins of horse-hide, about 23 cm in diameter and 28 cm long (Figure 30). It is held slightly aslant in front of the player, whose left hand

Figure 28 Ōdaiko, the *furedaiko*, 'message drum', of Ōashi (1997).

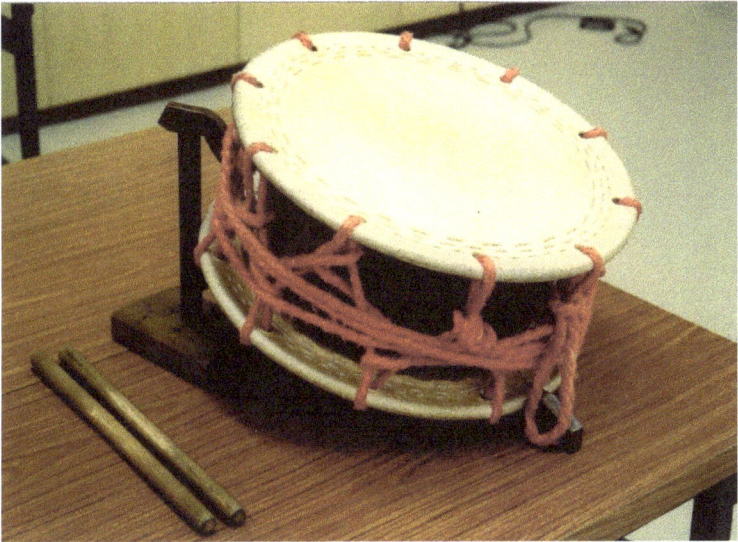

Figure 29 *Shimedaiko* or *kozuke* (Ōashi, Taketoyo 1997).

holds on to the edge of the drumskin. The right hand holds an approximately 40 cm long, thin, and flexible drumstick, often made from bamboo. The leaning skin is struck by a vertical movement with the stick, which thus strikes the skin at an angle. It produces a sharp and distinct hollow tone. In some places, a shorter non-flexible drumstick may be used. Less often it is struck with the bare hand. The same kind of drum is used in *nō* and *kabuki*, but it is then held on the left thigh and struck with the right hand. It is also called *ōkawa, tsuzumi, tsuzumi no dai*.

– *Kotsuzumi* or *tsuzumi* is a smaller hourglass drum with two skins, about 20 cm in diameter and 25 cm long (Figure 30). It is normally held in the left hand by which the laces, called *shirabe*, are twisted, which tightens the skins and varies the pitch. It is held so that the edge of the back skin rests on the right shoulder and the front skin – which is the one being struck – is slightly above the player's chest. It is struck with the right hand's fingers. Less often it is struck with a drumstick. When struck it is often moved slightly forward/downward, so that the drum's skin and the right-hand fingers meet. It may also be held in front of the player's chest and moved forward/downward when struck. The sound is rather high-pitched and moderately sharp, depending on the skill of the player and the tightening of the skin; but it is not as loud as the

Figure 30 *Ōtsuzumi* or *ōdo* with its drumstick (left) and *kotsuzumi* or *tsuzumi* (right) (Ōashi, Taketoyo 1997).

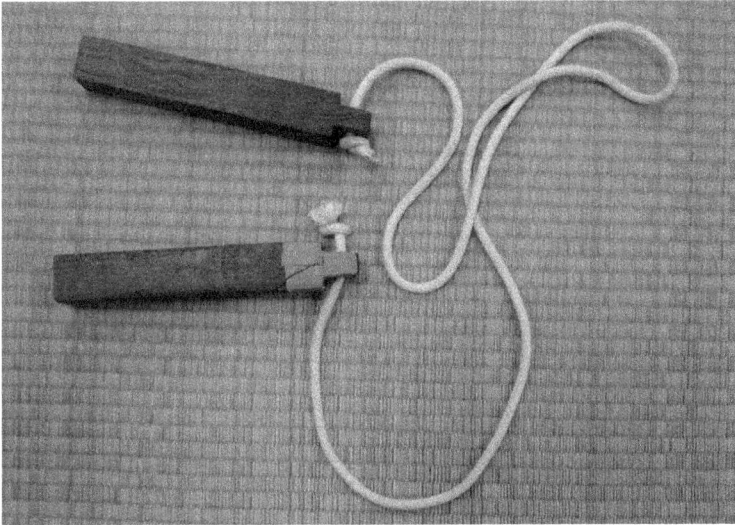

Figure 31 *Hyōshigi* (Tamanuki, Nagao 1 April 2016).

ōtsuzumi. As distinct from *nō* and *kabuki*, where different kinds of strokes are used, that possibility seems not to be utilized in the ensembles. Sometimes the *kotsuzumi* is combined with the *ōtsuzumi*, forming a drum-pair normally struck with a drumstick.

- *Kane* refers to gongs that may differ in size, form, and playing technique. Gongs are rather rare in the ensembles of Chita Peninsula.
- *Chappa* is a pair of small cymbals, about 10–15 cm in diameter. It is seldom used in the *dashibayashi ensembles*. It is also called *surigane, changiri.*
- *Hyōshigi* is a pair of wooden clappers, often tied together with a rope (Figure 31). They are about 40–50 cm long and are struck rapidly together as a signal for starting or stopping the float. They are handled by a man some distance in front of the float, and sometimes behind it; but they are rarely used in *dashibayashi ensembles. Hyōshigi* may also consist of two separate clappers. *Hyōshigi* are used in *geza ongaku*, the offstage music of *kabuki*, to signal the opening and closing of the curtain and other occasions during a play.[2] It has also had folk uses, for example by night watchmen or to call attention to *kamishibai*, 'paper theatre'.

---

2 Brandon 1978, p. 107. *Geza ongaku* is performed by musicians separate from the ordinary *kabuki* ensemble, called *debayashi*, and illustrates the situations of the play in various ways, a kind of 'special-effects department'

The musical instruments are expensive. Some of them are old; some large drums may be from the eighteenth century. Others have been recently bought from an instrument maker, or from shops specializing in festival instruments. How many instruments a neighbourhood owns depends on the age of its festival tradition, whether the instruments have survived fires and wars, and how much money the neighbourhood could raise for repairing or buying new instruments.

The music and its functions

The music used for festivals in the Komukae neighbourhood in Nagao, Taketoyo, is well documented. As early as the beginning of the 1950s, the people engaged in the music had an interest in documenting and preserving their repertoire. One copy of the very first recordings on 78 rpm lacquer records made in 1953 that still exists has deteriorated and can no longer be played.[3] New recordings were made on open reel tapes in April 1959 on the occasion of the wedding of the then Crown Prince Akihito.[4] This tape has later been copied to cassette tapes and CDs. In the period 1987–1990, a complete graphic notation was also made, with tablature for flute and special signs for the drums. That is an efficient way of notating this music, since it does not have the limitations of ordinary notation regarding pitches, rhythm, and measures of irregular beats. It is instructive to the instrumentalists and produces an immediate spontaneous visual understanding of the sound.

(Malm 1963, p. 108). The performers, who cannot be seen by the audience, are seated behind a screen in an area called *kuromisu*, also called *kuromisu ongaku*. That instruments occur in *geza ongaku* does not necessarily mean that they spread from there to the folk traditions. In some cases, they may have come from folk traditions. *Invitation to Kabuki: Guidance for Japanese traditional performing arts Kabuki* 2019; *Kabuki A to Z: the Japan Arts Council's Culture Digital Library* 2018 (Internet sources).

3 *Bishū Nagao Komukaegumi Hōōsha: sōken hyakugojisshūnen kinenshi* [The festival float Hōōsha of the neighbourhood Komukae, Nagao district, Owari province: memorial magazine for the 150th anniversary of its construction] 2013, p. 41.

4 This refers to the Emperor Akihito, who abdicated on 30 April 2019 and received the title Emperor Emeritus.

The notations were made by the leading flute players in Komukae at the time: Aoki Yoshinobu and Sugisaki Shōji.[5]

Combined, the notation and the recordings are, above all, a valuable historical documentation, particularly since Chita Peninsula was hit by the big Ise Bay typhoon, *Isewan taifū*, in September the year that the recordings were made. After the typhoon, many festivals in Chita Peninsula were discontinued, and it took years until they could be resumed. In Nagao, floats were not pulled to Takeo jinja until April 1968, when the centenary of the Meiji restoration was celebrated. At that time, the floats of four neighbourhoods took part: Age, Ichiba, Komukae, and Shitamo. The existing music documentation certainly played a role when Komukae needed to resume the *dashibayashi music*, and it still does – at a rehearsal in 2016, the tune *Yūkagura*, which had not been played since before the typhoon, had been reconstructed and was now performed again.[6]

The notation contains all the different tunes that are performed in the recording. In total, the notated repertoire consists of 40 tunes.[7] They are organized under the following headings:

1. *Matsuribayashi 1*: *Dashi no michiyuki*, approximately 'parading the float' (13 tunes, of which one seems to have been added to the list of contents at a later point).
2. *Matsuribayashi 2* (3 tunes).
3. *Matsuribayashi 3*: *Keigo no bu*, 'respectful section' (14 tunes).

---

5 *Taketoyo-chō Komukae-ku: Matsuribayashi 1–4* [Taketoyo town, Komukae ward: festival music 1–4] 1987–1990. Aoki Yoshinobu and Sugisaki Shōji (eds) [Unpublished reference]. Mr Sugisaki kindly introduced me to this notation and presented me with a copy when I attended a music rehearsal at Komukae in 1992. See also *Bishū Nagao Komukaegumi Hōōsha* 2013, p. 43.

6 *Yūkagura* is a widely spread tune and appears in many different spellings in Japanese. In the one used in Komukae, 'yū' has the meaning 'evening'; *Bishū Nagao Komukaegumi Hōōsha* 2013, p. 34.

7 While I have found 40 notated tunes, *Bishū Nagao Komukaegumi Hōōsha* 2013, p. 42 says that there were 36 tunes handed down in 1959. The tunes can be counted in different ways. In my counting I have included the tunes that belong to puppet performances, one of which is purely vocal. 10 tunes are performed differently in *michiyuki* and *isami* and both have therefore been counted, which adds up to 20f. The recordings from 1959 lack one of the tunes in the notation, namely the one under '*Matsuribayashi 1*' that appears to have been added at some point. The categorization in the notation and the recordings is basically the same, though there are some minor differences.

4. *Isamibayashi no bu*, in literal translation approximately 'courageous music section' (10 different tunes, which are all variants of tunes in *Matsuribayashi 1*).

Although the categorization is not totally consistent, this practice is generally applied in Taketoyo and many other places in Chita Peninsula. *Keigo* means respect or respectful. Written with a different character it has the meaning of protecting or guarding, in this case guarding the deities, *kami*. It is believed that the float tradition in Chita goes back to the guarding of *mikoshi* or palanquins that carried a deity or a person of high rank.[8] There is no simple translation of the word *isami*.[9] Judging from what people believe and from the situations when this kind of music is performed, it seems to have the connotations of encouragement, courage, gratitude, and protection. Some tunes in the repertoire are played when honouring a deity or a person; they are often called *hōnōgaku*, *hōnō* meaning approximately 'offering'. In the following, the categories are illustrated with examples mainly from Tamanuki, which is the most recent neighbourhood in Nagao to have a float. In the mid-1950s, the Tamanuki *dashibayashi* players learnt from masters in Komukae and Shitamo.

Michiyuki music is the part of the repertoire that is played when the float is pulled along. It may also be called *michibiki* or *dōchūgaku* 'parade music'.[10] The music of this category has the important functions of supporting and coordinating the practical work in the different situations that occur when the float is transported (Figure 32). The main part of this music is calm and with a steady beat. When passing up or down a slope, the very slow piece *Shinguruma* is often played. The most dramatic piece is *Shagiri*, which is played when the float is turned, for instance at crossroads or when entering a shrine.

A distinctive characteristic in Nagao and Ōashi is the use of three *kotsuzumi* drums and the rhythm they create in the *michiyuki* music. In *Shagiri*, the rhythm is markedly different, and so is the tempo. *Shagiri* starts slowly, and the tempo gradually increases

8 Tatematsu 1994, p. 27; *Bishū Nagao Komukaegumi Hōōsha* 2013, p. 33.
9 According to *Bishū Nagao Komukaegumi Hōōsha* 2013, p. 42 'the origin and meaning of *isami* is unknown' but in documents it can be interpreted as 'offering of tunes'.
10 *Taketoyo-chō shi: shiryō-hen 2* [Handbook of Taketoyo: reference material 2] 1983, p. 310.

Figure 32 The float *Gyokushinsha* of Tamanuki paraded along a street in Taketoyo. This is when the *michiyuki* repertoire is played by the ensemble in the float (only the top of a *kotsuzumi* drum with its red strings can be seen) (10 April 2004).

until it is fast enough for the float to be pulled around a corner at high speed.

Hōnōgaku (or *hōnōbayashi*), 'offering-music', is performed when the float stands still before starting and when stopping to celebrate a person along the road, or a deity in front of the shrine building. The procedure of celebrating a person, called *iwaikomi*, differs according to the object of the celebration. Thus, for a general celebration the float may be stopped and the lively tune *Ochazuke* played. Traditionally, this is done for members of the steering board of the festival, or for celebrating those who are 42 years of age, which is considered an unlucky age for males; but others can be celebrated in this way, too.[11] For the higher degree of celebration, the float is turned towards the object and three lively tunes

---

11 Hardacre 2016, pp. 477–478, explains that the forty-second year in the life of a man and the thirty-third for women are regarded as particularly inauspicious and requiring ritual to avoid misfortune.

are played: *Ochazuke*, *Komenari*, and *Sagariha*. Those who are celebrated in this way will offer food and drink in return to the people who toil with the float. *Hōnōgaku* is normally performed by the *dashibayashi ensemble* while seated in the float, but the *tsuzumi* drums are not used.

Keigo means 'respectful performing arts'. This category contains music as well as puppet performances made in front of the altar of the Takeo jinja building. The music contains both instrumental pieces and pieces including song, *utabayashi* or 'singing piece'.[12] Floats that are equipped with puppets or perform dances have separate pieces of music for these different performances.

Isami, literally 'courageous music', is sometimes also referred to as *futsū kagura*, 'general *kagura*'.[13] *Isami* is performed on many occasions during the year by an ensemble without *tsuzumi* drums, which exists separately from the festival floats. It is different from the *michiyuki music*, but the two categories do overlap: in Nagao the *isami* repertoire is largely the same as *michiyuki*, though the tunes are performed differently. They are like variants of each other. In *isami*, the flute melody is generally on a higher pitch level and the tunes are faster, with lively drumming by *ōdaiko* and *shimedaiko* only.

In Komukae in Nagao, the number of occasions when *isami* is performed has diminished compared to the late 1920s, but it is still regularly performed on certain calendrical occasions as well as on occasions in the life cycle. Thus, *isami* may be performed on the first of each month at the *kōminkan* or at a local shrine. In certain situations, it is connected to strengthening and encouraging, for instance at the ceremony for men at an inauspicious age – particularly those who are 42, but 25 is also considered unlucky. Households that have a member over 60 years of age, and households that have had an accident, may also be the object of *isami*.[14] Such occasions may occur during the festival days, too.

The most important first day of a month is New Year's Day, when all the six neighbourhoods of Nagao take turns to perform *isami* in front of the Takeo jinja main building. A small group of

---

12 *Bishū Nagao Komukaegumi Hōōsha* 2013, p. 33–44. According to *Taketoyo-chō Komukae-ku: Matsuribayashi 1–4* 1987–1990, the term is '*utaibayashi*'.

13 *Bishū Nagao Komukaegumi Hōōsha* 2013, pp. 21–22.

14 This information is summarized from a description of situations for *isami* in the ward of Komukae in 1927, as well as today's practice, in *Bishū Nagao Komukaegumi Hōōsha* 2013, p. 43.

men from each neighbourhood walk up to the shrine area while playing and then perform *isami* tunes there. When they leave, the next group arrives, and so on. On this occasion the instruments are flutes, *shimedaiko*, and *ōdaiko*. *Isami* is also performed at the shrine when the festival is over. On that occasion, one aim with *isami* is to thank the deity and to ceremonially close the festival. About a month after the festival, too, some neighbourhoods – like Tamanuki – travel to the important shrine Ise jingū on the other side of the Ise Bay to make *isami* there.

In Ōashi, *isami* is performed at Toyoishi jinja in the afternoon of the second and final festival day after the float has been returned to its storing house (Figures 33–34). This is called *orei isami* 'thanking the deity', *isamibayashi* 'courageous music', or *isamidaiko* 'courageous drums'. The tune that is played is called *Kanemaki*. It is believed that this tune came from Atsuta jingū in Nagoya, but that people play it in their own way here. The ensemble consists of 2 *yokobue* (flutes), 1 *ōdaiko* called *dadaiko* (large drum), and 1 *shimedaiko* (called *kodaiko*). The *tsuzumi* drums are not used on this occasion. Only the musicians and three or four other people take part. After playing in front of the shrine building, they walk – still playing – out through the shrine gate, *torii*, across the street to the Hotta inari jinja where the instruments will be stored. The ceremony is not considered to have any ritual connection to the Hotta inari jinja, so this relation is purely practical.[15]

Music situations during the festival

The general term for performances made as offering to deities is *kagura*, a term which encompasses performing arts such as music and dance. Performances by puppets placed on a float, *karakuri-ningyō*, are sometimes accompanied by the *dashibayashi ensemble*, sometimes by other instruments, by song, or recitation – and sometimes the puppets themselves sound drums or rattles or something similar. The Ichiba neighbourhood has a large ensemble performing the music for the dance *Sanbasō*. The repertoire thus differs from one neighbourhood to another, depending on whether they have dances or puppets or even what kind of puppets they have.

---

15 Observed 23 July 1995 and 21 July 2002. In Ōashi there is an old lion's head and its 'house', *yakata*, once used for *orei isami* (*Taketoyo-chō shi: shiryō-hen 2* 1983, p. 287). This is similar to Fuki, as mentioned in the previous chapter.

Figure 33 *Orei isami* at Toyoishi jinja, Ōashi. The *ōdaiko* is placed in front of the shrine and beside it the *shimedaiko*. Behind them there are two flute players (23 July 1995). (● **2a**)

Figure 34 The *isamidaiko* players returning from Toyoishi jinja, Ōashi, still playing (23 July 1995).

Table 1, 'Music at different points of the festival', is a translation from the Japanese and marks the music used at the most
important parts of the float parade, being based on the Komukae
tape-recording from April 1959.[16] The comments were made by
Mr Iida Katsuji, who was among the recording members, as were
Mr Nakagawa Kinroku and others. (• 1c)

Table 1 Music at different points of the festival in 1959.

Ochazuke	When leaving the *sayagura* ['garage']	*Ochazukebayashi* means prelude to *kagura* offering. It is played to purify from evil and to make people willing to do something.
Michiyuki	When parading *Shinguruma* *Komenari* *Yaguruma kuzushi* *Shinpo* etc.	*Shingurumabayashi* is a music that empowers the steep up- and downhill pulling. Contributing an element of elegance to the steering of the float, it is the best and most original piece in our district [Komukae] to be presented in front of the shrine building. *Shingurumabayashi* is played both up- and downhill along the slope behind Takeo jinja.
Ochazuke, Oharusa, Komenari, Tōka ebisu, etc.	For *hōnō* ['respectful offering']	
Shagiri	When leaving the shrine	
Michiyuki	On the way back [to the *sayagura*] *Shinguruma* *Komenari* *Yaguruma kuzushi* etc.	
Ochazuke	When entering the *sayagura*	When the float is to be placed in the *sayagura*, it is pulled around in front of it while *Ochazuke* is played loudly as a culmination of the festival.

Source: Saitō and Saitō 2008: 2–7.

16 The Japanese-language original is printed in Saitō and Saitō 2008, pp. 2–7.

Each of the six neighbourhoods in Nagao has its version of *Shagiri*, which is generally played when the floats are turned at a road crossing. The Age and Ichiba neighbourhoods also use *Shagiri* while parading on a straight street, usually in combination with a tempo change from walking speed to running. Being equipped with two *shimedaiko*, the drumming of the Age float is quite rich.

Shagiri is always played on the Saturday evening during the festival, when the six floats parade from Takeo jinja and one by one pass a crossing before assembling in an open space by the JR Station with their lanterns lighted. On the Sunday, the festival day, the players again pull the floats uphill on the sloping road to the shrine playing *Shinguruma*. Before entering the shrine area, one by one, each float plays the slow beginning of *Shagiri* and then enters at a high speed. Once a float is placed in its designated area facing the shrine building, they play *Ochazuke*.

The *michiyuki* repertoire that is used when the floats are paraded is basically the same for all the six neighbourhoods, even though the versions differ to some degree and tunes may occasionally have different names in the respective neighbourhoods. Other music that is performed during the festival, for instance music that belongs to puppet or dance performances, is unique to the respective neighbourhood.

The musical categories are basically the same in all of the Chita Peninsula, although there are many variations regarding names and usage. In each location, too, there are traditional practices for the choice of tunes that are to be played, as well as for their linkage with certain stages during the parading of the floats.

Learning and practising

The ensembles are ideally made up of young people – traditionally boys only, but recently girls may join as well, initially only for playing the flutes but later also for drums. New children are recruited every year, and they practise in advance, usually in the neighbourhood community house, *kōminkan*. These organized rehearsals are important for involving the young in the festival music, serving to minimize the effects of young people moving away to major cities. Generally, this is not a great problem in the Chita Peninsula, but it is necessary to work actively for recruitment to the festivals. In some places care has been taken to involve girls in this early training, while other communities consider this as being against tradition. The training is basically built on oral learning. It exposes children and teenagers to traditional rhythms and musical scales as well as to the function, meaning, aesthetics, and oral transmission of a traditional music style.

According to Linda Fujie, who studied festival ensembles in Tokyo, oral learning through imitation has the advantage of ensuring that pupils become used to the whole of the musical style by being exposed to it for a long time. On the other hand, learning by pedagogic means, such as vocalizing, tablature, graphs, notation, and even recordings, has the advantage of making sure that a repertoire is learnt faster. She found that in Tokyo, the development was towards the use of various pedagogical tools.[17] A similar process is going on in the Chita Peninsula, but the traditional oral learning by imitation continues to have a strong emphasis.

Nagao, Taketoyo

The youths are seated on the floor practising various musical instruments. The youngest children, of about six to eight years of age, are learning the *kotsuzumi* held by the shoulder. Those who are a little older play the larger *ōtsuzumi*, which is held aslant on the floor in front of the player. Some in their upper teens work at the *shime-daiko*, or at the suspended *hiradaiko* with red and yellow ribbons tied to the drumsticks. The oldest youths play the flutes.[18]

Each group of instrumentalists is sitting together, and each group has one or more adult leaders on its specific instrument. All groups practise the same piece simultaneously, thus forming a large ensemble. Leaders and learners are normally facing one another as they play together, the beginners imitating the leaders. When the number of instruments is insufficient, they take turns in playing. Those who have no instrument beat the rhythms in the air or do the fingering without flutes. Some do not blow their flutes but just hold them and try to copy the fingering. Similarly, both flutes and drums can be practised without an instrument; this is also a way for beginners to memorize the movements.

In this manner the children learn the repertoire by watching and imitating the leaders. Most of them have started with the

---

17 Fujie 1986b.
18 These observations were made at rehearsals in the community halls of Shitamo and Komukae in 1992, of Tamanuki and Komukae in 2016, and of Age in 2018.

Figure 35 Practising in Tamanuki. Left: flutes; centre: *ōtsuzumi*; right: *kotsuzumi*; back centre: *hiradaiko* and *shimedaiko* (31 March 2016).

kotsuzumi, and when they are able to start playing the flute, they have learnt each of the different drums during previous years. The flute is considered the most demanding instrument, since it leads the ensemble by signalling the beginning and end of tunes and often also signals tempo changes.

More than twenty years after my first visit to the training sessions, nothing had changed in principle, but some new tunes had been added. The most noticeable difference was that of Tamanuki. This neighbourhood had only resumed participation in the *Nagao no harumatsuri* in 1981, and at the outset they had depended on teachers from Komukae. Now they had built up quite a crew of players, with their own leaders and a stable number of participants for rehearsals and for taking part in the ensemble (Figure 35).

Ōashi, Taketoyo

There is a similar practice in Ōashi. An association was formed for the organization of the festival music in the mid-1970s, one of its aims being to encourage children and youths take an interest in the music of *Shintō*.[19] The children themselves decide whether they want to join the ensemble. Recruited from the years 3–6 in primary school, those who want to continue the activity while they are growing up can do so. The children start by playing the *kotsuzumi* drum, whereupon they move on to *ōtsuzumi*, *shimedaiko*, and *hiradaiko*. When they are able to start playing the flute, they already know all the drum rhythms. Some two or three children out of ten continue all this way.

The work on developing the organization appears to have borne fruit since I first observed the *Ōashi Jaguruma matsuri* in 1994. At that time there were few young people who joined the festival, the percentage of older people in the ensemble being quite high. By 2001, though, the number of youths who attended was considerably higher, and the ensembles consisted mainly of young boys and youths. It seems as if a functioning continuity between the age groups had been achieved.

There are rehearsals every Sunday evening during May and June and every day in July, up to a mid-July weekend when the festival takes place. In 1997, ensembles were practising in the community house beside a new *sayagura* which had been built in 1993.[20] There were some 30 children and about 10 adults who functioned as teachers. About 20 young boys were learning the *kotsuzumi*, three at a time could play the instrument, while the others beat the rhythms clapping their hands (Figures 36–40).

Learning in other places

The learning situations are organized in similar ways in most places, but they vary according to practical circumstances such as the size and strength of the festival organization and the number of children and youths available.[21] In Kitagumi in Kōwa, there were four groups of boys and girls learning to play the flute.[22]

---

19 *Kagura hozonkai*, Kagura preservation association, according to oral information (*kagura* '*Shintō* music', *hozon* 'preserve'). Formally *Ōashi kagura hozonkai*, cf. *Kōhō Taketoyo* [Public relations brochure Taketoyo] 2019.
20 This was Sunday 14 July 1997.
21 This passage is built on visits to training sessions in Higashibata (Utsumi) 2002; Hon-Itayamagumi (Itayama, Handa) 2003; Ichiba (Tokoname) 2002; Kitagumi (Kōwa) 2002; Nishinokuchi (Tokoname) 2003; Uemura (Futto) 2002.
22 This was Monday 18 March 2002.

Figure 36 Rehearsing in Ōashi *kōminkan*. To the right in front are the flutes, and behind them first the *shimedaiko* and then the *hiradaiko* (partly hidden by a player standing up); to the left of them (not visible) are the *ōtsuzumi* and to the far left children with *kotsuzumi* (14 July 1997).

Figure 37 The flute section rehearsing in Ōashi.

Figure 38 Two *shimedaiko* (front left) and *hiradaiko* (right). In the background (left), the skins of a *kotsuzumi* are being stretched. Ōashi (14 July 1997).

Figure 39 Two *hiradaiko* (left) and two *shimedaiko* (right). The boy to the far left is learning the *hiradaiko* by copying the older boy on his right. They are seated so that the learner can watch the movements of the leader. Ōashi (14 July 1997).

Figure 40 In the foreground two boys with *kotsuzumi* drums while other boys clap the rhythm with their hands. Centre right the *ōtsuzumi*, held aslant leaning on a chair. Ōashi (14 July 1997).

The teachers were comparatively young and had themselves not learnt the flute until after they finished school. For about ten years, children had been recruited through the school, and there was now a steady participation of younger children. A young university student demonstrated how to teach the flute by ear: he sat in front of the children with his back towards them, so that they could learn by watching his fingering from behind without having to mirror his finger movements. This young teacher had played the flute since he was in school and now played it once a month in *Shintō* rituals. He liked pop music but could appreciate the traditional style as well. The children practised once a week starting in the beginning of March, about one month before the festival. The aim was to integrate as many young children of both sexes as possible, and the atmosphere was informal and relaxed.

In Ichiba in Tokoname, the youngest children started practising at 8 p.m.[23] The flute players sat in two parallel rows, the beginners facing the youths whom they were supposed to follow. There were two to three children per leader. They practised tempo changes, in particular, so that they would be well prepared for that at the festival. There were two *hiradaiko*, the largest of which was played by a youth while the children took turns playing the smaller one that was placed slightly behind it, so that the children could see and follow their leader. The *shimedaiko* players were of various ages and seated in a row. After 45 minutes the youngest children stopped their practising, and now the youths assumed the role of learners, and the oldest that of teachers. The best players would eventually learn all instruments.

Learning is predominantly by ear through imitation. In some places vocalizing, *shōga* or *kuchishōga*, is used for tone-names and drum patterns.[24] This was the case in Ichiba in Tokoname and Hon-Itayamagumi in Itayama, Handa, while a notation in the form of a graph and tablature is used by Komukae in Nagao (see further Chapter 9).

---

23 27 March 2002.
24 For examples of *kuchishōga*, see Hayakawa 2003b, p. 14.

5
Ensembles in the Chita Peninsula

Musical ensembles consisting of combinations of drums and flutes, gongs, and/or scrapers have been used for performances connected with religious rituals and festivals involving the offering of music to the *kami* ever since the Heian period, around the year AD 1000, and probably earlier than that.[1] In Chita Peninsula, the core of the *dashibayashi ensembles* is similar to the ensemble of transverse flutes, two types of hourglass-shaped drums, and a flat laced drum used in *nō* drama and *kabuki*.[2] The three-stringed lute *shamisen* that is used in *kabuki* is, however, not generally used in the Chita Peninsula.

Ensemble types

The composition of musical instruments in *dashibayashi ensembles* in the Chita Peninsula differs from place to place, but they are quite stable in each location. Variations may occur from year to year depending on the number of people available for the ensemble, and in some cases also depending on their age and which instruments they are able to play. This chapter compares the ensembles in the Chita Peninsula, the purpose being to define the main types of ensembles and map their geographical distribution.

There is also variety with regard to how ensemble members and their instruments are placed inside the float. Some musicians may sit on its rear edge, being visible from the outside. To a

---

1 Groemer 2002, pp. 599–606.
2 The song and dance drama *nō* contains *nō* plays and shorter comic plays called *kyōgen*. Both categories are covered by the term *nōgaku*, but for practical reasons I will use the commonly accepted English '*nō* drama' or '*nō* theatre' except when necessary to include *kyōgen*.

certain extent the placement depends on the size and construction of the float; but since that is fairly stable in each location, it also represents local tradition and may indicate possible historical connections. The following comparative study deals with instrumentation and placement of ensemble players, with a special focus on the hourglass drums and on instrumentalists seated on the rear edge of the float (for locations, see Maps 2 and 3).

Drums and flutes ensemble

The type of ensemble used in most parts of the city of Handa, which has been a local centre for festivals in Chita for a long time, is widespread in the peninsula. It consists of one *hiradaiko*, one *shimedaiko*, and three or more flutes. The *hiradaiko* is placed crosswise farthest to the front of the float and the *shimedaiko* is placed on the floor behind it, closer to the rear of the float (Figure 41). The *shimedaiko* player normally faces sideways; but in the neighbourhoods of Nishiyama in Okkawa (Handa) and Daigone in Agui, the *shimedaiko* player is seated in the centre of the float facing backwards. Closer to the rear are the flute players,

Figure 41 *Hiradaiko* and *shimedaiko* inside the float *Yokosha yamaguruma* of Yokomatsu in Agui just north of Handa (26 April 2015).

Figure 42 The float *Nansha* of Minamigumi in Narawa, Handa. Two flute players facing each other. The *hiradaiko* is in the front of the float. The *shimedaiko* is hardly visible (10 April 2016).

and usually two or three of them are seated on the rear edge – it might be two sitting sidewise or three facing backwards (Figure 42). Sometimes during the festival, one or two flute players may also sit on the shafts in the back of the float.

The four districts of Agui, just north of Handa, have the same type of ensemble. In Yokomatsu, however, one person plays both the *ōdaiko* and the *shimedaiko*, which is characteristic of the so-called *Miyaryū style*.

This is also the standard ensemble in Koba, Taya, and Yata in Tokoname, as well as in Ōta in Tōkai city to the north. In the south it occurs in Okuda, Noma, and Kitagata (all in Mihama), as well as in Yamami (Minamichita), where the *hiradaiko* is suspended at an angle in the front left corner of the float. In Morozaki on the southernmost tip of the peninsula, there are five floats with the *hiradaiko* suspended at an angle or in the front part of the float parallel to one side.

The basic *drums and flutes ensemble* with its variations may be summarized as shown in Table 2.

The neighbourhood called Itayama, located in the far west of Handa, close to Tokoname city, has variations of this pattern. The four floats in Itayama all share the common trait that the

Table 2 Basic *drums and flutes ensemble*.

Instrument	Number	Comment
Fue	3 or more	*Shinobue*, *nōkan* etc. are used
Hiradaiko	1	*Ōdaiko* may be used. Occasionally 2 *ōdaiko*
Shimedaiko	1 or more	

hiradaiko – which is also called *ōdo* – is placed crosswise on an upper level (Figure 43). There are two or three *shimedaiko*, called *kodaiko*. In Hiyakugumi, three *shimedaiko* players sit beside one another along the left side of the float facing towards the left, while the three remaining districts have the three *shimedaiko* players sitting beside one another close to the front of the float and facing backwards. Two or three flute players are seated in the far back facing backwards, and more are seated inside the float. Similarly, the float of the Yamakata district in Tokoname has a *drums and flutes ensemble* with the large drum placed on an upper level.

Occasionally, there will be an *ōdaiko* – a barrel-shaped large drum – instead of the *hiradaiko*. This is the case in Nakagumi and

Figure 43 The float *Asahiguruma* of Koitagumi in Itayama (Handa) has three *shimedaiko* beside one another. The *hiradaiko* is placed on a 'bridge' which creates an upper level. The arrow shows the lower edge of the drumskin that can be seen at the top of the photograph (15 April 2017).

Minamigumi in Yokone, Ōbu, in northeastern Chita. An *ōdaiko* is placed in a stand that fixes one of its skins over the rear end of the float, so that the drum is protruding in the back. The player is seated inside the float. Here the flute players stand upright inside the float.

In Ogura in the northwest, the float also has an *ōdaiko* protruding over the rear end. A smaller *ōdaiko* is placed a little farther into the float. The flute players are seated still farther in, close to the front. In Kitakasuya, located north of Ogura, the large *ōdaiko* is also placed on a stand in the back, but a little farther into the float so that the person playing it can be seated between the drum and the rear edge. Still another variant exists in the south in Ōi, Minamichita, where the *hiradaiko* is suspended in the rear of the float and is struck from the outside by a player walking behind it, by a player sitting inside the float, or by both at the same time.[3] North of Ōi, the ensemble of Kitagumi in Kōwa has a small gong called *surigane* and wooden clappers, called *hyōshigi*, to set the tempo. They use an *ōdaiko*, a barrel drum.

Drums, flutes, and kotsuzumi ensemble

Some ensembles also contain one or more *kotsuzumi*, which are sometimes used for specific musical pieces only, particularly the *michiyuki music* played when the float is pulled along. In some places the *kotsuzumi* seems to be optional, which means that if there is no player available one will do without it. Sometimes this has to do with the recruitment and availability of young girls or boys who can learn to play the *kotsuzumi*.

Table 3 The *drums, flutes, and kotsuzumi ensemble.*

Instrument	Number	Comment
Fue	3 or more	*Shinobue, nōkan* etc. are used
Hiradaiko	1	*Ōdaiko* may be used
Shimedaiko	1 or more	
Kotsuzumi	1–3	

---

3 I did not have the opportunity to visit Ōi where there is a summer festival in July with one float. The information here has been gathered from *Ōi natsumatsuri: Minamichita-chō* ... [Ōi summer festival, Minamichita town ...] 1–3 (Internet reference).

Figure 44 *Honmachigumi dashi* in Yokosuka, Tōkai, has two *kotsuzumi* players in the back. One of the flute players can be seen between them a little farther into the float (26 September 2015).

In Nishinokuchi in the northwest, the *kotsuzumi* and flute players may be seated in the rear of the float.[4] The exact number of players may vary. Farther north in Yokosuka, Tōkai, two *kotsuzumi* is a common variant. The two players may either sit facing each other in the rear or be seated on the very rear edge of the float facing backwards (Figure 44).

In Nakagumi, Okada (Chita city), the *hiradaiko* is placed crosswise on the right side of the front of the float. It is suspended in a frame standing on the middle shelf on which the drummer is also seated (Figure 45). The flute players are seated inside and in the back. On an upper level, there were two *kotsuzumi* and a three-stringed lute called *shamisen*.[5]

In Higashibata, Utsumi, in the southwest of the peninsula, there are two flutes in the rear, the players being seated so that they face

---

4 For instruments and tunes in Nishinokuchi, see Fukaya 1996.

5 These instruments could not be heard during the *michiyuki* parade on 16 April 2017 and were perhaps only used for accompaniment to a puppet performance.

Figure 45 The float *Ameguruma* of Nakagumi in Okada, with
the *hiradaiko* placed to the right above the middle level. Below it
is a *shimedaiko*. The ceiling seen in the picture is also the floor of
the third level (16 April 2017).

each other. Inside the float, there are two *shimedaiko* players who
face each other as well. The *hiradaiko* is suspended diagonally
front right. The ambition was to have two *kotsuzumi* in a complete
ensemble.

In some places, the *kotsuzumi* are not always used owing to a lack
of players. In 2002 there were *kotsuzumi* players in the rehearsals
in Higashibata, Utsumi, but they were not seen in the *michiyuki* in
2017. Conversely, the two floats in Nishinokuchi that had loosely
organized *kotsuzumi* in 2003 had a stable ensemble with two
kotsuzumi each in 2016, and the float *Saihōsha* had three in 2017
when joining the festival in Ōno.[6] Fluctuations like these may occur
during the course of one festival and even depend on which tune is
played, but they also vary over a longer period of time depending
on the recruitment and training of players.

---

6 In 2017 the three floats and a boat-float of Ōno joined the two floats of
Nishinokuchi in the spring festival in Ōno. This happens every two years.
Saihōsha also had three *kotsuzumi* in a *michiyuki* tune at a festival music
concert in Tokoname in 2002.

Drums, flutes, and ōtsuzumi ensemble

Another common type of ensemble in the Chita Peninsula is identical to the basic *drums and flutes ensemble* with the addition of the *ōtsuzumi*.

The *drums, flutes, and ōtsuzumi ensemble* is the dominating one in the six floats of Tokoname town (the old town area of Tokoname city). The *hiradaiko*, *shimedaiko*, and flutes are generally placed as in the *drums and flutes ensemble*. There are two and sometimes three *shimedaiko*. In some cases, the flute players will sit in the back and the *ōtsuzumi* will be just inside the float. In other cases, the *ōtsuzumi* will be in the centre of the rear edge with one flute player on either side (Figure 46). Flute players sometimes sit on the shafts

Table 4 The *drums, flutes, and ōtsuzumi ensemble.*

Instrument	Number	Comment
Fue	3 or more	*Shinobue*, *nōkan* etc. are used
Hiradaiko	1	*Ōdaiko* may be used
Shimedaiko	1 or more	
Ōtsuzumi	1	

Figure 46 The float *Horakusha* of Hōji in Tokoname, with *ōtsuzumi* in the back together with flutes (8 April 2017).

in the back and the *ōtsuzumi* player will sit there as well, particularly when approaching the shrine at the climax of the festival.

The ensemble of Okujō in Ōtani, just south of Tokoname City, is of the same kind, with the *ōtsuzumi* placed on the upper level. Satogumi in Okada in the northwest uses *ōtsuzumi* for *michiyuki music*; on one occasion the *ōtsuzumi* player walked behind the float.

Variants include Kitajō in Tokoname, which – like Itayama in Handa – has the *hiradaiko* on the upper level, in this case on a 'bridge' across the middle of the float. Ichiba in Tokoname also has a gong, *kane*, suspended in a hand-held frame and struck on the inside of the rim by a metal stick with a small ball on the end.[7]

Drums, flutes, and two tsuzumi ensemble

A *drums, flutes, and two tsuzumi ensemble* is characterized by the simultaneous use of *kotsuzumi* and *ōtsuzumi* (Table 5). This is the standard ensemble in Nagao and Ōashi, Taketoyo. It occurs in the neighbourhoods Fuki, Fuki-Ichiba, and Higashi-Ōdaka, and in Futto a little bit to the south of there. This kind of ensemble may consist of many people. In Nagao, for instance, there may be one *hiradaiko*, one to two *shimedaiko*, three (or more) flutes, one *ōtsuzumi* and three *kotsuzumi*, in total nine to ten persons plus possible additional flutes. In comparison, most places in Handa have one *hiradaiko*, one *shimedaiko*, three (or more) flutes, in total five persons plus possible additional flutes. To accommodate that many musicians in the *Chita-type* float calls for practical solutions, which result in quite varied practices for placement inside the float.

In some places, two *tsuzumi* drums – *ōtsuzumi* and *kotsuzumi* – are held together by one player and thus become one instrument. This is the case in the southern-central part of the peninsula in Sakai and Kaminoma. In Kosugaya, too, the two drums are played by one person for some tunes, and in the children ensemble they are

---

7 Formerly a deer horn attached to a wooden stick was used, which provided a suitable sound and some degree of flexibility; but the horn would quickly become worn out. Not many know how to play it nowadays, and therefore the manner of playing has been simplified. The gong could not be heard in 2017, though in a festival-music concert in Tokoname in 2002 it was used in the tune *Tokiwashabayashi* (named after their float), and in rehearsals in 2002 it was used for several tunes.

Table 5 The *drums, flutes and two tsuzumi ensemble*.

Instrument	Number	Comment
Fue	3 or more	*Shinobue*, *nōkan* etc. are used
Hiradaiko	1	*Ōdaiko* may be used
Shimedaiko	1 or more	
Ōtsuzumi	1	
Kotsuzumi	1–3	Occasionally more than 3 *kotsuzumi*

Figure 47 It is common for a *kodomobayashi*, 'children ensemble',
to perform at festivals. This picture shows the *drums, flutes, and two
tsuzumi ensemble* of Kosugaya. The *ōtsuzumi* and *kotsuzumi* are made
into pairs played by one player with a drumstick (4 April 2010).

tied together (Figure 47). As in Nagao, the *ōtsuzumi* is called *ōdo*
and the *kotsuzumi* is called *tsuzumi*.

General principles of the placement inside the float

The placement of the largest drum – in most cases a suspended flat
drum, *hiradaiko* – is fixed once the drum is fastened in the float. It
may be suspended crosswise in the front part of the float so that

the skins are at straight angles with the direction of the movement, but it may also be suspended diagonally in one of the front corners. Other variants are lengthwise with the skins parallel to one of the sides of the float, either close to its front, in the middle, or close to its rear. In some cases, it is placed in the very back of the float, either crosswise or diagonally in one of the back corners.

Since the placement of the *hiradaiko* is fixed, it affects the placement of the other instruments. The second largest drum is normally the *shimedaiko*, and it is usually placed close to the *hiradaiko*, either just behind, beside, or in front of it. If the *hiradaiko* is placed along one of the sides, the *shimedaiko* may be opposite to it by the other side. In the case where there is more than one *shimedaiko* – two or three are not unusual – the players are either seated opposite or beside each other.

Most other instruments are more flexible when it comes to placing. These are the flutes, the *ōtsuzumi* and *kotsuzumi* drums and other smaller instruments, such as gongs and cymbals, when they are present. Normally the players will either be seated inside the float or on the rear edge, in the latter case either opposite each other or facing backwards.

In most cases, the seating is fairly consistent within the same neighbourhood and within the same town; but it may vary from time to time as far as the more flexible instruments are concerned.[8] Stability may be said to be the rule rather than the exception. The seating of the players is thus not based on practical reasons alone but also on tradition, which says something about historical relationships.

A crucial place in the float is the rear, where the instruments may be seen and heard from the outside (Figures 48–49). It is quite clear that the most common seating in the rear of the float are flutes, or flutes in combination with *ōtsuzumi* or *kotsuzumi*. All six floats in Nagao and the one in Ōashi have three *kotsuzumi* in the back, and this is a norm that does not change (Figure 50).

---

8 The seating of musicians and placement of instruments inside floats are seldom commented on in the literature. An exception is Alaszewska 2012, p. 205, where a practical solution concerning the Chichibu night festival is described.

Figure 48 In the float *Honwakasha* of Fuki in Taketoyo, there is one flute player and two *ōtsuzumi* players in the very back of the float facing backwards. One of the *ōtsuzumi* players would change to *kotsuzumi* for certain tunes (7 April 2019).

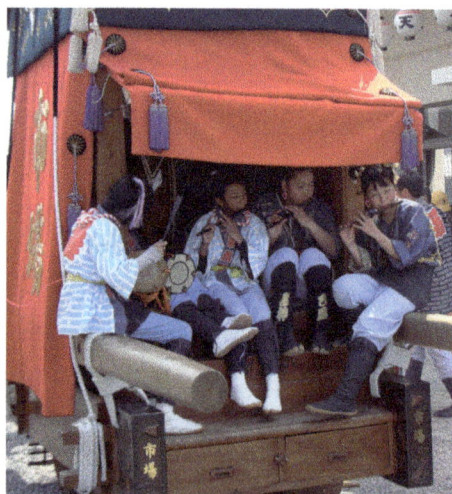

Figure 49 In the float *Tennōmaru* of Fuki-Ichiba in Fuki, Taketoyo, an *ōtsuzumi* player and a flutist are seated on the shafts. A *kotsuzumi* and two flutes are seated in the rear (6 April 2019).

Figure 50 The float *Gyokushinsha* of Tamanuki in Nagao with three *kotsuzumi* players in the back. Behind them, two flute players and the *hiradaiko* can be seen. The *ōtsuzumi* will be on the middle level and the *shimedaiko* below it (8 April 2016).

The geographical distribution of the ensemble types

When this information is gathered and mapped geographically, a distinct pattern emerges (Map 3). Obviously, the *drums and flutes ensemble* is a basic and dominant variety, particularly consistent in Handa and Agui but present in all of Chita Peninsula. In the southern-central part, there is a clear dominance of the *drums, flutes, and two tsuzumi ensemble*, with both kinds of *tsuzumi* drums in combination. The *drums, flutes, and ōtsuzumi ensemble* is concentrated in the same area, but it also appears in the northwest (though with regard to some places, it is uncertain whether the *kotsuzumi* is in fact still in use).

The placement of the musicians or instruments in the float can be used for tracing more local differences. Particularly prominent are the variants of seating on the back edge of the floats, where two models stand out: that of all flutes, and that of *tsuzumi* drums with or without flutes (Appendix 1: Tables 7–8). The latter, of course, only occurs in the ensembles that have *tsuzumi* drums, and Nagao and Ōashi in Taketoyo are the only ensembles that always have three *kotsuzumi* drums in the back.

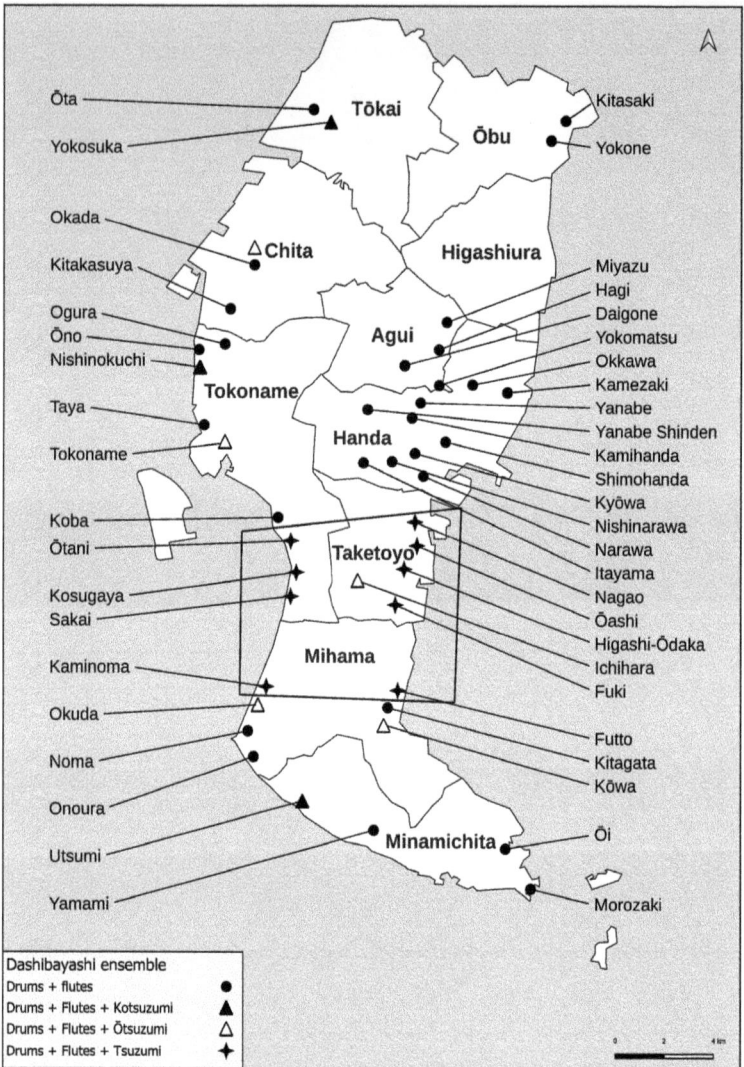

Map 3 The ensemble types in the Chita Peninsula. With the exceptions of Onoura and Ōi, all this information is based on observations during fieldwork. Onoura's float is boat-shaped. According to *Mihama dashimatsuri* [Mihama float-festival] (AV reference), it took part in the city float-festival in 2015, but with no musicians or instruments. *Aichi dashi zukan* [Picture-book of the festival floats in Aichi] (Internet reference) informs that it is not in use at present. The rhomboid-shaped area represents the area that will be referred to as the southern-central part of the peninsula. Courtesy of Jakob Cederblad.

6
Ensembles in Nagoya and Owari

The smaller hourglass drum, the *kotsuzumi*, is quite common in *dashibayashi ensembles* in Nagoya and the rest of Owari. It is a widely held view that the *dashibayashi music* of Chita Peninsula spread there from Nagoya. For this reason, the present comparison will be widened to include a selection of festivals in Nagoya and the remainder of Owari. The comparison will take the ensemble types in Chita Peninsula as the starting point, with a particular focus on the presence and placement of the *kotsuzumi* and *ōtsuzumi* drums.

Ensembles in Nagoya

In present-day Nagoya, there are several festivals that include floats. Even though about 20 floats are reported to have been destroyed, mainly in the Second World War, there are still at least 35 that take part in several festivals in different parts of the city. The *Nagoya matsuri* that occurs annually in October is a modern city float-festival that was arranged for the first time in 1955. It is a big event with many activities, including a parade. In recent years, the nine floats of Dekimachi (three), Tsutsui-chō (two), Wakamiya Hachiman Shrine (one), and Old Hiroi Village, the current Nagoya Station Area in Nakamura-ku (three), have been included in the Nagoya festival (for locations in Nagoya, see map 4).[1]

The *drums and flutes ensemble*

Some areas in Nagoya, like Ushidate in Nakagawa-ku in the western part of the city, use the *drums and flutes ensemble*. The *Ushidate Tennōsai* takes place in July. In 1997 it was raining when

---

1 See Tajima 1983 concerning the floats in Wakamiya Hachiman Shrine.

the summer festival of Ushidate took place, and the float was protected by a plastic canvas with an opening only for a puppet, so that it could be used and seen. After the puppet performance, the float was only pulled to just outside the shrine area and back again. Therefore, the *hayashi* musicians were not seated inside the float but on a stage nearby with a roof (Figure 51). Accompanying the puppet show from there, they also played *michiyuki music* and *kagura* pieces. The ensemble consisted of three flute players and an *ōdaiko* that was played together with one *shimedaiko* by one player, typical of the *Miyaryū style* or more precisely of the *Owaridaiko style*, in which the drummer twirls one of the two drumsticks in the air when there is no stroke for that hand. The audience mainly consisted of middle-aged or older people and young children. It was felt to be important that the youngest children should grow up with the festival.

With minor variations regarding seating, and most often with the flute players seated in the back of the float, the same type of ensemble is used in Hira, Honji, Toda, and Tsutsui. A similar arrangement is found in three of the four floats in Narumi Urakata, with one exception in which the two drums are played in the *Miyaryū style* by one person who is seated to the left and facing right, while the flute players are farther inside the float (Figure 52).

Figure 51 The ensemble of Ushidate in Nakagawa-ku. The drummer to the right handles both the *shimedaiko* and the *ōdaiko* (27 July 1997).

Figure 52 The float *Hanai* of Narumi Urakata, Midori-ku, showing one
player handling a *hiradaiko* and a *shimedaiko* (9 October 2016).

One float has a small gong suspended from the left vertical pole in
the rear of the float. It is played by a person walking behind it.

The *drums, flutes, and kotsuzumi ensemble*

Several districts in Nagoya use *kotsuzumi* drums in their ensembles.
The old Tōkaidō road that connected Edo with Kyoto passed
through Narumi in Midori-ku, in the eastern part of Nagoya,
which used to be an important station along the road, with many
inns. Around the year 1700, their festival was split into two, which
are now related to two different shrines and take place on succes-
sive weeks in October. In Narumi Urakata, four floats gather at
Narumi jinja. In one of them (*Kinomoto*), one flute player and one
kotsuzumi player are seated in the back, partly facing each other
and partly facing backwards.[2]

Another festival in Narumi Omotekata has five floats, four of
which are of the *hayashi yatai type* that is common in Mikawa
along the old Tōkaidō road.[3] This is a rectangular wagon with one

---

2 This was the case in 2015. In 2016 I did not see a *kotsuzumi* player, but
there were two flute players in the back facing each other.
3 Den 2017, p. 56.

floor and wheels of wood, iron, or rubber. It is covered by a roof, curved like that of a shrine, and there is a kind of balcony along the open sides which are partly covered by *shōji*, or sliding doors. This construction leaves the ensemble and its instruments visible from the outside. Generally, there are two *shimedaiko* players placed beside each other in the front, facing forwards, while the *hiradaiko* is suspended behind them on the right or left side (Figure 53). All these floats have one, two, or three *kotsuzumi* in the back; but in some cases this varies from year to year, or even from time to time during the festival. The musicians seated on the rear edge can be either two flutes, two flutes and one *kotsuzumi*, two *kotsuzumi*, or – in the float *Sakumachi* – three *kotsuzumi* (Figure 54). The remaining float (*Karakosha*) was bought from Onoura in Mihama, Chita Peninsula, and was rebuilt to become a *Nagoya type*. At least on one occasion, there was a *kotsuzumi* and a flute player seated in the back.

Not far from here lies Arimatsu, Midori-ku, which is also located along the old Tōkaidō road. Arimatsu has three *Nagoya-type*

Figure 53 The float *Sakumachi* of Narumi Omotekata, Midori-ku, with two *shimedaiko* players in the front and the *hiradaiko* suspended behind them (18 October 2015).

Figure 54 Three *kotsuzumi* players in the back of Narumi Omotekata's
float *Sakumachi* (18 October 2015).

floats, with the *hiradaiko* suspended in front along one of the
sides. Flutes and three *shimedaiko* are inside. The float *Hoteisha*
had four *kotsuzumi* players in the rear, three on folded legs facing
backwards, and one, seated further inside, facing sideways. The
remaining two floats had two to three *kotsuzumi* players seated in
the back, partly face to face and partly facing backwards.[4]

The three floats of Dekimachi in Higashi-ku north of the
castle area participate in *Nagoya matsuri* with *kotzuzumi*. The
hiradaiko is suspended in the front part along one of the sides,
while flutes and *shimedaiko* are placed inside and the *kotsuzumi*
players are seated on the rear edge facing backwards. The float
Kashikajinsha had two *kotsuzumi*; *Kasuisha* had three adult, male
kotsuzumi players dressed in *yukata* (Figure 55); and *Ōgishisha*
had three young players of both sexes wearing short jackets, *happi*.
Sometimes there may be as many as four *kotsuzumi* players in the
back.

---

4   *Arimatsu dashimatsuri: mukei minzoku bunkazai* [The Arimatsu float-
festival: an Intangible folk cultural property] (Internet reference).

Figure 55 The float *Kasuisha* of Dekimachi during *Nagoya matsuri* with three adults dressed in *yukata* seated in the back playing the *kotsuzumi* (19 October 2014).

The float of *Wakamiya matsuri* in Naka-ku, the castle area, has the *hiradaiko* in front along the right side and three or even four *kotsuzumi* on the rear edge. Old Hiroi Village in Nakamura-ku has three floats, each with three *kotsuzumi* in the back; this is also the case in Ōmori in Moriyama-ku.[5]

Ensemble types in Nagoya

The existing ensembles in Nagoya are either *drums and flutes ensembles* or *drums, flutes, and ko-tsuzumi ensembles*. In Nagoya, the musicians are seated on the first level of the float, with the *hiradaiko* usually suspended in the front. It may be placed crosswise or diagonally, but often it is parallel to the sides. When there are more than one *shimedaiko*, the players are normally

---

5 This information stems from *Owari no dashimatsuri* [Float-festivals of the Owari province] → *Ōmori Tennōsai* [Ōmori Tennō festival] 2014 (Internet reference).

seated beside each other inside the float. The flute players are seated inside, but some of them may also sit in the back.

In the case of *drums and flutes ensembles*, some flute players are generally seated in the back or on the rear edge. That is the rule for this ensemble type in the Chita Peninsula, too. In the back of floats with *drums, flutes, and kotsuzumi ensembles*, there may be a combination of flutes and *kotsuzumi*. In several cases, though, there are only *kotsuzumi*, usually 2–4, an arrangement which also has parallels in the Chita Peninsula.

In Map 4 the number of floats in the respective festival districts are noted, and the number that use *kotsuzumi* are marked with an 'X'. It should be remembered, however, that this analysis is based on present-day practice alone. Since several floats have disappeared as an effect of war or accidents, a study of historical documents would add important information. For instance, *kotsuzumi* drums were used in the ensembles of Tsutsui-chō before the Second World War. When the festival was restarted in 1949, there was no one who could play the instrument. Since then, attempts have been made to restore the *kotsuzumi* tradition.[6]

Today, floats with *kotsuzumi* exist in many parts of Nagoya. There is some concentration to the castle area in Naka-ku which neighbours Atsuta-ku, where the large shrine Atsuta jingū is located. Another such area is Midori-ku in the southeast, where Narumi and Arimatsu are located along the old Tōkaidō road.

In the *hayashi yatai type* of float, flutes and/or *kotsuzumi* players are also seated in the back or on the rear edge. However, *hayashi yatai* floats differ in many other respects. The most characteristic trait is that two *shimedaiko* players are seated beside each other in the very front of the *yatai*, facing forward, while the *hiradaiko* is suspended behind them. This placement of two *shimedaiko* in front is also common in *hayashi yatai* in festivals in Mikawa, close to the old Tōkaidō road to the southeast of Nagoya.

Ensembles in other parts of Owari

The *drums and flutes ensemble* is common here as well. This is the case with the *Inuyama matsuri* in the northernmost part of Owari, where there are 13 floats. All except one of these floats have three

---

6 *Nagoya jōka no dashi gyōji chōsa hōkokusho: Nagoya no dashi gyōji sōgō chōsa* [Survey report of festival float events in the castle town Nagoya: a comprehensive survey of Nagoya festival float events] 2018, p. 419.

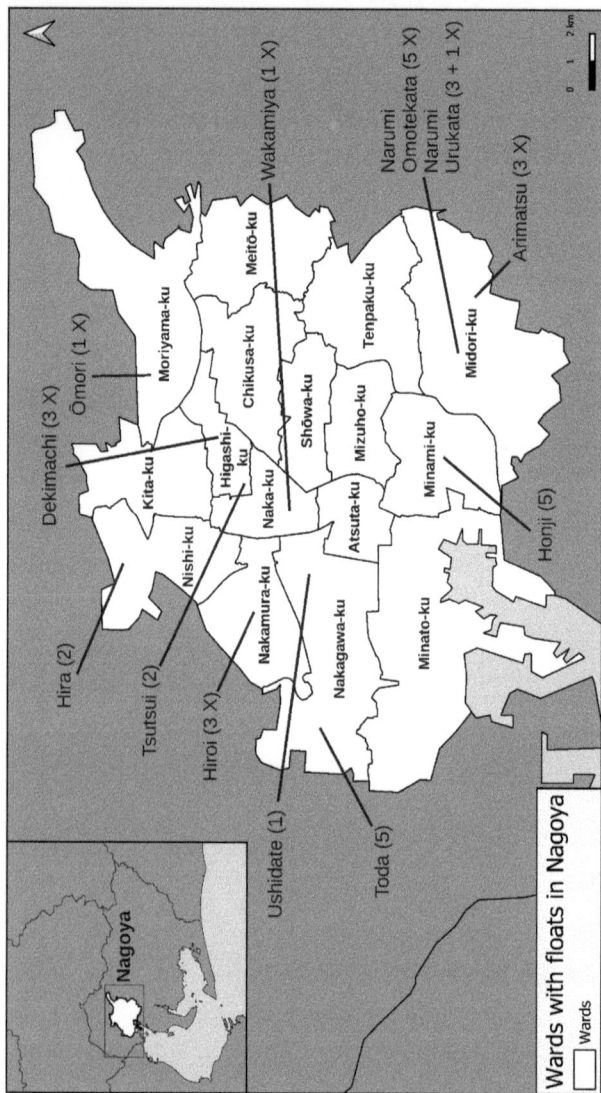

Map 4 Districts with floats in Nagoya. The Nagoya castle is in Naka-ku and the shrine Atsuta jingū in Atsuta-ku. Numbers in brackets show the number of floats in a district. A number followed by an 'X' shows the number of floats that have *kotsuzumi* for *michiyuki* ('parading'). These are – except in the case of Hira – results of observations during fieldwork. Therefore, all that may be said is whether or not *kotsuzumi* were present on the occasion of the fieldwork visits. Courtesy of Jakob Cederblad.

storeys, and they are taller than the *Chita type* and the *Nagoya type* of float. A *hiradaiko* is normally suspended in the centre of the float, parallel to its sides. In front as well as in the back, there are 2–3 *shimedaiko* players facing towards its centre.

Some festivals in the vicinity of Nagoya feature the *drums, flutes, and kotsuzumi ensemble*. A festival that took place in Iwakura north of Nagoya in July 1997 included three large and wide floats that were equipped with puppets. There were two drums, suspended in the two front corners: one *hiradaiko*, here called *gakudaiko*, and beside it on a stand an *okedaiko*, which is a laced barrel drum, here called *shimedaiko*.[7] Together they created a rich and loud drum sound. There were also ordinary *shimedaiko* and flutes. When parading back after the puppet show, one of the floats had six flute players seated on the back edge and two *kotsuzumi* players a little farther into the float (Figure 56). According to oral information, *Nakahonmachi dashi* also used to have *kotsuzumi*, but the players had grown too old to take part. There were not many teenagers or young people. On the other hand, there was a significant number of children playing the flutes, particularly young girls. The impression was that a generation shift was going on in these three districts, at slightly different stages. This was the first time in years that all three floats joined the parade and puppet shows.[8]

In Tsushima to the west of Nagoya, there is the old and influential summer festival *Owari Tsushima Tennō matsuri*, which includes six boat floats called *danjiri*. There is also an autumn festival called *Tsushima akimatsuri* with 16 floats.[9] Three of them belong to

---

7 The festival name presented on the Poster was *Iwakura dashi natsumatsuri*. The description of the festival of Iwakura is mainly based on my fieldwork. The information on the festival dates and the musical instruments is based on material received from Mr Yamauchi Hiroyuki (18–22 May 2023) and Ms Suzuki Nanami (15–22 May 2023) at the Iwakura city hall, *Iwakura no dashi* [Festival floats in Iwakura] 1991, and on *Dashi to karakuriningyō: Iwakura-shi shitei yūkei minzoku bunkazai* [Floats and mechanical puppets: The city-designated tangible cultural property of Iwakura city] n.d.

8 Since 2019, they have again become two separate festivals, one on the day before the first Sunday in August and the other on the fourth weekend in the same month. The first festival is the *Gionsai* with the floats *Nakahonmachi dashi* and *Shimohonmachi dashi* and the second is *Tennōsai* with *Ōkamiichiba dashi*.

9 Two floats did not take part during my fieldwork in 2014 and 2017, namely *Ōnakagiriguruma* and *Onozaguruma*. According to oral information, the former was cancelled because the people involved had become 'too old'.

Figure 56 Six girls playing the flute in the back of the float *Ōkamiichiba dashi* of Honmachi in Iwakura when it starts to return to its storing place after finishing the puppet performance. A large *okedaiko* drum can be seen inside the float to the right (19 July 1997).

Kamori town where *ōdaiko* are used. Four *Ishidorimatsuri-guruma* take part as well, with an *ōdaiko* placed in the back and two large gongs suspended at either side of the drum and with three musicians walking behind. This type of wagon with its very loud music has a background in the *Ishidori matsuri*, 'stone-taking festival', of Kuwana city in Mie prefecture.[10]

Most of the floats in *Tsushima akimatsuri* have *kotsuzumi* (Figure 57–58). The most common placement of the instruments inside the floats was with the *hiradaiko* suspended diagonally in the right front corner. On the left side were one *shimedaiko* and one *kotsuzumi* and on the right side one *kotsuzumi* and one *shimedaiko*, thus forming a diagonal cross. Flute players were sitting on the rear edge of the float.

Nishibiwajima is located to the southwest of Nagoya, just outside the city border. There is a festival with five floats that takes place in June with *drums, flutes, and kotsuzumi ensembles*. The seating of the musicians seems to vary, but there are examples of

10 Lancashire 2011, pp. 178–179.

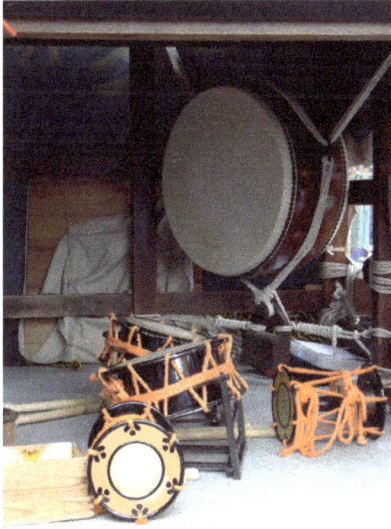

Figure 57 The drums of the float *Fuyamachiguruma* of Tsushima with *hiradaiko* (top), two *shimedaiko* (middle left) and two *kotsuzumi* (front and right) (4 October 2017).

Figure 58 The float *Asahimachiguruma* of Tsushima on its way to Tsushima jinja with puppets in its front and on its top. The *ensemble* is seated inside the float, and below the folded cloth the skin of one *kotsuzumi* is barely distinguishable, indicated by an arrow (4 October 2017).

kotsuzumi and flutes or three *kotsuzumi* being placed in the back of the float.[11]

Comparison with Chita Peninsula

The *dashibayashi ensembles* of Nagoya and the remainder of Owari that are employed in this comparison are dominated by the *drums and flutes ensemble* and the *drums, flutes and kotsuzumi ensemble*. The composition of the ensembles is consistent with what is seen in the Chita Peninsula, which suggests a historical relationship. Another aspect that points in this direction is the spread of the rather large *Nagoya-type* float in the northern part of Chita Peninsula which is closest to Nagoya. Further to the south, the Handa-type float is the most common one, and several ensembles – in contrast to Nagoya – include the larger hourglass drum *ōtsuzumi*.

---

11 I was not able to conduct fieldwork in Nishibiwajima, Kiyosu city. The information is based on *Owari Nishibiwajima matsuri a–b* [The Nishibiwajima festival in Owari province a–b] and *Aichi-ken shōgai gakushū jōhō sisutemu: Manabi-netto Aichi* [Aichi prefecture lifelong learning information system: Learning-net Aichi] 2018 → *Owari Nishibiwajima matsuri: Yoritomo-sha no matsuribayashi* [The Nishibiwajima festival in Owari province: the music of the festival float, *Yoritomo-sha*] (Internet reference).

7
Ensembles in Mikawa and parallels in Chita

To the east of Nagoya lies the area called Mikawa, which is further divided into West and East Mikawa (see Map 1). The ensembles in this area are generally composed of a larger number of musicians, and multi-level floats to accommodate the ensembles are common. The *kotsuzumi* frequently occurs, normally in combination with the *ōtsuzumi*. Many ensembles also include the three-stringed *shamisen* lute (see Figure 63), and gongs or cymbals are occasionally present. There are historical connections between the Chita Peninsula and Mikawa including trade, not least across the strait between West Mikawa and the eastern coast of the Chita Peninsula with the towns Handa and Taketoyo. There are therefore good reasons to investigate how the festival ensembles in Mikawa relate to those in Chita. This comparison has a special focus on the joint presence of the *kotsuzumi* and *ōtsuzumi* drums and on the placement of the musicians inside the multi-level floats.

Ensembles in Mikawa

The *drums and flutes ensemble*

The westernmost parts of Mikawa are geographically very close to the east coast of the Chita Peninsula with the cities Handa and Taketoyo, only divided by the narrow Mikawa Bay. Nowadays, the cities of Handa in Chita and Hekinan in Mikawa are connected by a bridge and a tunnel. Before that, contact was by boat (for locations in Mikawa, see Map 5). Hekinan has three floats. Two of them were bought from Kamezaki in Handa in 1788 and 1864 respectively. The ensemble of the float in the Shinkawamachi (*Tamaguruma*) district is a *drums and flutes ensemble* like many in Handa, with the difference that some musicians sit on an upper level inside the float.

The *drums, flutes, and two tsuzumi ensemble*

In Hekinan, one float in the Ōhamanaka district (*Nakanokirisha*) has a *drums, flutes, and two tsuzumi ensemble*. The *hiradaiko* is placed in the back parallel to the left side of the float and is handled by one player, facing forward, who also plays a *kodaiko* in the *Miyaryū style*. In front of the drummer there is room for two *kotsuzumi* players, but only one was present at the time of observation. The flute players were seated on the right side of the float, one of them in the very back beside the *hiradaiko* and *kodaiko*. Two *ōtsuzumi*, called *ōkawa*, were placed on the third level, but could not be seen from outside. The other float in the area (*Urashimasha*) had no musicians at the time, but recorded *michiyuki music* was played.

Just north of Hekinan lies Kariya with two floats. In April, there is a festival in the Ogakie district with one float accommodating an ensemble consisting of one *hiradaiko* (called *ōdo*), two *shimedaiko*, one *kotsuzumi*, one *ōtsuzumi* (called *ōkawa*), and flutes. In the parade, this float is followed by a smaller wagon with an ensemble of children that employs the same instruments, with the addition of two *shamisen*. The same float takes part in an autumn festival with the same arrangement of musical instruments.[1]

Farther to the northeast, close to Toyota, lies Shiga. Shiga jinja is located high up on a hill with a steep road along which the float is brought down and up again in the evening of the autumn festival.[2] There is one float that was, according to oral history, bought from Chita Peninsula in the mid-Meiji period. However, since it is not a *Chita type* it was probably rebuilt.[3] It has a special solution for the placement of the musicians. The *hiradaiko* is placed in the back along the left side, and along the same side there are two *shime-daiko* beside each other farther into the float. The players are seated with their backs towards the inside of the float. The flute players are

---

1 A picture of an ensemble from around 1924 shows the same instruments (Kōno 2015, p. 82).

2 This festival is also called *Shiga jinja kigansai* according to *Aichi dashimatsuri zukan* [Web-version] 2020, p. 69 (Internet reference).

3 Oral information during the fieldwork at Shiga jinja in Shiga-chō, Toyota (4 October 2015) and *Owari no dashimatsuri* [Float-festivals of the Owari province] (Internet reference) → *Mikawa no dashikan: Shiga jinja sairei* [Festival float museum of Mikawa: the festival of Shiga shrine in Shiga town, Toyota] (Internet reference).

Figure 59 The float *Gankake dashi* of Shiga, Toyota. Seated on the upper level are the *kotsuzumi* player (left) and the *ōtsuzumi* player (right) (2016 October 23).

seated along the right side. The *kotsuzumi* and *ōtsuzumi* players are seated on top of the float (Figure 59).

The city Gamagōri on the southern coast by Mikawa Bay is the location of *Miya matsuri* in October. This is an annual grand festival for the two shrines, Yatsurugi jinja and Wakamiya jinja. The festival is known for its climax when the floats are pulled through the water. I chose, however, to gather my material in the early afternoon, when the five floats – one of which is boat-shaped – assemble at the Yatsurugi jinja. An *ōdaiko* is placed in the centre of the upper level with its skins parallel to the sides of the float, and it is covered by cloth suspended on all four sides. It is played by four players, two on each side. They alternate striking the skin of the drum and its wooden side, which creates a contrasting, snappy sound. Because of this proceeding, and because of the involvement of several cymbals, called *changiri*, the short melodies employed have distinct rhythms. The ensemble is visible, seated on the balcony on the upper level. A trait common to all the floats is that two – or sometimes one – *shimedaiko* is placed in the front, while the instruments on the other sides are combinations of flutes and small cymbals, *changiri* (Figures 60–61).[4]

The *drums, flutes, two tsuzumi, and shamisen ensemble*

The festival in Chiryū to the southeast of Nagoya takes place at the beginning of May – every second year (the even year) is *honmatsuri* with five floats, and every other year (the odd year) is *aimatsuri* with five smaller wagons called *hanaguruma*. The ensembles consist of flutes, *shamisen, kane, kotsuzumi, ōtsuzumi, shimedaiko,* and *hiradaiko*.[5] 2017 was the year of the *aimatsuri,* but it had been decided to show all puppet performances this year, because the *dashibunraku* and *karakuri* puppets of Chiryū had been labelled with UNESCO Intangible cultural heritage status the previous year. This included four floats with *dashibunraku,* which are puppet performances on a stage in front of each float in the same style as the traditional *bunraku* puppet theatre, with accompaniment by vocal recitation and *shamisen*. The *Nishimachi dashi* with its *karakuri* puppet was also included. The assembling of this float took place by the *kōminkan* and was open to the public.

This float has an upper level, and the musicians would be seated on both levels. The actual seating may change according to the situation, but generally flutes are placed on the upper level.[6] This is the case in, for instance, the Takaramachi neighbourhood. The instruments include *hiradaiko* and two *shimedaiko* placed inside the float in the far back. Farther inside are the *shamisen, ōtsuzumi,* and *kotsuzumi*.[7]

The city of Toyota – called Koromo before 1959 – is located to the east of Nagoya. *Koromo matsuri,* which takes place in the autumn, has eight floats. On the same day, another float is paraded in a separate festival.[8] The shafts in the back of these floats are curved upwards, and the *hiradaiko* is placed crosswise in the back

---

4 Mr Uchida Shōgo, Tourism Division, Gamagōri City Office, personal communication 1 November 2022.

5 Hayakawa 2003b, p. 50. There is a photo of an ensemble practising in *Chiryū matsuri, Chiryū festival* 1990, p. 5.

6 Oral information at Nishimachi *kōminkan* 28 April 2017, when the float was assembled.

7 *Chiryū matsuri: Shigaku 4–5* [Chiryū festival: the 1st day of the festival 4–5] (Internet reference).

8 This is *Miyamae-chō sairei*.

Figure 60 *Miya matsuri*, Gamagōri. *Hana no yama* of Naka-ku with the *ōdaiko* on top, indicated by an arrow. Most of it is hidden behind a purple cloth (15 October 2016).

Figure 61 *Sangaikasa no yama* of Kita-ku, showing part of the ensemble with two *shimedaiko* players in the front. On each side there are two flutes and two pairs of cymbals (only partly seen) (15 October 2016).

Figure 62 The rear of *Nishimachi dashi* of Koromo jinja, Toyota, with curved shafts. A *hiradaiko* is seen to the right. The boy sitting on the left is playing the *shimedaiko* (18 October 2014).

(Figure 62). On the left side there may be one *shimedaiko* player or two seated beside each other, while the flute players are seated on the right. In the front inside the float there are two *shamisen* lutes. The players are seated on the bottom level below a middle board, facing backwards. On the middle board there are *tsuzumi* players, normally two *kotsuzumi* and one *ōtsuzumi*; but there may be three *kotsuzumi*, too (Figure 63).[9] Some of the districts use a bugle for military-like signals, which are not part of the ensemble, but the bugle player walks beside the float or stands on top of it.

Not far away, to the northeast, and within Toyota township, lies the shrine Hirai Hachimangū. There are two floats. One of them belongs to the Hirai district and was originally bought from Tsushima or Higashibiwajima, but it has been rebuilt and now resembles those in *Koromo matsuri* in Toyota.[10] The second float

---

9 *Koromo matsuri to dashi* [The Koromo festival and floats] 1981, p. 150, lists one *taiko*, one *ōkawa* (= *ōtsuzumi*), two *shamisen*, three *kusabue*, three *nōkan* and two *tsuzumi*.

10 Oral information during the fieldwork at Hirai Hachimangū in Toyota (4 October 2015) and *Owari no dashimatsuri → Mikawa no dashikan*:

Figure 63 The front part of the inside of *Nishimachi dashi* of Koromo jinja, Toyota, displaying two *shamisen* below the middle board and three *kotsuzumi* drums above it (18 October 2014).

belongs to the neighbouring district of Dōdo and is a modified *Chita type*. According to tradition, it was bought from Handa and rebuilt to fit the local style. They both take part in a festival in the beginning of October. The seating inside these floats is much like that of Toyota with a *hiradaiko* (called ōdaiko or ōdo) in the back (Figure 64).

In Miyoshi, located to the west of Toyota, two floats take part in a festival in October.[11] The musicians are seated partly inside the float and partly on the balcony on the upper level. A *hiradaiko*, called ōdō, is suspended inside the float at an angle a little bit behind the front. Two *shimedaiko*, called *kobachi*, are placed beside each other in the middle of the float, and the flute players sit towards the rear. All these players are facing forward towards the

---

Hirai-chō Hachimansha sairei [Festival float museum of Mikawa: the festival of Hachimansha shrine in Hirai town, Toyota] (Internet reference).

11 '*Miyoshishimo no dashi*' *chōsa hōkokusho* [The festival wagon in Miyoshishimo ward. An investigation report] 1986, p. 19; '*Araya no dashi*' *chōsa hōkokusho* [The festival wagon in Araya ward: an investigation report] 1988, p. 21.

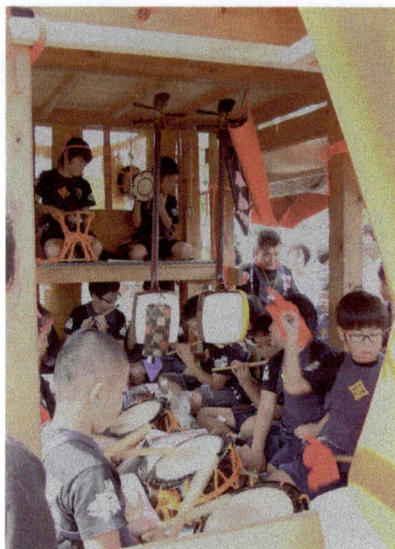

Figure 64 A part of the ensemble inside the float of Dōdo, Hirai, displaying the placement of three *shimedaiko* placed beside each other, flutes, one of the two *kotsuzumi*, and one *ōtsuzumi*. Two *shamisen* are suspended from the ceiling (4 October 2015).

hiradaiko. On the balcony around the float there are two to three *ōtsuzumi*, called *ōkawa*, and four to five *kotsuzumi*, called *tsutsumi* (Figure 65).[12] One of the floats (*Miyoshi Kamiku dashi*) also has a *shamisen* lute. The music has characteristic lively rhythms made up by alternating strokes on the different drums.

A major part of the Kō summer festival in Toyokawa to the east of Gamagōri is a parade along a street that is a part of the old Tōkaidō road. In Kō town, there are four floats of the *hayashi yatai type*.[13] They have three wheels, one in front and two at the back. The ensembles had both *kotsuzumi* and *ōtsuzumi* (Figure 66).

---

12 As elsewhere, instrument names may vary. This information is built on oral information (20 October 2019) and information from the Miyoshi City Hall, Industry Division, Environment and Economy Department, personal communication 15 November 2022.

13 Similar floats are used in the neighbouring Akasaka in Toyokawa. *Amagoi matsuri, junran gōkana kabuki gyōretsu: Heisei 29-nen 8-gatsu 20-nichi* [The Amagoi praying for rain festival, with a splendid kabuki procession, 20 August 2017] (Internet reference).

Figure 65 *Kotsuzumi* and *ōtsuzumi* players seated on the balcony of the float *Miyoshi Kamiku dashi*. The man farthest to the left plays the *ōtsuzumi* and the one in front of him the *kotsuzumi*, holding it in front of his chest (20 October 2019).

One or two floats had *ōtsuzumi* struck with a rather wide, stiff drumstick. Some *kotsuzumi* were also struck in this manner. Each ensemble used the same melody, played by the flutes in unison with two *shamisen*.

In nearby Goyu, there was also a summer festival parade along the old Tōkaidō road. It included a *mikoshi* and six three-wheeled floats of the *hayashi yatai type*. The music was the same as in Kō town, and the ensembles were similar. One of the floats (*Mikoguruma*) differed in several ways, though. There is an *ōdaiko* in the front right corner and two gongs in the front more to the left. Behind them are a *shimedaiko* and a flute, and there are three flutes in the back. *Miko* dancers are seated on an upper level.

Ensemble types in Mikawa

Even though there are large variations with regard to the ensembles in Mikawa, a common trait is the simultaneous use of *kotsuzumi* and *ōtsuzumi*. Apart from those already mentioned,

Figure 66 Like all floats in Kō, Toyokawa, the float of *Kamimachi* is
open. Three boys with *kotsuzumi* are seated on its right side. Behind
them inside the float, there is one boy playing a gong. The women farther
inside play the *shamisen*. A flute player and a *hiradaiko* are placed aslant
in the back, but the players are hidden behind a pillar. Two *shimedaiko*
players in the front and one *ōtsuzumi* cannot be seen in the picture
(27 July 2003).

this characteristic also occurs in other places in Mikawa, including
Asuke,[14] Okazaki,[15] and Tahara.[16] These findings go well with
Hayakawa's view that *ōtsuzumi*, *kotsuzumi*, and *shamisen* are
characteristic instruments of ensembles in Mikawa.[17]

The most consistent trait among the festivals in Mikawa is thus
the predominance of the *drums, flutes, and two tsuzumi ensemble*
and the *drums, flutes, two tsuzumi, and shamisen ensemble*
(Map 5). The *tsuzumi* drums may vary in number, but most often
there are three, for instance three *kotsuzumi* or two *ōtsuzumi* and
one *kotsuzumi*. The *tsuzumi* drums are either struck with the hand
or with a drumstick. The seating of the musicians varies with the

14 *Asuke-chō no matsuri to dashi* [Festivals and wagons of Asuke town] 1998,
　　p. 3.
15 *Nomi Shinmeigū taisai...* [Nomi Shinmeigū shrine's Grand festival,
　　Okazaki] 2022 (Internet reference).
16 *Tahara no matsuri...* [The festival of Tahara city] 1983 (Internet reference).
17 Hayakawa 2003b, p. 48.

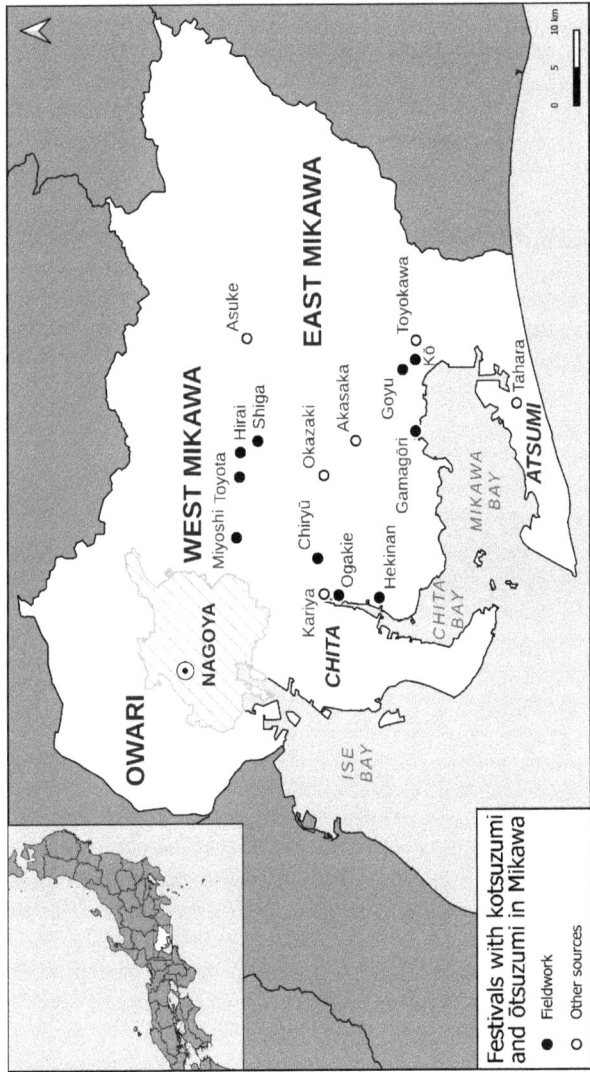

Map 5   Examples of festivals in Mikawa with *kotsuzumi* and *ōtsuzumi*. As indicated, the information is based on fieldwork and on the Internet or printed sources. Courtesy of Jakob Cederblad.

different types of floats in use. In tall floats covered with cloth –
like those in Nagoya and Chita – the *hiradaiko* is often placed in
the back. It is very common for the musicians to be spread out on
different levels inside the float.

Comparison with Chita Peninsula

In many respects, the ensembles of the Chita Peninsula are closely
related to those of Nagoya/Owari (Chapters 5–6). It was noted
that the ensembles of southern-central Chita stand out as slightly
deviant in this respect (Map 3) and share some of the traits typical
of Mikawa: the simultaneous use of *ōtsuzumi* and *kotsuzumi* and
the placement of the musicians on more than one level inside the
float. The use of multi-level floats increases the possible accom-
modation of musicians, and the different solutions tend to be stable
and quite consistent in each locality.

Multi-level floats and placing of the instruments

In Taketoyo and nearby places in the southern-central part of the
peninsula, a float usually has a middle level – or a 'shelf' – close
to its front. Many floats also have an upper level in the rear, and
then there is the top level, which is like a balcony around the float
with a low rail or fence. In Nagao, the *ōtsuzumi* is placed on the
middle level and the *shimedaiko* on the bottom level beneath it.
Immediately behind them is the *hiradaiko*, which is suspended
crosswise, and then come the flutes. On the rear edge, three
kotsuzumi players are seated facing backwards.

In Ōashi, however, the middle level is used for the *shimedaiko*
while the *ōtsuzumi* is on an upper level. In Fuki the *shimedaiko*
and a flute are on the middle level, the *hiradaiko* being suspended
along one side of the float or diagonally in one of the front corners.
The seating of the other instrumentalists is more flexible here, but
normally a combination of flute, *ōtsuzumi*, and *kotsuzumi* are
seated on the rear edge. An *ōtsuzumi* player, a *kotsuzumi* player,
and/or a flute player may be seated on the shafts in the back,
sometimes holding on to a corner beam by wrapping one arm
around it. The details of this seating may change during the festival.

There is a great variety, but also a degree of consistency in
the placing of the instruments. In most places, the *hiradaiko* is
suspended crosswise in the front of the float, either in the very front
or just behind the middle level if there is one (Figures 67–68).

Figure 67 In the float *Tōōsha* of Okujō, Ōtani, the *hiradaiko* is placed crosswise in the very front of the float and above the shelf that is the middle level, the front edge of which can also be seen just below the drum. The front opening will later be covered by a Venetian blind (1 April 2016).

Figure 68 The float *Gyokushinsha* of Tamanuki, Nagao, with *hiradaiko* suspended crosswise in the front, behind the middle level (8 April 2016).

The *hiradaiko* may also be placed lower than the middle level, which is the case in Yoshima, Kaminoma, or above it (Figures 69–70). In the latter case it could also be placed diagonally across one of the front corners, and the player would not be sitting but standing up. This is the case in Ochishima, Kaminoma. The *hiradaiko* can also be placed along one side of the float, either in the front or at the rear (Figures 71–72).

The other instruments are movable, and any of them may be found inside the float. Which drums are placed on the middle or upper levels – if any – varies and is summarized in Appendix 1: Tables 7–8. Kaminoma, Kosugaya, Sakai, and Ōtani in the southern-central part have the *tsuzumi* on the upper level. This is also the case in the Ichihara neighbourhood located in the western part of Fuki, very close to Kosugaya. Similarly, Ōashi has the *ōtsuzumi* on an upper level (Figures 73–74), which may be explained by the fact that Ōashi bought its float from Ōtani, so that it has the same construction as the other floats there. This type of float is sometimes referred to as the *Hōreki type* and is generally considered to be comparatively old.[18]

The floats in Fuki and Ichihara have the *shimedaiko* on the middle level in the front, and this is also the case in Ōashi. All floats in Nagao, on the other hand, have the *shimedaiko* on the bottom level in the front part of the float and the *ōtsuzumi* on the middle level (Figure 75).

In principle, then, the floats of Nagao, Fuki, and Kosugaya are obliged to employ the middle level for reasons of space. When another instrument than *shimedaiko* is placed there, the *shimedaiko* is normally placed on the bottom level; but in Kosugaya, where there are two flutes on the middle level, the *shimedaiko* is on the upper level. The floats of Kaminoma, Ōtani, and Sakai have a larger upper level which may accommodate most of the ensemble. The solutions are not purely coincidental. To some degree they depend on the construction of the float, but they also reflect geographic and historical relations between these localities.

Two tsuzumi drums and multi-level floats

Many ensembles in Mikawa differ from those of Owari and Chita Peninsula in their use of the *shamisen* lute. However, the presence

---

18 *Taketoyo-chō shi: shiryō-hen 2* [Handbook of Taketoyo: reference material 2] 1983, p. 227.

Figure 69 In *Yoshima no dashi* of Kaminoma, the *hiradaiko* is placed
below the middle level. The drummer sits to the left and a flute player
to the right. This photo was taken during a puppet performance.
The floor of the upper level can be seen in the upper part of the
picture (26 March 2016).

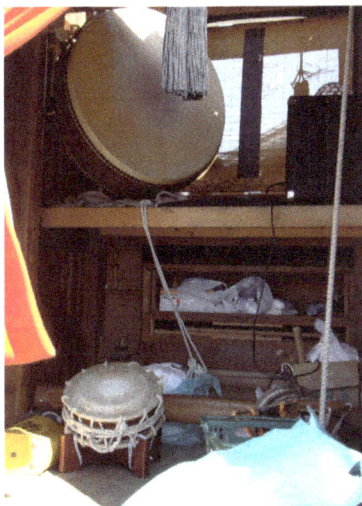

Figure 70 In *Ochishima no dashi* of Kaminoma, the *hiradaiko* is placed
diagonally in the left-hand corner and above the middle level, which
permits the drummer to be standing up (26 March 2016).

Figure 71 The *hiradaiko* in the float *Tennōmaru* of Fuki-Ichiba,
Taketoyo, is suspended along the left side of the float behind the middle
board. This photo was taken from the left side before the float was
draped in red cloth (1 April 2016).

Figure 72 In the float *Hakusansha* of Kosugaya, the *hiradaiko* is also
suspended along the left side, but in the rear part of the float
(2 April 2016).

Figure 73 The upper level of the float *Jaguruma* of Ōashi in Taketoyo. The upper part of the *ōtsuzumi* can be seen in the top left corner (arrow). Below in front, the *shimedaiko* can be seen on the middle level (cf. Figure 74 below) (19 July 1997).

Figure 74 The same float as Figure 73, showing the *shimedaiko* on the middle level in the front and the *hiradaiko* suspended below it (19 July 1997).

Figure 75 The inside of the float *Hachimansha* of Shitamo in Nagao, with the *ōtsuzumi* standing on the middle level (arrow). The *hiradaiko* is suspended just behind the shelf, with two drumsticks placed on the three white cushions for the players. The *shimedaiko* is seen below the *hiradaiko* (to the left). On both sides there are benches for the flute players (8 April 2016).

of both *kotsuzumi* and *ōtsuzumi* in most of them has a parallel in southern-central Chita Peninsula. Generally, though, the festival floats in West Mikawa are larger than those in southern-central Chita; they typically have several levels inside, which makes it possible to admit more ensemble members by spreading the instrumentalists out on separate levels.

As has been shown, the simultaneous use of *kotsuzumi* and *ōtsuzumi* and the use of multi-level floats are characteristics that set the *dashibayashi ensembles* in southern-central Chita apart from those in the rest of the peninsula (Map 3). They also differ from the ensembles of Nagoya and the rest of Owari in the same respects. Considering the historical maritime trade routes and historical contacts between Mikawa and southern-central Chita, a historical relationship with regard to festival-float construction and use of musical instruments seems likely.

8
The *tsuzumi* drums and folk performing arts

The *drums and flutes ensemble* is obviously a nucleus that is present in all the types of *dashibayashi ensembles* that were presented in the three previous chapters. Ensembles differ from one another according to which additional instruments they possess. It is evident that the *kotsuzumi* and *ōtsuzumi* drums play significant roles in the ensembles. This chapter deals with the background of these drums and their use in traditions in the Chita Peninsula other than *dashibayashi music*. One of these is the *manzai* entertaining tradition, which is not connected to festivals, whereas the mechanical or *bunraku-style* puppets and the *Sanbasō* performances are common in festivals.

Tsuzumi drums belong to the type called hourglass drums, because of their shape with two skins and a narrow waist. This type of drum is thought to have spread from India via China and Korea to Japan, where it is believed to have arrived about the seventh century. It is not known when the Japanese variants *ōtsuzumi* and *kotsuzumi* originated. In traditional arts, these two drums are used in *nō* ensembles in combination with the *taiko* drum and the flute *nōkan*. The same combination occurs in *kabuki*, with the addition of the long-necked three-string lute *shamisen*. In these ensembles, the *kotsuzumi* is held by the left hand and rests against the front of the player's right shoulder. It is struck with the right-hand fingers, and there are several different kinds of strokes. The *ōtsuzumi* is held by the left hand so that its back skin – which is not played – rests against the seated player's left thigh and its front skin is struck with the fingers of the right hand.[1]

In *dashibayashi ensembles*, the playing technique is different from the one employed in *nō* and *kabuki*. The *kotsuzumi* is

---

1 Hughes 1984a, 1984b, and 1984c.

normally held as in *nō* and struck with the bare hand, but there is generally only one kind of stroke. Occasionally a drumstick is used. The *ōtsuzumi* is held aslant with the thumb and opposite fingers holding the edge of the upper skin, which is of a larger diameter than the drum's body and thus protrudes a little on the side. It is usually played with a drumstick held in the other hand – a long, thin, and somewhat flexible stick – but several other types of drumsticks occur as well. It is also occasionally struck with the bare hand.

Tsuzumi drums are common in festival music in the Chita Peninsula and other parts of Aichi, as well as in Gifu prefecture; but they are not generally thought to be typical of *dashibayashi music* in other parts of the country, even though there are places where they are in fact in use. That is, for instance, the case in the *Sawarabayashi* of the summer and autumn grand festivals in Sawara, Katori city, Chiba prefecture.[2] There the *ōtsuzumi* is struck with a bamboo stick while a few *kotsuzumi* in each float are held on the player's lap and struck with the bare hand.

It is generally believed that the widespread use of *tsuzumi* drums in *dashibayashi ensembles* in Chita Peninsula and Aichi stems from *nō* and *kabuki*, which seems fairly likely.[3] Even so, there are particular uses of *tsuzumi* drums in Chita Peninsula and Mikawa, and they may have added to its popularity in these areas.

Manzai

The *manzai* are traditional entertainers. They used to range from wandering performers to well-organized ensembles. One function of the *manzai* was to visit households at New Year to entertain and to spread good luck and well-being. This is believed to stem from door-to-door greetings for longevity and prosperity in the Nara region, which in turn possibly dates back to festive greetings at the Imperial court. In the late thirteenth century, the practice had spread to Owari, where it took root on the north-west coast of the Chita peninsula, and to Mikawa. Three types of performances

---

2 By way of oral information from a flute player in Kawagoe in 2002, I was informed that *kotsuzumi* were not used in Kawagoe, but that they were in Sawara. See slso *Sawarabayashi: Tokushū* [A feature article on Sawarabayashi, Chiba] 2014 (Internet reference).

3 Hayakawa 2003a, p. 16, discusses the relation between *dashibayashi music* and the music of *nō* and *kabuki*.

are now recognized: *kadozuke manzai*, 'door-to-door *manzai*', performed at the gates of individual households; *goten manzai*, 'parlour *manzai*', performed in the parlour of a household or at house-buildings; and *sankyoku manzai*, 'three instruments *manzai*', using *tsuzumi*, *shamisen*, and *kokyū*.[4]

Manzai from the Chita region travelled around villages and cities as far away as Tokyo and Osaka, and the art spread across the country. One reason behind the flowering of *manzai* in Chita was probably a need to provide income during the agricultural off-season. It is said that around 200–300 artists went on door-to-door performances several months a year in the decades around the turn of the century, 1900. Later, especially in the 1960s, the number of manzai decreased drastically. The performer Kitagawa Kōtarō (b. 1933) has been labelled the last *manzai*. He learnt the art from his father, who ran a fish-shop and worked as a *manzai* three months a year. During Kitagawa's career a *Chita manzai hozonkai* was formed about 1957, and *Chita manzai* was designated an Aichi Prefecture Intangible Cultural Property. In 1996, the name was changed to *Owari manzai hozonkai* when it became a Nationally designated important intangible folk-cultural property.[5]

In 1970, the actor Ozawa Shōichi discussed the idea of investigating itinerant performers such as 'street performances and door-to-door greetings' with the Victor record company, and together with the producers he began to 'gather information and make recordings'.[6] In 1971, the result of this research was released as a box of LP records. *Manzai* were included and also participated in performances staged in Tokyo in 1974.[7] Ozawa's motivation for the research was to confirm 'the soil of origin of Japanese entertainers by searching the characteristics of performing arts among Japanese jongleurs, itinerant performers and other

---

4 The *kokyū* is a vertically held fiddle with a square body covered with skins, in a manner similar to the *shamisen* lute.
5 Takahashi 1975; Hikawa 2011; Lancashire 2011; Chita City Museum, Ms. Ōya Minori (personal communication 26–27 November 2024). *Iwau gei kara no hajimari* [Originating from a blessing art]; *Anjo City Museum of History* → *Mikawa manzai*; *Owari manzai: an important intangible cultural asset*; and *Cultural heritage online* → *Owari manzai* (Internet references).
6 Suzuki 2023, p. 60–72.
7 Ozawa, Ogawa, and Ichikawa 1971; Ozawa 1974; and *Ozawa Shōichi ga maneita Nihon no hōrōgei* [Wanderers' performing arts in Japan invited by Ozawa Shōichi] 1974.

wandering entertainers'. He referred to their art as *hōrōgei*.[8] This was an early recognition of *manzai* as a folk performing art. As late as the 1980s, single *manzai* with *kotsuzumi* could be seen on the streets of Handa visiting shops and other places, and *manzai* shows are still staged in the town of Chita and on stage in city float-festivals. A group called *Itayama manzai* has appeared in *Handa dashimatsuri*,[9] and a group of *Yata manzai* has been included in the *Tokoname dashimatsuri*.[10]

In *manzai* performances, the *kotsuzumi* is held in one hand in front of the player's chest and struck with the other hand, much like the playing technique of *kotsuzumi* in some festival ensembles such as those of Miyoshi in Mikawa. In combination with dance movements, *manzai* performers often move the *kotsuzumi* in different poses (Figure 76).

Puppets

There are many activities containing music during festivals. Sometimes a float is preceded by a parade including, for instance, drums and flutes. In many places, *gagaku* or *kagura music* is performed for certain ceremonies as part of the festival. Dances accompanied by *kagura* ensembles, such as the *shishimai*, 'lion dance', of Narawa in Handa and Kosugaya, are also performed, usually at a *kaguraden*, a special stage in the shrine.[11]

Most performances of puppets take place on the float, the musicians being placed inside or immediately behind it. Puppets placed in an opening in the float's front, which is usually covered by a straw curtain, are called *maedana-ningyō*, and puppets on the top are referred to as *uwayama-ningyō*. Puppets are controlled from below or behind by ropes that are hidden from view, and some are equipped with intricate mechanical devices. These are the *karakuri-ningyō*, 'mechanical puppets'. Other puppets are similarly constructed to the ones in the puppet theatre *bunraku*, and they are operated directly by three persons who are usually hidden from view. Whenever a term for them is necessary for the purpose

---

8 The term *hōrōgei* appeared in connection with Ozawa, Ogawa, and Ichikawa 1971. See also Gunji 1971, 1973.

9 *Warau kado niwa fuku kitaru* [Fortune comes in by a merry gate: welcome to Itayama *manzai*] (Audiovisual reference, hereafter AV reference).

10 Observed in 2019.

11 For the lion dance and its music, see Kárpáti 2000.

Figure 76 *Mikawa manzai* from an *ukiyoe* print by Utagawa Hiroshige dated 1852. The actor to the right is the *tayū* holding a fan while the *saizō* plays a *tsuzumi* drum here caught in movement, holding the drum as an extension of his arm (By permission from the Museum of Fine Arts, Boston).

of specification, they will be referred to below as *bunraku-type puppets*. In everyday language, all kinds of puppets on a float are frequently called *karakuri-ningyō* or just *karakuri*, regardless of performance technique. The puppet shows are mainly scenes from plays or from traditional myths and legends.

> In 1662 Takeda Ōmi opened a theatre in Osaka to present plays featuring the mechanical puppets he made. Takeda's theatre thrived for about a century. The tradition of mechanical puppets is now carried on via puppet-equipped festival floats, especially in the area around Nagoya.[12]

Puppet performances have a musical accompaniment containing special instrumental pieces or songs. When such performances are based on scenes from *nō* drama, adaptations of the corresponding *nōgaku* are normally used as accompaniment.[13] The ensembles for puppet performances usually differ from the *dashibayashi ensembles*, although some musicians may actually be the same. The musical instruments employed in connection with puppet shows may also differ from those of *dashibayashi ensembles*. *Tsuzumi* drums are thus often used although they are not part of the *dashibayashi ensemble*, for instance in Handa. Another example is the *shamisen* lute used for puppet performances by Satogumi in Okada, Chita. In Ōtani, Tokoname, the small barrel drum referred to as *kankaradaiko*, played with two long and flexible sticks, is used by Hamajō for a piece that precedes a *Sanbasō* puppet performance when the float is standing still. It is placed in the back of the float together with two *shimedaiko*, drummers and flute players standing together behind the float. This drum belongs to the offstage *geza* music of *kabuki*.

In Nagao, performances of puppets and music belong to the category of *keigo*, meaning respect or respectful. As a climax on the main festival day, all six floats line up facing the main building of Takeo jinja and simultaneously perform *keigo*.[14] Since all musicians produce sound at the same time, some of the music is drowned

---

12 Thornbury 1997, p. 30.
13 Hayakawa 2003a, p. 16.
14 A detailed description of *keigo* and the music of the puppet performances in Komukae can be found in *Bishū Nagao Komukaegumi Hōōsha: sōken hyakugojisshūnen kinenshi* [The festival float Hōōsha of the neighbourhood Komukae, Nagao district, Owari province: memorial magazine for the 150th anniversary of its construction] 2013, pp. 33–40.

in the totality, which is a part of the festive atmosphere. Three of the floats in Nagao have puppets. There are two *maedana-ningyō* of the *bunraku* type: *Sanbasō* in the Age neighbourhood, with its special accompaniment, and *mikomai*, the 'shrine maiden dance', in Komukae, performed to the tune *Mikobayashi* played by an ensemble without *tsuzumi* drums. *Emperor Ōjin* in Shitamo is a *maedana-ningyō* operated by strings from behind. The float of Shitamo also has an *uwayama-ningyō*: *Jingū Kōgō*, the mother of *Ōjin*, in a scene that is an act of divination, where she is fishing in the presence of the legendary statesman *Takenouchi no Sukune*. Komukae has a pair of *uwayama-ningyō* that are *karako*, 'China-child puppets'. One scene relates to the *nō* play *Shōjō* about a *sake*-drinking mythological figure represented by a big puppet which is able to change its face mask from white to red and is accompanied by the *nō* chant *Shōjō*.[15] A smaller puppet that cannot reach a suspended flat drum climbs onto the larger puppet's shoulder. At the end it strikes the drum, and the sound is integrated with the accompanying music (Figures 77–78).[16] The whole performance is accompanied by a sequence of tunes played by flute, *shimedaiko*, and *ōtsuzumi*.

The *Sanbasō* character

Sanbasō literally means 'the third old man', a figure who appeared in medieval dance and theatre as a third player after *Chichi no jō* and *Okina*, both of whom represented old men. The performance with the third dancer, originally a prayer for a rich harvest, has developed into the sacred ceremonial *nō* dance *Okina*.[17] *Okina* that opens a formal *nō* programme is the

> most ancient and sacred of *nō* plays... Technically, it is not a *nō* play at all but rather a plotless *Shintō* ritual performance, possibly created in the 10th century and possibly in Okinawa (its origins are not clearly known) for presentation at a shrine, before *nō* itself was created. It is referred to by Zeami as *Shiki Sanba* ('Ceremony

15 *Taketoyo-chō Komukae-ku: Matsuribayashi 3* [Taketoyo town, Komukae ward: festival music 3], 1987–1990.

16 The puppets are described in *Taketoyo-chō shi: shiryō-hen 2* 1983, pp. 318–326.

17 *Nihon minzoku jiten* [Japanese folklore encyclopedia] 1975, p. 298; *Takayama matsuri no yatai* (The floats of Takayama Festival) 1991, p. 12; Plutschow 1996, p. 66.

Figure 77 Rehearsing the puppet performance in the *kōminkan* of the Komukae neighbourhood. The puppets are operated from below with strings and wooden handles. The smaller puppet in a green jacket is holding a drumstick, while the larger puppet in a red jacket is making a one-hand handstand, drinking *sake* from a bucket whereupon his face turns red (4 April 2016).

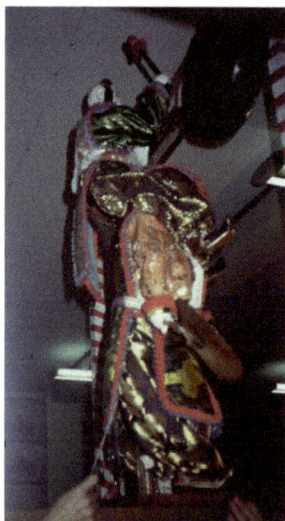

Figure 78 The smaller puppet strikes the suspended flat drum sitting on the shoulders of the larger puppet (7 April 1992).

of Three Numbers'). Performed only on felicitous or memorial occasions, it is – for all its solemnity – intended to be joyous.[18]

Nō theatre includes *nō* plays and *kyōgen*, which are shorter comic plays. Both categories are covered by the term *nōgaku*. The *Okina* character is played by a *nō* actor and the *Sanbasō* character by a *kyōgen* actor. All the actors observe purification rituals before the performance. A difference between *Okina* and *nō* plays is that the former consists of dance only, without dialogue.[19]

In *nōgaku* as well as in *kabuki* theatre, all actors are traditionally male, and both male and female roles are performed by male actors. This practice was particularly implemented during the *Edo period*. During the twentieth century, however, these powerful traditions were relaxed, so that there are now female troupes both in *nōgaku* and *kabuki*. Even so, female actors are still a minority.[20]

During the 1600s *Sanbasō* became a regular feature in the traditional puppet theatre, which was later called *bunraku*, and it became common practice for puppet shows to begin with a dance called *Shiki Sanbasō*, 'Ceremonial *Sanbasō*'.[21] In the early *Edo period*, *Sanbasō* dances were also included in *kabuki*. Several *Sanbasō* scenes were then developed.

> Many non-realistic dance plays – some say over 100 – were based on the *Sanbasō* characters... They all differed from the nō treatment, in which the lead character (*shite*) was Okina, the secondary character (*tsure*) Senzai, and the *kyōgen* character *Sanbasō* by making the latter the leading figure. The emphasis on the comical *Sanbasō* rather than the solemn Okina exemplifies the difference between the spirit of nō and kabuki.[22]

The music ensemble used for *Sanbasō* differs from the ordinary *nō hayashi* in that it has three *kotsuzumi* drums instead of one. The instruments are: one *nōkan* (flute), one *ōtsuzumi*, and three *kotsuzumi*.

The use of *Sanbasō* puppets in rites in general life has survived into modern times. In several cases, it has actually been revived. When investigating pre-War traditions on Awaji Island, Jane Marie Law found two different performance situations. *Sanbasō* was performed at the beginning of something, for instance in the

---

18 Leiter 2006, p. 288 (slightly edited).
19 Komparu 1983, pp. 3–4, 96; Fujita 2008, p. 127.
20 Miyanishi 2005; Edelson 2009; Suzumura 2013; Koyano 2020.
21 Leiter 2006, p. 290.
22 Leiter 1997, p. 547.

New Year, at a wedding party, or when the main pillar of a house went up. The performances took place at the sites of those festive occasions. This was *Kotobuki Sanbasō*, *kotobuki* meaning felicity or auspiciousness. Another situation consisted of performances that took place before shrines at New Year or in rice-seedling nurseries in the spring. These performances were *hōnō*, meaning consecration or worship, and were directed to the divine.[23]

Sanbasō's dance is a prayer for good fortune, for a plentiful harvest, or – in fishing areas – for a big catch of fish. It has traits that seem to go back to the *dengaku* field rituals that historically preceded the *nō* drama, and the movements 'clearly [suggest] the actions both of demon-quelling and of farming activities'.[24]

> During the Tokugawa period, every kabuki program began at dawn with a sophisticated ritual dance featuring the character of Sanbasō. Performed by a low-ranking actor the dance was built around three short scenes (*dan*): 'waving sleeves and stamping' (*momi no dan*), the conventional 'jumping like a crow' (*karasutobi*) and the 'bell-tree' (*suzu no dan*), in which the dancer shakes a wand covered with small bells... Today the dance is performed regularly for the New Year's production, and occasionally at other times as well.[25]

The 'bell-tree' refers to *kagurasuzu* or *suzu*, which is a hand-held rattle normally made of twelve metal bells organized in the shape of a pyramid. It is a sacred ritual implement for purification also used by *miko*, the dancing shrine maidens.[26] *Sanbasō* usually holds a *kagurasuzu* in one hand and a fan in the other (see Figure 84).

Sanbasō at festivals

Sanbasō has come to be seen as a bringer of good luck at festival performances and occurs in different forms: as a live dance, as *karakuri-ningyō*, or as a *bunraku-type* puppet.

Sanbasō *dance*

Some *dashimatsuri* include a *Sanbasō* dance by children, called *kodomo Sanbasō* in some districts. The dancer usually holds a fan.

---

23 Law 1997, p. 171.
24 Komparu 1983, p. 4.
25 Brandon and Leiter 2002, p. 52.
26 Reader 1991, p. 78.

The dance is relatively long – around 10–15 minutes – and incorporates different sections symbolizing rice cultivation. In most cases, it is accompanied by a rather large instrumental ensemble. In Yokone, Ōbu, children from each of the three *kumi* perform *Sanbasō*. When the three festival floats have arrived at the shrine, they are moved and placed side by side at a straight angle to the shrine building, more precisely the worship hall. A stage is then built in front of them for this occasion (Figure 79). The dances are accompanied by ensembles consisting of flutes, two *shimedaiko*, and one *kotsuzumi*. Each dance performance is preceded by an instrumental piece including an *ōdaiko*. The performance is quite intricate and consists of several sections with the instrumental music and *utai* singing in *nō* style.[27]

In Kamihanda, Handa, there are two neighbourhoods: Kitagumi and Minamigumi. Each neighbourhood has one ordinary float and one boat float called *Chintorobune*, which resembles the *danjiri* of Tsushima. The *Chintoro matsuri* takes place in April. In the evening, the two *Chintorobune* covered with lanterns circulate on a pond and take turns in moving towards land in the direction of the shrine. When a *Chintorobune* faces the shrine, where an audience is waiting, a child performs a *Sanbasō* dance. This is accompanied by a rather large ensemble including several flutes, *ōtsuzumi*, and *kotsuzumi*. The footsteps of the dancer are emphasized by a wooden clapper.[28]

The child dancers who perform *Sanbasō* are treated as deities and their feet should not touch the ground. On the evening before the festival, the child dancer of Kitagumi was, after a period with several rehearsals, dressed up as *Sanbasō* and carried around in the neighbourhood on the shoulders of one of the men. The procession was accompanied by the tune *Chintorobayashi*, played by the same ensemble that would be inside the float during the

27 *Ōbu-shi bunkazai chōsa hōkokusho 1: Ōbu-shi shitei yūkei minzoku bunkazai Fujii jinja, Yamano jinja sairei dashi 1* [Report on the investigation of Ōbu city folk cultural properties. 1: The city-designated tangible cultural property: Fujii shrine, Yamano shrine festival floats 1] 1996, pp. 65–66; Hayakawa 2003a, pp. 54–55 and note section 98–99; Ōbu City History; Folklore Museum, Ms Takaba Nozomi, personal communication 17 November, 4 December, and 8 December 2022; *Yokone Fujii jinja: sairei dashi, Sanbasō* [Fujii shrine in Yokone, Ōbu city: festival floats, *Sanbasō* dances].
28 Documented on 7 April 2001.

Figure 79 *Sanbasō* dancer and ensemble of Nakagumi in Yokone, Ōbu. The front of a float is seen to the right, and the roof of the worship hall is seen in the upper corner far left (12 October 2014).

festival. Consisting of flutes, *hiradaiko*, and *shimedaiko*, it was thus different from the ensemble which would accompany *Sanbasō*'s dance.[29] On the day of the *matsuri*, each of the two child dancers was carried to the shrine for ceremonies.

Kitagumi has a male-style *Sanbasō* dance whereas Minamigumi has a female-style *Sanbasō*, both performed by young boys. The dances differ not only in style but also in respect of the dancers' facial paint.[30] The music that accompanies a *Sanbasō* performance is generally called *Sanbasōbayashi*. The performance starts with the tunes *Sagaribana* (Kitagumi) or *Sagariha* (Minamigumi),[31] whereupon the music that accompanies the dance section follows. It consists of short rhythmic motifs, which are units of sounds that make up and

---

29 I was kindly invited to observe the *Sanbasō* rehearsals of Kitagumi in April 2004.

30 Mr Fukumoto Takahisa, Ichiba, Taketoyo town, personal communication 17 November 2022.

31 *Handa-shi shi: sairei minzoku hen* [Handbook of Handa city: festival and folklore] 1984, pp. 223–224.

Figure 80 The dancing *Sanbasō* of Ichiba in Nagao (11 April 2004).

characterize the tune. The short rhythmic motif is repeated with little or no variation, lasting until the relevant section of the dance is finished. Then follows a short interlude with a different melody and rhythm. When a new dance section starts, the short rhythmic motif is played again; a new interlude ensues, and so on.[32]

Ichiba in Nagao has a *Sanbasō* dance. It was learnt from Kamihanda in 1931 and is hence a female-style dance performed by a young boy. On the evening before the main festival day the *Sanbasō* dancer is carried to Takeo jinja with music including small hand cymbals, called *chappa*, for a ceremony, after which he is treated as a deity and must not touch the ground. On the main festival day – the Sunday – the six floats of Nagao are lined up beside one another facing the shrine. The *Sanbasō* dance is performed on a stage built for this occasion in front of Ichiba's float. The *Sanbasō* ensemble is basically the same as that of Kamihanda and normally consists of four flutes, one *ōtsuzumi*, three *kotsuzumi*, and a wooden clapper (Figure 80).[33] Since 2014, it has been preceded by

---

32 There is a full transcription of the *Sanbasōbayashi* of Kitagumi in Hayakawa 2003a; note section pp. 38–39.
33 Documented on 12 April 1992 and 11 April 2004.

Figure 81 Three *Sanbasō* dancers – one of whom is hidden from view – of Ōike in Futto (3 April 2004).

a *miko* dance performed by three girls accompanied by the same ensemble, except that a *shimedaiko* is used instead of the *ōtsuzumi*. The performance begins with the instrumental piece *Sagariha*, which accompanies the *miko* dance; *Enbukyoku* follows, accompanying the *Sanbasō* dance.[34]

In Ōike, Futto, two or three boys perform a *Sanbasō* dance on a stage made of a wooden board placed across the front shafts of the float (Figure 81). The performance is preceded by an instrumental piece called *Getō* – performed by an ensemble consisting of one *hiradaiko*, two *shimedaiko*, one *ōtsuzumi*, one *kotsuzumi*, and about seven flutes – while the dance is accompanied by a recorded folk-song, *minyō*.[35]

---

34 This information about Ichiba comes from Mr Fukumoto Takahisa, personal communication 4 October and 17 November 2022, and from *Jingūsha sairei no ayumi: Ichiba-ku* [History of the Jingūsha float-festival: Ichiba ward] 2007, pp. 8 and 10. *Nagao-bu harumatsuri [Taketoyo]: Sanbasō, Mikomai tokubetsuhen* [The spring festival of Nagao district, Taketoyo: special edition of Sanbasō and Miko dances] (AV reference) is a documentation of the dances.

35 Documented on 3 April 2004.

Karakuri Sanbasō

There are several examples of the importance of *Sanbasō* in *dashi-matsuri*. In many places, there is an instrumental tune called *Sanbasō* or *Sanbasōbayashi*, which is played as *michiyuki* or *kagura* and is different from the music of *Sanbasō* performances. In Tsushima, the tune called *Sanbasō* or *Momi no dan* is often played when a float is starting.[36] The tune *Sanbasō* used for the float *Fuyamachiguruma*, for instance, is a *kyōgen* version that was adapted to *kagura* style by a musician who has now passed away. Recreated from his notation, it is now played as an introduction to *karakuri* performances with their puppets, which do not include *Sanbasō*. In *Takayama matsuri* in Gifu prefecture, there is a float named *Sanbasō* that is believed to have been built over two hundred years ago, and a *Sanbasō* puppet belongs to it.[37] Similarly, a float in *Hida Furukawa matsuri*, not far from Takayama, with a female *Sanbasō karakuri*, was also named *Sanbasōtai*. This float was destroyed in a fire in 1904, but the puppet itself was saved. No longer in use, it is currently on display in the Hida Furukawa Festival Exhibition Hall. The bottom part of the float (*yatai*), *Sanbasōtai*, was renewed in 2009 and has again joined the *yatai* parade with the name-banner raised on it.[38]

Sanbasō mechanical puppets are normally *uwayama-ningyō* placed at the top of the float (Figure 82). The movements contain several sections that are derived from the most common *Sanbasō* dances. The picture in Figure 83 was taken in the *kōminkan* of Kosugaya on a rainy festival day when the performance was moved indoors, a common procedure in the case of rain. Like most *karakuri* puppets in Chita, this *Sanbasō* puppet is controlled by strings. In this case the ropes run through a square wooden tube, called *detoi*, which also serves as the base for the puppet's dance.[39] It was handled by young boys and girls, as is often the case in *Sanbasō* performances. The ensemble consists of a flute and a combined *kotsuzumi/ōtsuzumi* handled by one player. There is also

---

36 Kuroda and Yokoi 2013, p. 216.
37 *Takayama matsuri no yatai* 1991, pp. 12–13.
38 Schnell 1999, pp. 80–81, 150; *Hida Furukawa matsuri: Sanbasoutai* [Hida Furukawa festival: the festival float Sanbasōtai] 2019 (Internet reference); Hida City Hall, Commerce and Tourism Division, Ms Ishihara Rena, personal communication 25 November 2022.
39 Senda 2006, p. 251; Tokoname City Hall, Commerce and Tourism Division, personal communication 26 May 2020.

Figure 82 The *Sanbasō karakuri-ningyō* in an outdoor performance
at the shrine in Kosugaya (2 April 2017).

Figure 83 Indoor performance in Kosugaya. The strings that control
the karakuri run through a square wooden tube called *detoi* (compare
Figure 82). The boy between the puppet and the large drum uses a stick
to play an ōtsuzumi and a kotsuzumi held together in his left hand
(7 April 2013).

a wooden clapper. During most of the performance, formulae are chanted together with the instrumental music (• 3a–b).

The *Sanbasō karakuri* of Nakagumi in Kōwa is of a different construction. When the dance is finished, the puppet folds into a house representing a shrine building. The shrine building then unfolds, and the puppet's dance and its transformation are repeated a few times. The dance with swirling movements is accompanied by an ensemble inside the float, and behind it a group of children with an adult leader chant a formula (Figure 84).

Daimongumi in Yokosuka, Tōkai city, has a similar *Sanbasō* puppet, which also transforms into a shrine. The *Enbukyoku* dance tune is not used in Kōwa or Yokosuka, and the puppet movements differ from the ordinary *Sanbasō* dance. In Yokosuka, the transformation of *Sanbasō* into a shrine building is accompanied by an ensemble inside the float playing the tune *Sagariha*. When the shrine building unfolds and the puppet has emerged again, the music moves into the tune *Hayabue* followed by *Shagiri*, which leads to *donten* when the float is turned around full circle, with the front wheels lifted from the ground.

Figure 84 *Karakuri Sanbasō ningyō* of Nakagumi in Kōwa with a *kagurasuzu* in its right hand (2 April 2017).

Puppet Sanbasō

The *bunraku-type* puppet *Sanbasō* is normally a *maedana-ningyō* played in an opening in the front of the float. For the performance, the bamboo curtain that generally covers the opening will be exchanged for a curtain of cloth. A puppet is handled by three puppeteers who are not, in principle, visible from the outside. In central Chita, one of them controls the puppet's neck and body; one controls both its hands; and the third controls its two feet (Figure 85).[40] There are three puppeteers in *bunraku* as well, but it differs in that one handles the puppet's head and right hand, one handles its left hand only, and the third operates both its feet.

The performance is usually accompanied by flutes, percussion instruments, and the singing or reciting of a short formula. Most commonly the scene is comical, and in many cases the young people

Figure 85 Young players in Okujō in Ōtani. Two players are clearly visible. The arms and one hand of the third player, who handles the puppet's feet, can be seen in the lower part of the picture (31 March 2016).

---

40 *Taketoyo-chō shi: shiryō-hen* 2 1983, p. 321.

who pull the float will be seated or standing in front of it and respond to the puppet's movements.

In Nagao, the neighbourhood called Age has a *Sanbasō* puppet (Figures 86–87). The climax of the performance is when the *Sanbasō* puppet is jumping from side to side and finishes with its

Figure 86 The *maedana* opening in the front of the float, covered by a curtain for a *Sanbasō* puppet performance with the first sign of the name Age. Age, Nagao (9 April 2006).

Figure 87 The *Sanbasō* of Age in Nagao; the same float as Figure 86 with the curtain removed (9 April 2006).

Figure 88 *Sanbasō* waving its sleeves. This puppet can blink its eyes. The float *Honkosha* of Hon-Itayamagumi in Itayama, Handa (3 April 2006).

arms stretched out in its version of *karasutobi*, 'jumping like a crow' (Figure 87).

Other movements that are always present in the performances are *Sanbasō* walking with heavy steps and *Sanbasō* waving its sleeves (Figure 88). Certain *Sanbasō* puppets are constructed so that *Sanbasō* can blink its eyes (Figure 88) or stick out its tongue (Figure 89). The latter is called *Shitadashi Sanbasō* and originates in a humorous dance developed within *kabuki* theatre in the early nineteenth century.[41] The great majority of the *Sanbasō* puppets are male, but female *Sanbasō* puppets do exist (Figure 90).

Sanbasō music

While there are different accompaniments to *Sanbasō* performances, *Sanbasō* is very often accompanied by *kotsuzumi*, *ōtsuzumi*, and a short flute melody that is repeated with variations. The combination of instruments shows similarities to the ensemble used for

41 Brandon and Leiter 2002, pp. 52–53.

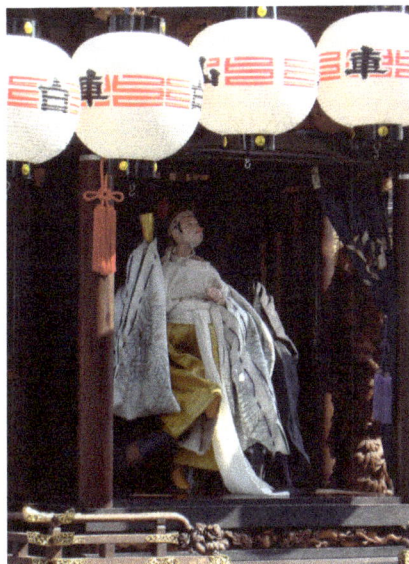

Figure 89 *Sanbasō* sticking out its tongue. The float *Hakusansha* of Sunagogumi in Kyōwa, Handa (15 April 2017).

Figure 90 Female *Sanbasō* of the float Ameguruma, Nakagumi in Okada, Chita city (16 April 2006).

Sanbasō in *nōgaku*. The music and ensemble for *Sanbasō* in Chita are quite easily recognizable even though there are variations. The following are recurring features, all or some of which may be used in the individual case:

- The performance is preceded by a tune, tunes, or a tale that functions as a prelude.
- The start of the performance is signalled by strokes on a large drum.
- The music starts with a high-pitched flute tone.
- The music of the initial section is slow in free rhythm, while the following dance section is rhythmic. Free-rhythmic passages may also occur within sections of the dance and at the end of the performance.
- A formula is chanted, most commonly a phrase that starts 'Ōsaiya ōsaiya'.[42]
- The dance section is accompanied by a short flute melody built on the rhythm used by the accompanying *kotsuzumi* and *ōtsuzumi* drums. The short melody is repeated with variations. It is sometimes called *Enbukyoku*, 'dance tune'.[43]
- The footsteps of the puppets or the dancer are emphasized by strokes on a wooden clapper.
- At times during the performance, the participants – often including younger ones seated in front of the float and functioning as an audience – chant or respond to the movements.
- The music and performance ends with a high-pitched flute tone.
- The end of the performance is signalled by a stroke on a large drum.
- The *dashibayashi ensemble* continues with some other tune.

The flutes. A flute signals the start and end of the music, and one or more flutes play the melody. In live dances, the full ensemble is usually standing or seated on a stage behind the dancer. In the case of a *karakuri* or *bunraku-type* puppet performance, it may be inside the float and/or outside it.

The tsuzumi drums. The two *tsuzumi* drums produce a rhythmic pattern when struck in alternation. The rhythm pattern used for

---

42 The phrase as chanted in Kamezaki, Handa, is transcribed in Hayakawa 2003b, note section p. 18. One interpretation is 'What luck! What luck! Let there be joy. Let there be joy. I will not let it go away from here'. Like the *Sanbasō* character itself, this phrase has parallels in *nōgaku*, *kabuki*, and *bunraku*.

43 *Jingūsha sairei no ayum* 2007, p. 8.

the dance section – *Sanbasō* or *Enbukyoku* – is basically the same as the rhythm of the flute melody played during the dance. In most cases one person plays the *kotsuzumi*, beating it with one hand, and another person beats the *ōtsuzumi* with a drumstick. In some places, one person handles both drums and strikes them alternately with a drumstick. In this case, the *kotsuzumi* may be held while the *ōtsuzumi* stands on the floor in front of the player. Otherwise, the two *tsuzumi* drums are held together by the red ropes by which their skins are tightened, normally in the player's left hand. In some places, the *shimedaiko* is employed instead of the *ōtsuzumi*.

The clappers. Wooden clappers of various kinds are used to loudly illustrate the steps of the *Sanbasō* dancing, like the *tsuke* in *kabuki* theatre. The *tsuke* consists of a wooden board and two beaters. Often, a pair of wooden beaters are struck against each other or against a solid wooden board. It also happens that a pair of beaters are struck against the base floor of the float, or against a wooden beam inside it. Since there is so much variety, such instruments will henceforth be referred to by the term *wooden clapper* in the *Sanbasō* context.

The dance tune Enbukyoku

Though the movements of the puppets are largely the same, there is also a great deal of variation with regard to how the dances are executed, not least regarding tempo. The same goes for the accompanying ensembles and their music. The music is dominated by the dance tune *Enbukyoku*, and the ensembles generally include flute, *ōtsuzumi*, *kotsuzumi*, and some kind of wooden clapper. The placement of the ensemble varies. The players may be seated inside the float, most commonly in its back, and on the shafts (Figures 91–92). Age in Nagao has most of the instruments inside the float while three *kotsuzumi* players are seated facing outwards from the rear, just as they are for parading. Quite often the ensemble stands behind the float, and sometimes even in front of it (Figure 93). When puppet play is performed outside the float, the players will occasionally be seated or standing close to the puppet.

The puppet *Sanbasō* goes through introductory movements to musical and/or vocal accompaniment. The dance section is rather short and repeated several times. Consequently, the main part of the music for the dance only consists of one short rhythmic and melodic motif – a unit of sound that characterizes the tune – which

Figure 91 Accompanying *Sanbasō*. The float *Miyamotoguruma* of Kamezaki, Handa. *Ōtsuzumi* (left), *hiradaiko* (center), *kotsuzumi* (right). The floats in the Kamezaki district are called *yamaguruma*. One person is holding a microphone, so the music is run through an amplifier and speaker (4 May 2017).

Figure 92 Accompanying *Sanbasō* of Daigone in Agui. The wooden clapper is in the centre (11 April 2004).

Figure 93 *Sanbasō* of Yokomatsu in Agui, performed in front of a private house. The ensemble is standing in front of the float so they can see the puppet's movements. From left to right: wooden clapper, two *ōtsuzumi*, two *kotsuzumi* (one partly hidden), four flutes (23 April 2017).

is repeated throughout the performance. In Age, Nagao, as in Kamezaki, Handa – which is believed to be the origin of Age's *Sanbasō* performance – the motif accompanying the dance consists of a unit of four beats (Example 1). As can be seen from the examples 1A–B, the two patterns are very similar; this comparison hence supports the common opinion that Age learnt their *Sanbasō* performance from Kamezaki.[44]

If such a pattern is called '*a*', the performance would be *a – a – a –* and so on. Many of the puppet performances adhere to a similar pattern, while some use two four-beat patterns where the second four-beat pattern is a variant of '*a*' with a slightly different melody '*a*ᵛ'. In those cases the performance could be written as follows: *a aᵛ– a aᵛ – a aᵛ –* and so on.

---

44 *Taketoyo-chō shi: shiryō-hen 2* 1983, p. 321.

Example 1 Patterns for accompanying the dance of the *Sanbasō* puppet in A) Kamezaki in Handa and B) Age in Nagao. The melodic motifs are the same, whereas the roles of the *kotsuzumi* and *ōtsuzumi* are shifted. The sign '∧' denotes an upward turn. (• 3a–b)

A)

B)

As is usually the case in music at festivals, there are local versions and the tunes are seldom exactly the same. However, the melodic motif and rhythmic pattern accompanying *Sanbasō* puppets are fairly stable from one place to another. The rhythm pattern is very similar to the rhythm used for *momi no dan*, the first of two *Sanbasō* dances in *nōgaku*, where the flute also plays a short melodic motif that is repeated throughout the dance.

The geographical distribution of *Sanbasō*

The occurrence of *Sanbasō* during *matsuri* includes live dances, *karakuri*, and puppet performances (Appendix 1: Table 9.). The kind of *maedana Sanbasō* puppets handled by three persons, and with the musical accompaniment mentioned above, is also found in Hekinan on the other side of the narrow Mikawa gulf, just east of Handa. The float *Nakanokirisha* in Ōhamanaka-ku and *Tamaguruma* of Tsurugasaki in Shinkawamachi both have such *Sanbasō* puppets. The music is basically the same as that described above, though the former is played notably faster than the latter.

Both areas have had close contacts with Kamezaki in Handa and bought their floats from there, so it seems reasonable to regard them as representatives of the same *Sanbasō* tradition as Handa and its surroundings in Chita. Hekinan is therefore included in the table.

Sanbasō also appears as a part of a unique *bunraku* tradition related to floats in Chiryū, located in West Mikawa. The so-called *dashibunraku* was designated UNESCO Intangible Cultural Heritage status in 2016. It consists of proper *ningyō-jōruri* performances accompanied by the long-necked lute *shamisen* and the kind of vocal recitation called *jōruri*. The narrator and the *shamisen* player are seated inside the opening in the front part of the float and are visible from the outside. Three puppeteers handle the puppets in the area just in front of the float that forms a stage surrounded by a low fence. They are visible, but dressed in black robes with their faces covered.[45] The *Sanbasō* performance of Chiryū thus employs different techniques and different musical accompaniments in comparison to the Chita Peninsula, where puppeteers are partly hidden behind a curtain and the musical accompaniment generally consists of flute and *tsuzumi* drums.

There is an unusual *Sanbasō* puppet in Ōmori in Moriyama-ku, Nagoya, which was made in 1960 by the rebuilding of a *karako* puppet, 'Chinese-style puppet', from nearby Seto. The *Sanbasō* puppet is placed on the top front of the float, and while it has all the attributes of *Sanbasō* – the hat, a fan, a *kagurasuzu* bell chime – it moves like a so-called *zaifuri-ningyō* or 'commander puppet' (as the float is pulled along, such a puppet turns its body, turns its head, and waves its arms with flags like military commander signals). In this case, though, the puppet waves a fan and a *kagurasuzu* bell chime.[46]

When patterns are plotted on a map, it becomes evident that there is a concentration of *Sanbasō* in and around the town of

---

45 This information is based on a *dashibunraku* performance show in Chiryū in 2010 and on *Chiryū no dashibunraku to karakuri: UNESCO mukei bunka isan tōroku kinen tokubetsu jōen* [A special performance of Chiryū festival float, puppet theatre, and mechanical puppets, in commemoration of the registration as UNESCO Intangible Cultural Heritage] 2017 (Internet reference).

46 *Owari no dashimatsuri* [Float-festivals of the Owari province] → *Ōmori Tennōsai: Nagoya-shi Moriyama-ku* [Ōmori Tennō festival in Moriyama-ward, Nagoya city] (Internet reference).

Tōkai

Kitasaki

Ōbu

Yokone

Ōta

Yokosuka

Okada

Chiryū

Chita

Higashiura

Kitakasuya

Miyazu

Hagi

Ogura

Daigone

Ōno

Agui

Yokomatsu

Nishinokuchi

Okkawa

Tokoname

Kamezaki

Taya

Yanabe

Handa

Tokoname

Kamihanda

Koba

Hekinan

Ōtani

Shimohanda

Taketoyo

Kyōwa

Nishinarawa

Kosugaya

Narawa

Sakai

Itayama

Nagao

Kaminoma

Ōashi

Mihama

Higashi-Ōdaka

Okuda

Ichihara

Fuki

Futto

Noma

Kitagata

Onoura

Kōwa

Utsumi

Minamichita

Ōi

Yamami

Morozaki

Distribution of Sanbasō

Puppet Sanbasō	▲
Karakuri Sanbasō	△
Sanbasō dance	✦
Dashibunraku Sanbasō	✧

0   2   4 km

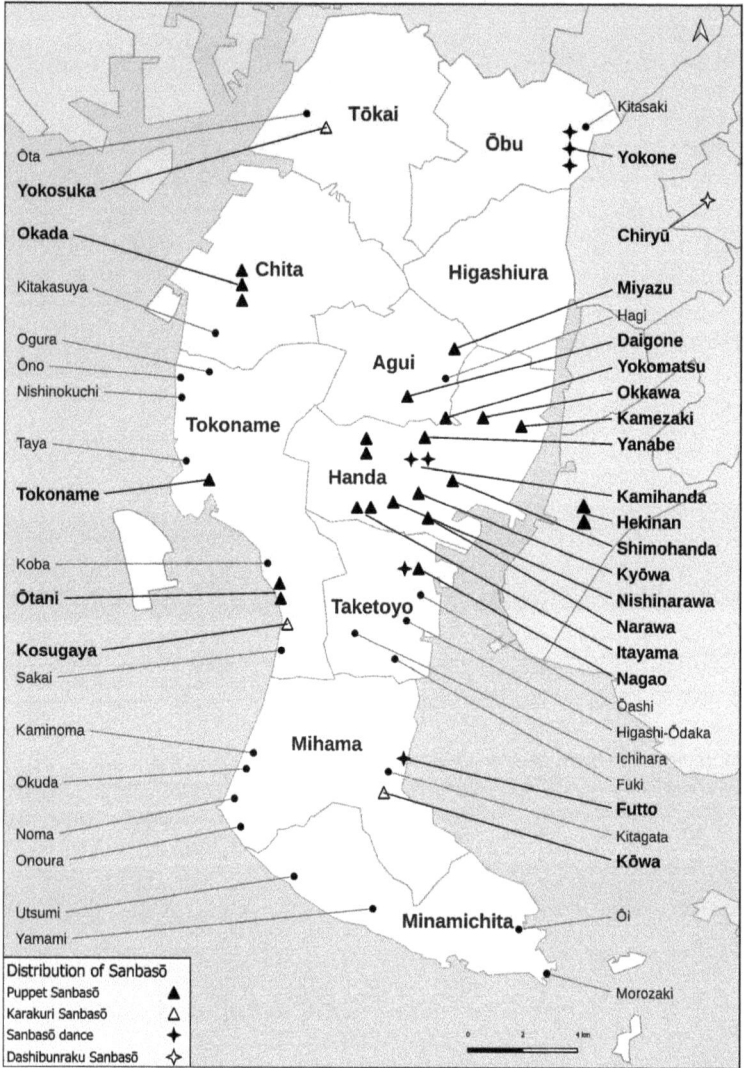

Map 6 Distribution of *Sanbasō* performances in the Chita Peninsula and the adjacent part of Mikawa (based on the list in Appendix 1: Table 9.). Courtesy of Jakob Cederblad.

Handa (Map 6). Yasuko Senda, who has studied the *karakuri* of Aichi and Japan at large, maps not only the *Sanbasō* but also the *Miko* puppets, since they too are handled by three persons.[47] The map in her overview shows a concentration of *Sanbasō* and *Miko* puppets in Handa and the neighbouring parts of the central Chita Peninsula. Evidently, Handa has served as a local centre not only for the *Chita type* of float but also for this type of puppet performance.

The combination of *kotsuzumi* and *ōtsuzumi* is present in the great majority of *Sanbasō* performances in the Chita Peninsula. The neighbourhoods Age and Ichiba in Nagao seem to be exceptional in that they use the two drums both for *Sanbasō* and *dashibayashi ensembles*. Age also differs from other *Sanbasō* performances by using three *kotsuzumi* as in *nōgaku*.

The simultaneous use of *kotsuzumi* and *ōtsuzumi* is a possible link to the combination of these two drums in many *dashibayashi ensembles*. The typical way in which *manzai* performers hold the *kotsuzumi* in front of them also has parallels in *dashibayashi ensembles*.

It is interesting to observe that even though the cities Handa and Agui house the majority of the *Sanbasō* performances, these drums are *not* used in their *dashibayashi ensembles*. This fact has sometimes been explained by a lack of people able to play these drums. The concentration of *Sanbasō* performances in Handa and Agui seems to contradict this interpretation, since there are clearly many persons who know how to handle *tsuzumi* drums. This means that there might be another reason.

---

47 Senda 1997, p. 37 and 2006, p. 263.

9

The musical repertoire

One initial question for this study concerned the use of the *kotsuzumi* drum in Nagao, Taketoyo. Through comparison with *dashibayashi ensembles* in Chita, Nagoya, and West Mikawa, the composition of the ensemble of Nagao has been placed in a wider context. There are parallels with Nagoya in the use of *kotsuzumi* and with Mikawa in the combined use of *kotsuzumi* and *ōtsuzumi*, as well as in the presence of floats with more than one internal level or floor. The *tsuzumi* drums are also used in connection with *manzai* and *Sanbasō*. In these cases, the music is quite different from the *dashibayashi music*; but the playing techniques involved display similarities.

The second initial question concerned the music in Nagao. The musical genres and their functions have been reviewed above. *Michiyuki* is played while the float is pulled along, *hōnōgaku* when a person or deity is celebrated, *keigo* in front of the shrine altar, and *isami* on special occasions, also apart from festivals. This chapter discusses these matters in greater detail.

People who are involved in *dashibayashi music* often say that the origin of individual tunes is unknown, or that a tune was learnt from a festival nearby. The most consistent comment in oral history, however, is that a tune stems from Atsuta, which is a place nowadays included in Nagoya city with the influential shrine Atsuta jingū.

A comparison based on tune-names confirms that about one third of the Komukae's *dashibayashi* tunes are in common with the repertoire of *Atsuta kagura* (Appendix 1: Table 10). Apart from this overlap, there are correspondences between the *dashibayashi* tunes of Nagao and those of Kamezaki and Kamihanda on the one hand and Ōtani, and Kaminoma in southern-central Chita Peninsula on the other. These resemblances are concentrated in the tunes *Shinguruma*, *Shagiri*, and *Seme*, which will be discussed in this chapter.

Tune-complex as an analytical tool

The general structure of the *dashibayashi music* and of most *kagura music* is *heterophonic*, much like the traditional Japanese music in *gagaku*. This means that all melody instruments – in this case the flutes – play the same melody with minor simultaneous variations. This is combined with percussive patterns – in Nagao these are synonymous with drum patterns, since gongs or cymbals are not used in *dashibayashi music* there. These patterns coincide with phrases or sections in the music, and their endings are often marked by a distinct rhythmic figure.[1] Many of these patterns are quite extensive, the percussion instruments moving on in repetitive arrangements. These will be called *longitudal percussive patterns*. There are also patterns that are comparatively short, percussion instruments interacting so as to weave a tight rhythmic figure. These will be called *interlocking percussive patterns*.

Individual tunes vary in length and tempo. A common musical form of the melodies is *aabb...* where each letter stands for one musical flute phrase which coincides with one breath.[2] Even though the tunes may have changed substantially through oral transmission and further development, there are in many cases some character-istics in the overall form of tunes or in units of sound, so called motifs, that are typical of a certain tune, so that it can be identified on fairly safe grounds. A complicating factor is, however, that these characteristic motifs may move and be combined with other tunes.

Since there are good reasons to assume that many tunes have spread to Chita from Atsuta jingū in Nagoya, and that several variants of each melody eventually developed, it would seem relevant to look at them as *tune families*, a concept often used in ethnomusicology. This approach usually aims at finding a common denominator by comparing numerous variants that seem to belong together, a proceeding which leads to the construction of a theoreti-cal archetype.[3] The establishing of the archetype thus emphasizes historical development and origin. In the present context, the term *variant* refers to tunes which may on fairly safe grounds be assumed

---

1 There are some parallels with *colotomy* and *heterophony* in Japanese court music, mentioned by Malm (1959, pp. 45, 98), and with percussive patterns of Southeast Asia, described by Becker (1968).

2 *Handa-shi shi: sairei minzoku hen* [Handbook of Handa city: festival and folklore] 1984, pp. 210–212.

3 Nettl 1983, pp. 105–109.

to be related. *Version* is, by contrast, used about tunes that are nearly identical, for instance a tune played by several neighbour-hood ensembles in the same community.

A method for comparison that focuses on the process of change and adaptation has been suggested by James Cowdery, who distinguishes three levels of comparison:

1. the 'outlining' principle, which focuses on similarities in the overall melodic contour;
2. the 'conjoining' principle, when some sections are in common while others differ;
3. the 'recombining' principle, whereby sections or whole melodies are compared without requiring a fixed overall contour.[4]

This approach takes account of common ways for musicians to develop melodies, and it is very much in agreement with the comparative method used in the *Atsuta kagura project*. Their experience is that new composition normally starts with borrowing from existing tunes. In the repertoire, there are tunes that are (1) almost identical, though they may sound different because of differences in tempo or between different kinds of flutes (with different scales and sounds); or tunes which display (2) many similarities in the melodies (form, melodic progression, motifs).[5]

In the following, I will use these approaches when listening for similarities or differences between tunes. I will group tunes together that are (1) nearly identical, that have (2) similar melody but different names, that have (3) similar names but different melodies, and that have (4) related functions. Such a group of tunes will be called a *tune-complex*. The tunes that belong to a *tune-complex* thus share some of the following aspects: musical characteristics, names, or function. They may be musically related or unrelated.

Three *tune-complexes* will be discussed in this chapter. The *Kanemaki tune-complex* serves as an example of what a *tune-complex* may be. This discussion, and that of the *Shinguruma tune-complex*, are concentrated in Nagao and the southern-central part of Chita. The discussion of the *Shagiri tune-complex* also covers the larger context of all Owari, including Nagoya.

The source material for this chapter consists of my own recordings, made at many festivals and rehearsals in the area

---

4 Cowdery 1984.
5 Mr Kanō Yoshio and Mr Hayakawa Makoto, personal communication 11 February 2023.

(see Appendix 2). In addition, audio and video publications in various formats are available on the website *Owari no dashimatsuri*.[6] The publications by Hayakawa Masao contain extensive material of notated tunes collected over a long period of time.[7] In the above-mentioned project based in Nagoya, *kagura* tunes stemming from Atsuta jingū are traced mainly in Aichi prefecture, and its website is my major source for the Atsuta repertoire.[8]

The *Kanemaki tune-complex*

Local variations in style sometimes make it difficult to even recognize tunes. This problem is further complicated by the fact that tunes have often been given local names – or that different tunes go by the same name. The lively tune *Ochazuke*, which is used in Nagao for honouring or celebrating, is a good example of this. Its name seems to be the same word as a popular dish, *ochazuke*, consisting of green tea, soup, or hot water poured over cooked rice with some topping. This may be a folk etymology based on sound similarity with the word *Shazuke*, as the name is written on the website of the neighbourhood Shitamo.[9] This would mean 'turn the float sideways', which is done when the float is halted to celebrate a person or a place, *iwaikomi*, during the parade along the city streets. The tune now called *Ochazuke* is in fact made up of two tunes, one of which is *Ochazuke* and the other is *Ōdakabayashi* (• **2a–c**).[10]

---

6 *Owari no dashimatsuri* [Float-festivals of the Owari province] (Internet reference).

7 Hayakawa 1984, 2003a, and 2003b.

8 *Atsuta kagura to Miyaryū kagura* [Atsuta kagura and Miyaryū kagura] (Internet reference).

9 *Shitamo Hachimansha kurabu: Bishū Nagao Shitamogumi* [The festival-float *Hachimansha* club of the neighbourhood Shitamo, Nagao district] → *Hayashi* [Festival music] (Internet reference).

10 *Handa-shi shi* 1984, p. 227 and *Bishū Nagao Komukaegumi Hōōsha: sōken hyakugojisshūnen kinenshi* [The festival float Hōōsha of the neighbourhood Komukae, Nagao district, Owari province: memorial magazine for the 150th anniversary of its construction] 2013, p. 43. The tune *Ochazuke* is included in the following AV references: *Komukae-ku Hōōsha: matsuribayashi* [The float Hōōsha of the Komukae ward: festival music]; *Tagakō kagura* [Kagura of the Taga shrine parish]; *Tamanuki no matsuribayashi: keigo* [Festival music of Tamanuki ward: *keigo* music], and *Tamanuki no matsuribayashi* [Festival music of Tamanuki ward].

A source concerning the neighbourhood of Banba in Nagao lists a tune called *Ochazuke* as *Ōdakabayashi*, a name that is also used for a tune in the *kagura* repertoire of Minamigumi in Narawa, Handa, which neighbours Banba to the north.[11] This type of name is normally used about a tune that is taken over from another area, in this case perhaps from Higashi-Ōdaka in Taketoyo, which used to be called just Ōdaka and in everyday language still is (*higashi* means 'east' and is used to distinguish this place from Ōdaka in Nagoya).[12] There are many examples of such borrowings of tunes. For instance, neighbourhoods in Nagao use a tune called *Ōashibayashi*, which stems from Ōashi. This is not to say that these tunes are known as *Ōdakabayashi* or *Ōashibayashi* in their original districts, where they – insofar as they are in use at all – might well go under other names.

In Ōashi, a tune called *Kanemaki* is performed as *isami*, 'gratitude music', when the *festival* is finished. It is also performed on various celebratory occasions during the parade: before the float starts out from the *sayagura*, when it is facing the shrine building, and when it has arrived at the *sayagura* at the end of the festival day. The melody is considered to have come from Atsuta. Musically, this *Kanemaki* has much in common with the tune called *Ochazuke* in Nagao.

A tune called *Kanemaki* is also used at a festival at Owari Taga jinja in Kariya, Tokoname, in a parade without floats which includes *ōdaiko*, *shimedaiko*, and flutes. Belonging to the *isami* repertoire, it is played while the parade climbs a long set of stairs that lead up to the shrine, and it is considered to facilitate the climbing.[13] This is a medium tempo piece that shows some resemblance to the first half of *Ochazuke* in Nagao: the melody has a pendulum movement between two pitches, and it ends with a motion to a higher pitch. They are far from identical, though.

---

11 *Taketoyo-chō shi: shiryō-hen 2* [Handbook of Taketoyo: reference material 2] 1983, p. 310 and *Handa-shi shi* 1984, p. 227.

12 *Taketoyo chiebukuro: Taketoyo chimeikō hoi* [Taketoyo wisdoms: supplemental information on place names in Taketoyo town] (Internet reference).

13 *Kanemaki* is listed under '*michiyuki, isami*', in *Kariya no matsuri* (AV reference). A list of tunes in *Tokoname-shi shi: bunkazai hen* [Handbook of Tokoname city: cultural assets] 1983, p. 569 mentions *Kanemaki* and *Kanemaki-modoki* (*modoki* approximately means 'variation') under the neighbourhood Hamajō in Ōtani which is used for *isami*. However, according to interviews these tunes appear not to be known now, and this is also the case in Okujō, Ōtani.

In Higashi-Ōdaka, too, there is a tune called *Kanemaki*. It is performed when the float enters the Chiryū jinja yard, which is a climactic moment of the festival. In addition, it is played as the very last tune when arriving at the *sayagura* at the final stage of the festival. In both cases it is played in a very quick tempo, with intense drumming, as the concluding piece in a set of fast tunes: *Shagiri – Hayabune – Kanemaki*. The *Kanemaki* melody consists of some rather short high-pitched motifs that bear some similarity to the first part of *Kanemaki* in Ōashi.

In Futto a few kilometres further to the south, a tune called *Kanemaki* is performed by the Hiratagumi neighbourhood. At one point, the three floats of Futto are lined up beside one another facing a steep road that leads up to a hill where the shrine is located. As the road is too narrow for the floats to pass, they cannot in fact proceed to the shrine. Just before they are to leave the area, Hirata's float will be pulled up the lowest part of the hill and then pulled down again backwards at full speed. This is when *Kanemaki* is played. This *Kanemaki* is a short and fast tune, more similar to the version in Higashi-Ōdaka than any of the others.[14] Hiratagumi's float is of the old type sometimes called *butsudansha*, 'Buddhist altar float', because its front resembles a Buddhist altar. Contrary to the rather austere fashion that characterizes floats made after the spreading of *state Shintō* in the Meiji period, the older floats often had colourful paintings or sculptures. This float displays a painted sculpture of a serpent writhing around a bell (Figure 94), which refers to the *Anchin Kiyohime legend* about Kiyohime, who was rejected by the priest Anchin. In a fit of fury, she turns into a fire-breathing serpent and burns Anchin, who has hidden in a temple bell, to death. The legend occurs in a classic *nō* drama which has also been adapted to *kabuki*. This float was bought from Okujō in Ōtani in the early Meiji period.[15]

In this rather small area, there are thus several versions of tunes called *Kanemaki*, *Ochazuke*, or *Ōdakabayashi*. The three names appear in different combinations with at least three melodies,

---

14 There is a transcription of Futto's *Kanemaki* in Hayakawa 2003a, note section p. 159.

15 According to a locally produced document signed by Sugiura Haruo in November 1998, an inscription in black ink inside the sculptured temple bell says that the float was built in 1807, and it names a carpenter and a sculptor from Chiryū. The legend is also present on the float of Banba in Utsumi, which has a bell and a writhing snake on top.

Figure 94 The front of the float *Tennōsha* of Hiratagumi in Futto, with the sculpture of a serpent writhing around a bell relating to the tune *Kanemaki*. An example of the colourful *butsudansha*, 'Buddhist altar float', dating back to the time before the *state Shintō* style had influenced float aesthetics (1 April 2018).

thereby forming the *Kanemaki tune-complex*. The tunes have slightly different functions in different areas; but it is significant that in none of these cases is it used for *michiyuki*, but exclusively for *isami* and *hōnō* celebrations at a *sayagura*, at a shrine, or for celebrating persons.

After barely having scratched the surface by looking at one *tune-complex* in a very limited geographical area, this example shows the complexity involved in recognizing and tracing different tunes belonging to the orally transmitted festival repertoire. While that complexity must be accepted, the individual tunes are nevertheless of great importance for the study of possible historical relationships.

The *Shinguruma tune-complex*

Shinguruma is a widely spread tune. The name means 'new float', but in some places the Chinese character for 'shin' is replaced by one meaning 'god'. In Nagao and Ōashi, it is combined with a special drum rhythm. This rhythm pattern dominates all of the slow or medium tempo tunes for *michiyuki* in all these districts.

Mitsubyōshi: *the three strokes rhythm*

This specific rhythm pattern is called *mitsubyōshi*, 'three strokes', and will be referred to as the *three strokes rhythm*.[16] It consists of consecutive strokes on the *shimedaiko*, *kotsuzumi*, and *ōtsuzumi*, in that order, followed by an empty stroke (or pause). The mnemonic *kuchishōga* syllables 'adapted to the sounds of the instruments'[17] for this pattern are *ten-kon-pan* (Ichiba, Komukae) or *tek-kon-pan* (Tamanuki). The sounds of *shimedaiko*, *kotsuzumi*, and *ōtsuzumi* are represented by '*ten/tek*', '*kon*', and '*pan*' respectively. The children in Tamanuki learnt the drum pattern by means of the phrase '*don'nan nā, tekkonpan*', meaning 'What's that sound? Tekkonpan'.[18] *Don* is the onomatopoetic word for the sound of the large *hiradaiko* drum. The *three strokes rhythm* has the following structure:

1st beat: a stroke on the *shimedaiko*,
2nd beat: a simultaneous stroke on the three *kotsuzumi*,
3rd beat: a final loud and high-pitched stroke on the *ōtsuzumi*,
4th beat: a pause.

Example 2 The *three strokes rhythm* of Nagao and Ōashi (A). The first *shimedaiko* stroke may coincide with a *hiradaiko* stroke (B). (• 4b–c)

---

16 The term *mitsubyōshi* is used in Kaminoma (Mr Isobe Toshihiko, Mihama Town Hall, Board of education, Lifelong learning section, personal communication 14 October 2022). In Ichiba, Nagao, this rhythm is referred to as *mitsuboshi*, 'three stars' (*Jingūsha sairei no ayumi: Ichiba-ku* [History of the Jingūsha float-festival: Ichiba ward] 2007, p. 8). *Mitsubyōshi* also appears as a term in *kagura music*, where it has a different meaning (Kárpáti 2008, 159–160).
17 Ido 2006, p. 181.
18 *Bishū Nagao Komukaegumi Hōōsha* 2013, p. 42; Mr Saitō Kiyotaka for the Tamanuki ward and Mr Fukumoto Takahisa for Ichiba, personal communication 16 April 2016 and 3 February 2023 respectively.

As was mentioned before (Chapter 4), *michiyuki music* is played by a *dashibayashi ensemble* seated inside a float, while *isami music* is performed by a different but similar ensemble (without *tsuzumi* drums) separately from the float and mainly at other times than the festival. In Nagao, these two genres are connected by the fact that they have several tunes in common. In principle, the tunes of the two genres are built on the same rhythm patterns of the larger drums (*hiradaiko* and *ōdaiko* respectively). However, the *three strokes rhythm* is not used for *isami*, which instead features fairly lively strokes on the *shimedaiko*. The result is that the *isami* versions are shorter and faster than the *michiyuki* ones. Another difference is a higher flute pitch in *isami*. All in all, *isami* tunes sound more strident than the more leisurely *michiyuki music*.

Drum rhythms of *isami* and *michiyuki* are compared in Example 3. Most tunes are dominated by rhythmic patterns that can be subdivided into 4-beat units. In the arrangement with the *three strokes rhythm*, one beat in *isami* corresponds to two beats in *michiyuki*. If there are syncopations or irregular beats in the *isami* version, this is compensated by extending a tone of the melody or by inserting a break, so that the *three strokes rhythm* can continue regularly. There is also a difference in tempo. One full repetition of the melody of the tune *Komenari* as performed by the Tamanuki neighbourhood in Nagao, Taketoyo, is 35 seconds in *isami* and 72 seconds in *michiyuki*, so the outcome is that *michiyuki* is about half the tempo of *isami*.

Shinguruma

All six neighbourhoods in Nagao play the slow *michiyuki* tune *Shinguruma* just before entering Takeo jinja. The floats are pulled along an uphill road leading there, except Age with their *sayagura* located on the same level.[19] In the notation (Example 4) one characteristic phrase of the tune is written out, also showing the drum accompaniment according to the *three strokes rhythm* (Examples 2–3).

The flute player, who is the leader of the ensemble, signals beginnings and endings of tunes. Some of these signals are unique to individual tunes while others may be used for more than one.

---

19 Nagao versions of *Shinguruma* are included in the following AV references: *Komukae-ku Hōōsha: matsuribayashi; Tagakō kagura; Tamanuki no mat-suribayashi: keigo*, and *Tamanuki no matsuribayashi*.

Example 3 A section of the tune *Komenari* showing the drum rhythm in its *isami* version (A) and the drum rhythm in its *michiyuki* version with the *three strokes rhythm* (B) transcribed from *Tamanuki no matsuribayashi: keigo* [Festival music of Tamanuki ward: *keigo* music] (AV reference). Tempi: A) *isami* ♩ ≈ 100, B) *michiyuki* ♩ ≈ 60. (• **4b–c**)

Example 4 A melodic phrase of *Shinguruma* consisting of a repetition of a high-pitched tone that characterizes the tune. The phrase is subdivided into two parts, 'c' and 'd' respectively. The percussive accompaniment is in the *three strokes rhythm*. Initial pitch ca. 1600 Hz. Transcribed from *Tamanuki no matsuribayashi: keigo* (AV reference). (• **1c**).

Melodic phrase c)

Melodic phrase d)

In this case, it is a high-pitched tone that descends and ends lower. The melody consists of phrases that are repeated two by two. These phrases are normally further subdivided into two symmetrical parts. This is the case with the most distinctive phrase of *Shinguruma*, which consists of a repetition of a high-pitched note (Example 4c–d). Sometimes phrases are identical when repeated and sometimes slightly varied. With regard to the melodic phrases, one stanza of this performance can be described as ab/ab, cd/cd, e/e, fg/fg). Paired phrasing is a fairly common form in festival music.[20]

The *three strokes rhythm* continues throughout the tune and the *shimedaiko* keeps an even and steady beat (Example 4). The *hiradaiko* is struck more seldom and at irregular intervals. When it is struck it coincides with a stroke on the *shimedaiko*. The three *kotsuzumi* and the *ōtsuzumi* follow. In performance, the three *kotsuzumi* drums are struck simultaneously, but often with a slight delay so that the sounding of them has the character of a rapid succession. There are some recurring drum patterns in the performance of *Shinguruma*. They differ in how often the *hiradaiko* is struck. Example 5a–b shows three such patterns that are sometimes varied. Phrase length and drum pattern length are closely interrelated. The end of a stanza is marked by three consecutive strokes on the *hiradaiko* (Example 5d)

When *Shinguruma* is played while the float is paraded, the melody and the corresponding drum pattern will be repeated several times. The total drum pattern of one full repetition may be described as A(ab)–A(ab)–B(cd)–B(cd)–C(e)–C(e)–D(fg)–D'(fg) where capital letters designate a drum pattern and lower case letters the corresponding musical phrases.

Shinguruma may serve as an example of how longitudal drum patterns are constructed in many of the tunes that are used in *dashibayashi music*. Similar constructions of drum patterns also occur in *kagura music* and in other traditional forms of music.[21]

Shinguruma *in the southern-central Chita Peninsula*

Within Taketoyo town, the *three strokes rhythm* can also be heard in the float *Honwakasha* in Fuki when the tune *Shinguruma*

---

20 *Handa-shi shi: sairei minzoku hen* 1984, p. 215.
21 Kárpáti 2008, p. 160 and *Atsuta kagura to Miyaryū kagura → Miyaryū kagura no taiko no uchikata* [How to play the drum in Miyaryū kagura] (Internet reference).

Example 5 Examples of drum patterns in *Shinguruma*. The drum patterns
'a–c' occur several times during the tune and are sometimes varied. Drum
pattern 'd' signals the end of a stanza. Transcribed from *Tamanuki no
matsuribayashi: keigo* (AV reference). **(• 1c)**.

Drum patterns:

a)

b)

c)

d (final pattern)

is played. Here, too, the *ōtsuzumi* is heard very clearly. A variant of
the same rhythm pattern is used by the Ochishima neighbourhood
in Kaminoma when the tune *Shinguruma* is played for *michiyuki*.
This is also the case in Kosugaya, where the same tune is used
on flat ground as well as when going downhill. It is moderately
slow, and the rhythm pattern is basically the same. *Tōōsha* of
Okujō in Ōtani has a variant of the same rhythm for *Shinguruma*.
Kaminoma, Kosugaya, Ōtani, and Sakai are located very close to

one another and typically share many characteristics in their music. In Uemura, Futto, just south of Taketoyo, the same rhythm pattern is used for *Shinguruma* as well as for the tune *Shinbayashi*.

In Kaminoma and Kosugaya, the *ōtsuzumi* and *kotsuzumi* drums may both be handled by one player and played with one drumstick. The two drums are either held together by the left hand or tied together into a double drum.

In Kaminoma and Sakai, tunes other than *Shinguruma* are used when going uphill or downhill. When going up the steep road to the shrine, the two floats of Kaminoma play *Seme*, which is a fast piece; going down, they play *Kyōgen*, which is extremely slow. In Sakai, too, the shrine is located on a hill, and the *sayagura* is just beside the shrine building. Before the float leaves the shrine yard in the morning, *Seme* is played. When it is pulled towards the exit, *Hayafune* will be played, and going downhill the ensemble play the slow *Kyōgen*. After that follows *Shinguruma* with the *three strokes rhythm*.[22] Before going uphill to the shrine on the way back in the evening, the musicians play the slow *Shinbayashi*, with a variant of the *three strokes rhythm*. *Shinbayashi* starts while the float is standing still, and it keeps on as they turn onto the road to the shrine. While the float goes up the hill, it is succeeded by a slow *Seme*, and when the float enters the shrine yard the lively *Hayafune* is played.[23]

Shinguruma *melodies*

Obviously, the drum rhythm – the *three strokes rhythm* – is shared by all versions of *Shinguruma* discussed so far. The relationship between the melodies is not as obvious. However, those of the six districts in Nagao and those of Ōashi and Fuki appear to be closely related. Those of Kaminoma, Kosugaya, Ōtani, and Sakai are slightly different, but resemble one another. Most versions share a slow tempo and a long high-pitched tone (Example 4), more

22 Included in *Sakai no matsuri Matsuo jinja hōnō* (*dashibayashi, kagurabayashi*) [Sakai's float-festival: Matsuo shrine offering (festival-float music and Shintō music)] (AV reference). According to *Sakai no ayumi to matsuri* [History and festival of Sakai] 2005, pp. 182–183, *Shinguruma* is nowadays called *Michiyuki* or *Michifuki* and is used when the float is paraded.
23 The information about Sakai comes from my own material and from *Sakai no matsuri* (AV reference), which contains recordings of tunes and comments.

melodical sections, and a final phrase dominated by a downward
motion. The version of Futto may be thought of as in-between
the versions of Kaminoma and Nagao. Taken altogether, all these
versions of *Shinguruma* are probably historically connected. A tune
called *Shinguruma* can also be found in Kamezaki in Handa, but its
melody sounds quite different.[24]

Shinguruma also occurs on the website of *Atsuta kagura* in
Nagoya under *Kasadera school*, after the name of the area where
the *kagura* masters resided in the southern part of Nagoya, also
referred to as *Saimeryū* after the founding master. Another branch,
Kantarōryū, is practised in Kamezaki (Handa, Chita) and Chiryū
(West Mikawa), where *Atsuta kagura* is called *Miyaryū kagura*.[25]
The *Kantarōryū Shinguruma* as performed in Kamezaki is quite
a lively tune. There are versions of it in Ōbu och Chiryū, too,
which are assumed to be derived from the tunes *Arimatsu* and
Hayame.[26]

The *Saimeryū Shinguruma* was taken over from the music of
a festival at Tsugata jinja, located not far to the east of Atsuta
jingū.[27] There was one large float, *Ōyamaguruma*, which was
destroyed in May 1945, near the end of the war. After the festival
had been kept up for many years, it was finally discontinued
in 1989. An engraving on a memorial stone states that 'Mister
Matsushirō' composed a new flute tune called *Shinguruma* in the
years 1844–1848. This *Shinguruma* was composed on the introduction of a new *karakuri* puppet. According to the memorial
stone, the new tune was 'startling' to people.[28] The first third of

24 *Kamezaki shiohimatsuri: matsuribayashi to Miyaryū kagura* [Kamezaki
shiohi festival: festival music and Miyaryū kagura] (AV reference).
25 *Atsuta kagura to Miyaryū kagura* → *Atsuta kagura, Miyaryū kagura no
rekishi: Atsuta, Kasaderakei* [A history of Atsuta kagura and Miyaryū
kagura: Atsuta and Kasadera lineages] → *Miyaryū kagura no bunrui*
[Classification of Miyaryū kagura] → *Sound source of Atsuta kagura
(Miyaryu kagura)*. The founding person of the *Kantarōryū school*, Kantarō,
may also be differently named. (Internet reference).
26 *Atsuta kagura to Miyaryū kagura* → *Kyoku no shōsaina kaisetsu* →
Shinguruma omote (Arimatsu, Hayame) (Internet reference).
27 Also referred to as *Tsukata jinja*.
28 *Atsuta kagura to Miyaryū kagura* → *Atsuta kagura: kanren no sekihi*
[Stone monuments related to *Atsuta kagura*]; → *Idota no Ōyamaguruma
(Tsugata jinja sairei)* [Floats of Idota district, Nagoya, Ōyamaguruma
(Tsugata shrine festival)] → *Tsugata jinja: dashi, ohayashi no yurai*
(Internet references).

the tune is very slow and similar enough to the *Shinguruma* of the southern-central Chita Peninsula to suggest a possible historical relationship.

However, the history of *Shinguruma* is still more intricate. There are two further local versions of *Shinguruma*.[29] One is used in Tsutsui-chō in Nagoya and one in west Owari, in the so-called *Owaridaiko style*, which is basically used west of Nagoya. On the basis of similarities with regard to melodic progression and the same fingering for the flute part, studies of *Atsuta kagura* indicate that all these *Shinguruma* tunes ought to be related. Some of them can be shown to be based on still older tunes. The similarities between the southern-central Chita *Shinguruma* and the *Saimeryū Shinguruma* might therefore be the result of both building on the same older tune. Though all details of the history are not known, it is likely that the southern-central Chita *Shinguruma* is a part of the Atsuta tradition.

The *Shagiri tune-complex*

Like several terms that occur in festival contexts, *Shagiri* also exists as a term in *kabuki* music, where it is commonly played between scenes. According to Leiter, *Shagiri* is

> a kind of ceremonial accompaniment, usually using stick drum (*taiko*), large drum (*ōdaiko*) and *nō* flute (*nōbue*), and played at the closing of the curtain. Some versions are heard at the beginning of plays. Each has its own name, such as *nibanme shagiri, kata shagiri, chakutō shagiri*, and so on.[30]

Shagiri has several meanings in the festival context:

- all *dashibayashi music* at a festival (for instance in *Nagahama hikiyama matsuri* in Shiga prefecture);[31]
- music played as a float is paraded, *michiyuki music* (for instance several districts in Handa);
- the process of turning the float (for instance Nagao and Tsushima, in many places called *donden* or *donten*);
- the music that is played as the float is turned (for instance Nagao and Tsushima).

---

29 This information about the history of *Shinguruma* comes from Mr Kanō Yoshio and Mr Hayakawa Makoto, personal communication 11 February 2023.
30 Leiter 1997, p. 570.
31 Nishikawa and Sazanami 2011, section 2.

Shagiri *in Nagao*

In Nagao and Ōashi, *shagiri* means turning the float – normally about ninety degrees at a road crossing – and it is also the name of the tune played during this process. In Nagao, all six floats also play *Shagiri* when they enter the Takeo jinja yard one by one at the climax of the festival.[32] The tune *Shagiri* starts slowly and increases in tempo until the speed is right for a fast turn. *Shagiri* differs in style from the general *michiyuki* tunes. Nevertheless, in the notation of Komukae it is listed in a separate section called '*Matsuribayashi 2*' together with two tunes of the category *hōnōgaku*, which are performed as celebrations. All these three tunes are played by the *dashibayashi ensemble* when the float is not paraded on a straight road, but either turning (*Shagiri*) or standing still when celebrating (*Ochazuke, Okamesan*). Being different from the general *michiyuki* tunes, *Shagiri* is performed by the ensemble without the large hourglass drum *ōtsuzumi* and without the *three stroke rhythm*. The rhythmic organization of Shagiri is based on a comparatively short pattern with cross-rhythms between the drums *ōdaiko*, *shimedaiko*, and *kotsuzumi*.

Shagiri starts with a characteristic flute signal: a high-pitched tone with a 'dip' in the middle followed by two drumbeats on the *hiradaiko*, one soft and the other strong (Example 6A). The *hiradaiko* is played with padded drumsticks. The strong beat is played with the right hand and the soft beat with the right or left hand.

The melody consists of one long phrase that is repeated several times (Example 6B). It has two parts: the first part is set at a high pitch level and the flutes slide slowly between a few pitches (B: a), whereas the latter part moves into a lower register (B: b) and includes a characteristic short melodic figure (compare Example 8a–c). The melody is accompanied by a percussive pattern by *hiradaiko*, *shimedaiko*, and *kotsuzumi*, which has the character of an interlocking short formula as the tempo increases (Example 7).

Shagiri also includes words of encouragement from those who handle the float. They shout '*sore!*', which may be translated as 'go, go!' or something similar. These shouts are rhythmically coordinated with the music of *Shagiri*.

---

32 For versions of *Shagiri* in Nagao, Handa, and Tokoname, see AV references marked 'S'.

Example 6 Shagiri flute part in a graphic transcription made by the software Melodyne as performed by Tamanuki in Nagao recorded on Tamanuki no matsuribayashi: keigo (AV reference). A) introductory flute signal, B) one whole section of the melody, C) final flute signal. Initial pitch ca. 2 320 Hz. (• 1a, 1d–f, 6a–b).

A

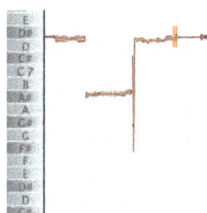

B a

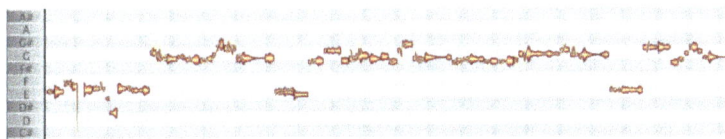

B b

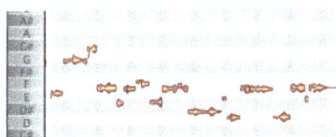

C

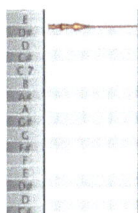

Shagiri is performed numerous times during the *Nagao no haru-matsuri*. In the late afternoon of the festival eve, the six floats leave Takeo jinja and parade along a straight road that leads to the JR Station area, where they will gather. Before they arrive there, they need to make a ninety-degree right-hand turn at a street corner.

Example 7 A percussive pattern of *Shagiri* section 'b' (see Example 6) as performed by Tamanuki in Nagao, transcribed from *Tamanuki no matsuribayashi: keigo* (AV reference). The instruments are *hiradaiko* (1), *shimedaiko* (2), and three *kotsuzumi* (3). (• **4a**)

On this occasion, the *dashibayashi ensembles* from six neighbour-hoods perform their respective versions of *Shagiri* one by one. The different versions adhere to the main outline in Example 6, but each has its own variants in respect of melody and rhythm.

Another occasion when the different *Shagiri* versions can be heard is when the six floats enter the Takeo jinja yard on the festival eve (the Saturday), as well as on the festival day (the Sunday). Then, however, on-lookers are gathered inside the shrine yard, and they will only hear and see the last part of *Shagiri* when each float is pulled in at high speed. There are many simultaneous sounds as well, which makes it hard to distinguish anything. Therefore, the following description of the Age neighbourhood's performance of *Shagiri* was documented at two different times: one observing the float from behind, outside of the shrine yard, and the other from the front, inside the shrine yard. In this way the complete process of *shagiri* could be documented.[33]

The float of Age is waiting outside the entrance to the Takeo jinja yard, which will be entered by means of a left-hand turn. Apart from the musicians and those who pull and steer the float, there are also active participants from the neighbourhood, dressed in *happi* coats for the festival. When the initial signal of a flute and the two drumbeats are heard (Example 6A), they all go completely quiet. They know that the process of turning the float and entering the shrine yard has started, and from now on full focus is on this process.

Shagiri starts out in a slow tempo. The first time that the B phrase is played, it lasts for 90 seconds. With each repetition the tempo is increased, until at the sixth time the B phrase only takes 10 seconds, which is quite fast. During this process, the musicians and the other participants, who chant *sore!* in rhythmic coordination with the music, have experienced the gradual increase in speed. At this point the drumming is very lively and exciting. About 3.5 minutes after the music started, the wooden clappers *hyōshigi* signal that it is time to move the float, which is then pulled forward into the shrine yard at running speed. The rhythmic shouting is now replaced by

---

33 The documentation from the outside was made on Sunday 9 April 2017. The one from inside the shrine yard was made on Wednesday 1 May 2019, which was when the floats of Age and Komukae were offered at Takeo jinja on the first day of the new Reiwa era.

free cheering and shouting. The B phrase is repeated over and over
at the constant high tempo (about 10 seconds per repetition). When
the float has been pulled some 50–60 metres it is turned sideways,
so that it faces the shrine building. A new clatter from the *hyōshigi*
signals that the float should be stopped. The music continues for a
little while until the final flute signal is sounded (Example 6C). The
whole process has taken about five minutes.

All the six floats go through the same, rather dramatic, process.
The music with the rhythmic shouting has the important function
of coordinating the activities of those who pull and those who
push and steer, as well as of those who hold on to ropes fastened to
the top of the float in order to prevent the heavy float from falling
over.

The geographical distribution of Shagiri

The *Shagiri* of Ōashi mainly belongs within the same musical frame
as that of Nagao, with the difference that rather than featuring
a gradual acceleration of speed, the beginning is an alternation
between slow and medium tempo sections until the fast part starts
and the float is pulled around a corner. The first natural location in
which to subject the *Shagiri* of Nagao and Ōashi to a comparison is
the city of Handa, which neighbours Taketoyo to the north.[34] The
district called Banba in Nagao actually pulls their float to the river
Ishikawa every year, just on the border between the two towns,
and there they meet the float *Kamiguruma* from the neighbouring
district of Narawa in Handa before the two floats continue their
separate routes.

In some neighbourhoods in Handa, *Shagiri* is sometimes a slow
to medium tempo tune used for *michiyuki*. However, there are
also neighbourhoods in Handa where *Shagiri* is used for increasing
speed, like Kamezaki, Kamihanda, and Shimohanda.

The *Shagiri* of Nagao and Ōashi, which Hayakawa calls *Nagoya-
type Shagiri*, has a characteristic melodic figure.[35] It occurs in many
other places in the Owari area as well, including Chita Peninsula.[36]

---

34 In Kamezaki, Handa, this tune is called *Hikioroshi* according to *Handa-shi
shi* 1984, pp. 218–219, and *Kamezaki shiohimatsuri*.
35 Hayakawa 2003a, pp. 46–47.
36 Examples from Owari include Hayakawa 2003a, note section p. 172
(*Akiba matsuri*, Komaki), p. 182 (*Kamori matsuri*, Tsushima), p. 185

Example 8 Characteristic melodic figure in *Shagiri*, a) Komukae in Nagao, b) Tsutsui in Nagoya, c) Minamigumi in Ōbu. Example 8a–c from Hayakawa 2003a, note section pp. 58, 14, 93. The transcriptions have been transposed to facilitate comparison. (• 4a)

a)

b)

c)

Example 8a–c shows three rather typical versions of this melodic figure from Nagao, Nagoya, and Ōbu respectively.

In some areas in Handa and nearby places, this melodic figure is less pronounced or not present at all. In most versions of *Shagiri* in Handa, the first section instead has a characteristic 'pendulum movement' between two tones in a high pitch area, with a stress on the higher-pitched tone (Example 9).

In Higashi-Ōdaka, Ōno, and Ōbu, for instance, *Shagiri* includes a pendulum movement, and the melodic figure is in equally prominent positions.[37] Looking at the whole Chita Peninsula and Owari, these melodic differences between local versions of *Shagiri* are more a matter of degree than of sharp contrasts. Another factor that ties the different *Shagiri* versions together is the commonly used introductory formula: a high-pitched flute tone followed by two drumbeats. This common feature suggests that these versions

(Iwakura), and Hayakawa 2003b, note section p. 49 (Tsushima), pp. 55/59 (Inuyama), pp. 73/74 (Asuke).

37 For Ōno, see Hayakawa 2003a, note section p. 105, and for Ōbu, see Hayakawa 2003a, note section pp. 93, 95, 96.

Example 9 Characteristic pendulum movement of *Shagiri* from
neighbourhoods in Handa: a) Kitagumi in Kamihanda, b) Nakagumi
in Shimohanda and c) Kitagumi in Narawa. Arrows indicate stressed
tones. Example 9a–b from *Handa-shi shi: sairei minzoku hen* [Handbook of
Handa city: festival and folklore] 1984, pp. 270–271 and c from Hayakawa
2003a, note section p. 49. The transcriptions have been transposed and
the rhythm notation adjusted to facilitate comparison.

can be understood as related, and related to the different versions
of Nagao, Ōashi, and Handa.

The characteristic pendulum movement of some *Shagiri* versions
mentioned above (Example 9) suggests a similar dominant motif
on the part of the tune *Hayakagura*, which is often played before
or after *Shagiri* in many localities.[38] *Hayakagura* and *Shagiri* may
be performed as one unit without a clear transition from one to
the other, so that one tune moves smoothly into the next one. This
technique is called *otoshikomi*;[39] in English, it is sometimes referred
to as a 'medley'.

---

38 See, for example, notation of *Hayakagura* and *Shagiri* as performed by
Narawa Kitagumi in Hayakawa 2003a, note section pp. 48–49, and *Shagiri*
by Okkawa Minamiyama in *Handa-shi shi* 1984, p. 265. For recorded
versions of *Hayakagura* in Handa and Tokoname, see AV references
marked 'H'.

39 *Handa-shi shi* 1984, p. 235.

In some districts, the slow initial part of *Shagiri* is presumed to be a different tune as compared to the latter part. In these cases, the slow part has a separate name while the fast part is called *Shagiri*. Both neighbourhood groups in the Kamihanda district, Handa – Kitagumi, 'north group' and Minamigumi, 'south group' – have *Shagiri* that move from slow to fast. In Kitagumi, the first slow part is called *Shagiri kuzushi*, '*Shagiri* variation'; it is followed by the uptempo *Shagiri*, which is used when the float is pulled backwards in the shrine yard.[40] Musically, this pattern closely resembles Nagao's *Shagiri*. In Minamigumi, however, the slow part is based on a separate though similar melodic material, a tune called *Kyōgen*. Both are examples of the *otoshikomi* or 'medley' technique.

Shagiri *and donden*

In many other areas in northern Chita and in and around Nagoya, the float is often turned more than ninety degrees – usually in a full circle, once or sometimes more than once. The front wheels are then lifted off the ground; but in some cases the back wheels are lifted instead, and it also happens that the float is turned while standing with all four wheels on the ground. Turning the float without lifting it is called *donden*, *donten*, or *shagiri*, and the music is generally a variant of *Shagiri*, sometimes in combination with other tunes.

In Arimatsu, Nagoya, turning is called *shagiri*, and both the float *Hoteisha* and its music shift tempo abruptly, slow–fast–slow–fast. The first sections are short, and the turning of the float starts on the last and fast section, which is played during the whole turning process and for a while afterwards, until the float is stopped.

Turning the float around several times is also practised in Tsushima, particularly at cross-roads, which were traditionally believed to be where 'malevolent spirits could pass'; it was believed that by rotating the float, the 'evil spirits could be driven out' (Figure 95).[41] Here this process is called *shagiri*. The tune *Shagiri* is played for as long as the rotating goes on. The *Babachō* float plays *Shagiri* in a steady medium tempo with heavy drumbeats. *Shagiri* is also used for parading without any increase in speed.

---

40 *Handa-shi shi* 1984, p. 223.
41 Kuroda and Yokoi 2013, p. 156.

Figure 95 *Kitamachiguruma* of Tsushima performing *shagiri*
(5 October 2014).

In Yokosuka, Tōkai town, *donten* is accompanied by three
tunes: *Hayabue – Shagiri – Hayakagura*, in that order. Each tune
starts with a high-pitched flute tone. *Hayabue* is rather slow.
Shagiri starts with the usual high-pitched flute tone followed by
two drumbeats. The young men handling the shafts in the back of
the float strike their hands twice on the shafts in unison with the
two initial drumbeats, and then press the shafts down so that the
front wheels are lifted from the ground. *Shagiri* is fast, and it is
played for as long as *donten* – the rotating of the float – goes on.
When it is finished and the front wheels touch the ground again,
a high-pitched flute tone signals the beginning of *Hayakagura*,
which is a moderately fast piece, sometimes decreasing in speed.
After this, a tune from the *michiyuki* repertoire will normally
follow. Similar practices occur elsewhere as well, for instance in
Kitajō, Tokoname, where the combination *Hayabue – Shagiri –
Yūshagiri* is played.[42]

---

42 *Shinmeisha Kitajō matsuribayashi* [The festival music of the float
   Shinmeisha of the neighbourhood Kitajō, Tokoname] 1991, booklet p. 3
   (AV reference).

While *Shagiri* is used for *donden* in most of Nagoya with sur-roundings, there are also other uses. In Nagoya, *Shagiri* in a medium tempo is often employed for *michiyuki*. In Iwakura, the parade is dominated by variants of *Shagiri* in a slow-to-medium tempo for all the three floats; and when a float is turned ninety degrees, the tempo increases to high. After the turn, it gradually slows down to the slow or medium tempo.

Seme, Hayabune, *and* Hayakagura

In other parts of southern-central Chita, other tunes are used for high speed in situations similar to *Shagiri* in Nagao: for turning and at special moments like leaving the *sayagura*, entering a shrine yard, or returning to the *sayagura*. The most common ones are *Seme*, *Hayabune*, and *Hayakagura*.[43]

Seme is characterized by fast drumming and rather short melodic motifs, most of which end with an upward slide at a high pitch. As the intensity and tempo increase, these motifs tend to become even shorter. Variants of *Seme* occur in Kaminoma, Futto (Mihama) and Kosugaya, Ōtani, Sakai, Segi (Tokoname) and Fuki, and Ichihara (Taketoyo).[44] According to oral information, many festival traditions in this area consider themselves to have learnt from Kaminoma, which has served as a local centre for festival music. In Uemura, Futto, the opinion was that *Seme* had been learnt from Kaminoma. This has been commented on by Hayakawa as well.[45] Regarding Uemura, the *ōtsuzumi* is used for some pieces of the *michiyuki* repertoire, particularly *Seme*, played when departing from the *sayagura* and entering into it, when a float is brought to movement after standing still, and when a float has entered the shrine yard. *Kotsuzumi* is used for *Seme* played when all three floats of Futto are going uphill to the shrine. It should be noted that some variants of *Seme*, particularly that of Kosugaya, feature the melodic figure that is characteristic of *Shagiri* (see Example 8). However, the music in Sakai is believed to have passed down from the neighbouring town of Fuki, Taketoyo. The tunes *Hayafune*,

---

43 In some districts in the area, the tune *Hayabune* is called *Hayafune*.
44 *Serakusha: Matsuribayashi* [Serakusha Festival Music, Tokoname-city, Segi ward] (AV reference) has the version of Segi, Tokoname.
45 Hayakawa 2003a, pp. 66–67. See also notations of *Seme* in the note section on pp. 156 and 160–161.

Seme, and *Shinguruma* resemble those used in Fuki while differing from Kaminoma.[46]

Hayabune occurs in most places in southern-central Chita Peninsula except Nagao and Ōashi. Most of the time, it is a fast tune with loud drumming. It frequently contains pendulum movements with high pitches, like some versions of *Hayakagura* and *Shagiri* (see Example 9). Some versions of *Hayakagura* and *Hayabune* have enough musical material in common to give the impression that they are the same tune with different names. In the fastest and most intense part, they may – as in Kaminoma – have similarities to *Seme*, with a short motif ending with an upward slide at a high pitch. *Hayabune* is sometimes used during parades as well – the people pulling the float may be running or walking at a moderate speed though the music is fast (Kaminoma), and in Higashi-Ōdaka *Hayabune* often follows after *Shagiri*. It is sometimes used for uphill movement (Sakai), when starting from the *sayagura* (Ichihara), or when entering a shrine yard (Higashi-Ōdaka).

Kaminoma and some neighbouring areas thus differ from Nagao and most areas north of there by not using *Shagiri*. Similarly, Nagao and the others do not use *Seme*, only *Shagiri*. The tune *Hayabune* has a geographic distribution similar to that of *Seme*. The variants of *Shagiri*, *Seme*, and *Hayabune* have the fast tempo in common and in most cases also the increasing tempo, from slow to fast; and the same goes for *Hayakagura*. By and large, they are also played in similar situations, where a significant factor is increasing the excitement for participants as well as spectators. Despite the similarities, however, these tunes are often different enough to be easily recognized as one or the other merely by listening. Still, the similarities in uses and function, and the cross-over of some typical motifs between them, justifies regarding them as belonging to the same *tune-complex*, here called the *Shagiri tune-complex*.

Main stylistic and functional traits

Most of the *dashibayashi music* is based on *longitudal percussive patterns*, which is in contrast to the music of the most famous festivals, like *Gionbayashi* (Kyoto) and *Kandabayashi* (Kanda, Tokyo),

---

46 *Sakai no ayumi to matsuri* [History and festival of Sakai] 2005, p. 186.

and also some in Mikawa, such as *Miya matsuri* (Gamagōri).[47] There, gongs are more prominent; and the parade music consists of rather short melodic flute phrases and repetitive rhythm patterns produced by drums and gongs, usually in a high tempo.[48] This brings to mind the interlocking percussive pattern in the up-tempo parts of tunes like *Shagiri* and *Seme*. At those festivals, however, slower and differently constructed tunes may also occur at other stages of the festival.[49]

In this chapter, the tunes *Kanemaki*, *Shinguruma*, and *Shagiri* were chosen for detailed discussion because of their frequent utilization and important functions during festivals. *Kanemaki* demonstrates how melodies and names of tunes may vary and brings out the close relationship between the festivals in southern-central Chita.

That *Shinguruma* is likely to have roots in *Atsuta kagura* corroborates the widespread opinion that the tunes of Chita *dashibayashi* stem from Atsuta in Nagoya. But the analysis also shows that the use of the *three strokes rhythm* points to a relationship between the local performance practice of Nagao and that centring around Kaminoma and Ōtani in southern-central Chita.

Shagiri represents a widely spread tune in the whole of the Chita Peninsula, Nagoya, and the rest of Owari, as well as in Mikawa and even in neighbouring prefectures. It illustrates how the *dashibayashi music* of Nagao is connected to this larger geographical area.

The *dashibayashi music* of Nagao thus mixes traits from Nagoya and from festivals in southern-central Chita, which accords with what was found in the comparison of the *dashibayashi ensembles*.

---

47 Own observations at Shijō-dōri in Kyoto on 17 July 1995; Hayashi 1992; *Gion festival, Saki-matsuri: twenty-three floats gorgeously parade through ancient capital's streets*. (Internet reference).
48 Fujie 1986a, pp. 105, 114.
49 Kurata 1997; *Sawarabayashi: Tokushū* [A feature article on Sawarabayashi, Chiba] 2014 and *Sawarabayashi no shinzui* [The essence of Sawarabayashi] (Internet references).

10

A historical perspective

It is, as was pointed out above, generally believed that many tunes in *dashibayashi music* have spread from Nagoya. The comparison of the ensemble types shows many similarities between Nagoya and Owari on the one hand and the Chita Peninsula on the other. Furthermore, an area in southern-central Chita Peninsula differs in some respects, something that also applies to ensembles in West Mikawa. The analysis of *tune-complexes* supplies further indications concerning the spreading of this music.

This chapter focuses on *how* the music spread from Nagoya: how it spread within the Chita Peninsula, how these factors have developed over time, and specifically how this has affected the *dashimatsuri music* in Nagao, Taketoyo.

The history of this music is closely tied to the history of shrine music, of the festivals themselves, and of festival floats. There are few overviews, so a large part of the relevant written material is scattered in local publications, information that has rarely if ever been put together before. Naturally, oral information has played a vital role, too.

The major *Shintō* shrines

The development of festival music in the Chita Peninsula depends to a large extent on the *kagura music* in the major shrines: Ise jingū in Mie prefecture west of Chita and Atsuta jingū in the southern part of Nagoya. *Shintō* music underwent major changes after the Meiji restoration in 1868. The main objective of the so-called *state Shintō* was to separate *Shintō* and Buddhism from each other, and the ceremonials at the shrines were reformed according to new standards.[1] The *kagura* music at the larger shrines was reformed as

---

1 Inoue 2003, pp. 163–164.

well. That the effects of these changes were considerable is evident in accounts about the important shrine in Ise:

> The *kora-ko*, female child dancers, were dismissed and replaced by young adult dancers, usually between sixteen and twenty-two, picked from the rural population... The new Ise *kagura* was staged in 1872 by Inokuma Natsuki... The new music was kept in the simplest style to symbolize the virgin age of the Yamato people. Such musical numbers as *Kami-oroshi*, *Yamato-uta*, *Sume-kami* and others were put together by the *gakunin* [court musicians], and the influence of *saibara* [a song genre] is evident.[2]

Initially *gakunin* were brought from Tokyo to Ise for major rituals, until local musicians had been trained and were able to perform this music.[3] In 1934, an attempt to recreate the old songs and dances turned out to be unsuccessful as they had dropped out of memory.[4]

The festival tradition at Atsuta jingū in Nagoya can be dated back to the eleventh century.[5] During the *Edo period*, the Atsuta yearly *matsuri* included three tall Ōyamaguruma that were about 20 metres high as well as six smaller floats called *danjiri*. When electricity and trams were introduced in the late nineteenth century, the Ōyamaguruma were too tall to be paraded in the streets, so they were used only very seldomly for celebrations of special importance. The remaining floats were destroyed during the Second World War. Since the final decades of the *Edo period* the musicians, who were also frequently priests, performed and taught their arts at other shrines in Nagoya as well as in the surrounding areas, such as the northern part of Chita Peninsula including Kamezaki in Handa.

The introduction of *state Shintō* led to a reorganization of the *kagura music*, and that took place at Atsuta jingū in 1875. The *kagura* at court was reformed and called *mikagura*, 'venerable' *kagura*, while 'all its variants outside it belong to "village", that is *satokagura*'. The *mikagura* repertoire superseded the older *kagura* sometimes referred to as *miyakagura*, 'shrine *kagura*', performed in

---

2 Harich-Schneider 1973, pp. 582–583.
3 Urita 2015, pp. 498–499.
4 Harich-Schneider 1973, p. 582.
5 Takamura 1982, pp. 40–41 and *Atsuta kagura to Miyaryū kagura* [Atsuta kagura and Miyaryū kagura] → *Atsuta kagura, Miyaryū kagura no rekishi: Atsuta, Kasaderakei* [A history of Atsuta kagura and Miyaryū kagura: Atsuta and Kasadera lineages] (Internet reference). The information on *Atsuta kagura* is primarily based on this site.

gagaku style, and 'local *kagura*', which used flute and drum.[6] The existing *miko* dances were replaced by new *miko* dances and music. However, some of the tunes of the old dances survived as instrumental tunes in *kagura* at other shrines in the area.[7]

Those who had performed *satokagura* at Atsuta jingū now had to find other means of earning their living. They increased their *kagura* performances and teaching at other shrines and continued their engagement in *michiyuki music* in the *Atsuta Ōyama matsuri* and other festivals. Kikuta Saime, who served Atsuta jingū around the middle of the 1800s, founded the head family of Atsuta *kagura*, often referred to as *Saimeryū*. Kikuta Kindayû became a maker of *gagaku* instruments and flutes for festivals and founded a shop that still exists in the vicinity of the shrine. Many *kagura* musicians moved to the neighbouring Kasadera district that became a base for their activities and thus spread the *kagura* music that had originated in Atsuta jingū to Owari (including Nagoya city), north Chita and west Mikawa.[8]

The Nagoya castle district

The festivals that started in the Nagoya castle district were another important source of *matsuribayashi music*. This goes back to 1603 when Tokugawa Ieyasu (1542–1616) was appointed *shōgun* and established the shogunate in Edo, which marks the beginning of the *Tokugawa period* (also called *Edo period*) that was to last until 1868.[9] He had a new castle built in Nagoya on the site of a previous

---

6 Kárpáti 2000, p. 153.

7 Garfias 1965; Takamura 1982, p. 39; *Handa-shi shi: sairei minzoku hen* [Handbook of Handa city: festival and folklore] 1984, p. 207; Hayakawa 2003b, p. 7; *Atsuta kagura to Miyaryū kagura → Atsuta kagura, Miyaryū kagura no rekishi; → Miyaryū kagura to ohayashi* [Miyaryū kagura and festival music. With English text] (Internet reference).

8 *Handa-shi shi* 1984, p. 244; *Atsuta kagura to Miyaryū kagura → Atsuta kagura, Miyaryū kagura no rekishi* [A history of Atsuta kagura and Miyaryū kagura: Atsuta and Kasadera lineages] (Internet reference). An account of the *kagura* family named Kikuta who were active during the late Edo and the Meiji periods can be found in Takamura 1982, pp. 56–57. Information on Kikuta Saime was also provided by Mr Kanō Yoshio, personal communication 29 January to 6 February 2023.

9 The last *shōgun* resigned in 1867, and 1868 is counted as year one of the Meiji period, *Nihon zenshi: Japan kuronikku: Japan Chronik* 1991, pp. 904, 908.

one on the northern side of the so-called Atsuta plateau.[10] His ninth
son, Tokugawa Yoshinao, became the first Owari *daimyō*, and
after his father's death he moved into the new Nagoya castle. A
Tōshōgū shrine was built in the castle area in 1619; there was also
a Tennōsha shrine, which nowadays is called Nagoya jinja.[11] Both
shrines were moved to their present locations in the late 1800s.

The festival *Tōshōgū sairei* is believed to have been first celebrated in mid-April 1618, with influences from *Gion matsuri* in
Kyoto and from the new festivals in the capital Edo. By the mid-
eighteenth century, the *Tōshōgū sairei* had nine floats. They were
still there in the early twentieth century but were destroyed during
the Second World War. The festival is now celebrated with court
music and dance, *bugaku*.

At Nagoya jinja, the *Tennōsai* had floats that were called *danjiri*.
One of them still exists and is brought out and decorated for the
festival, but not paraded. Instead *mikoshi* are used in parades to
Wakamiya Hachimansha. *Wakamiya matsuri* dates back to the
latter part of the 1600s and is the third of Nagoya's major early
festivals. Up to the Second World War there were seven floats, but
now only two of them are in use. At one time they were both sold
to Dekimachi. One of them was later bought back again, and this is
the float now in use in *Wakamiya matsuri*.[12]

In 1660 the so-called *Manji fire* destroyed a large part of the
castle town, which was then reconstructed. The town also expanded
towards the Atsuta area in the south. The festivals in the castle area
were strictly controlled by the Owari domain government, which
did not permit much spending. This was in line with the Edo government's contemporaneous policy of 'the spirit of simplicity and
frugality'. In 1730, Tokugawa Muneharu (1696–1764) became
the Owari domain *daimyō* and the seventh lord of the castle.

---

10 The old castle was built around the 1520s and the new one in the 1610s.
    Both are called Nagoyajō but are written with different characters. *Nagoya
    castle: special historic site: the zenith of early modern castle design and
    construction* (Internet reference).

11 Nagoya jinja is sometimes called Nagono jinja.

12 *Shinshū Nagoya-shi shi* [A history of the city of Nagoya] 2001, pp. 733–740;
    *Nagoya jōka no dashi gyōji chōsa hōkokusho: Nagoya no dashi gyōji sōgō
    chōsa* [Survey report of festival float events in the castle town Nagoya: a
    comprehensive survey of Nagoya festival float events] 2018, pp. 15–16,
    47–62, and Tajima 1983, pp. 183, 186, concerning the floats of *Wakamiya
    matsuri*.

He was opposed to the government's economic policy of cut-downs, martial spirit, and supremacy of law, holding the opinion that too many rules and too much economizing would be harmful to society. Instead, he promoted an active economic growth policy which included support to commerce and industry and the building of theatres.

Atsuta shrine on the southern side of the plateau had been enshrined in ancient times. Atsuta was the largest station on the Tōkaidō road. It had about 250 inns for travellers and two official guest residences for travelling people of high rank, including the Emperor's messengers, lords, court nobles, and upper-class *samurai*. Located close to the sea and with a harbour, it became a centre of prosperity due to shipping. It housed several fish markets, and rice taxes were transported there via the Kiso River. Together with Edo, Osaka, and Kyoto, Nagoya became a town of impor-tance, known for providing space for performing arts. Muneharu's open-trade idea led to economic development but was in opposition to the government and caused large budget deficits. In the end, he lost his position and was sentenced to confinement in the castle. Nevertheless, Muneharu had a strong and lasting influence on the culture of Nagoya and the Owari area, including its festivals, not least thanks to his reorganization of the *Tōshōgū sairei*, which was restored to its former grandeur.[13]

All of the three important leaders from the Nagoya area, Oda Nobunaga (1534–1582), Toyotomi Hideyoshi (1537–1598), and Tokugawa Ieyasu (1542–1616), had favoured *nō* drama, and the Owari domain also supported *nō*. Many *nō* musicians were employed, and many citizens were engaged in *nō*. Consequently, *nō* music – especially *michiyuki music* for floats arranged in *nō* style – spread extensively in the Owari area.[14]

In 1629, a *nō* flute player in Kyoto named Fujita Seibē Shigemasa (1600–1677) had been invited to the Owari domain by the Tokugawa family.[15] He is considered to be the founder of the *Fujitaryū*; and for generations after him, his descendants were *nō* flute players in Owari and carried on the name Fujita Rokurobyōe.

---

13 This whole passage about Nagoya is based on Hiraoka 2008, pp. 140–141; Kitagawa 2013, pp. 33–34, and *Nagoya jōka no dashi gyōji gyōji chōsa hōkokusho* 2018, p. 16.

14 *Nagoya jōka no dashi gyōj gyōji chōsa hōkokusho* 2018, p. 413.

15 Iizuka 1999, p. 112; *Nōgaku yōgo jiten → Noh Terminology: Fujitaryū* 2021 (Internet reference).

According to oral information, it is believed that he was given the task of arranging *dashibayashi music* in the castle district of Nagoya. This music is later supposed to have spread to Owari and the Chita Peninsula. That assumption is supported by the fact that much of the *dashibayashi music* of Nishibiwajima was taught by *Fujitaryū* flute players.[16] Similarly, some of the music taught in Kamezaki, Handa, by a priest from Atsuta jingū in the late *Edo period* was based on the *nō* music of *Fujitaryū*.[17]

The festivals in the Chita Peninsula

There are some records of early float-festivals in the Chita Peninsula. It is said that eighteen fleeing *samurai* households from Kyoto came to Kamezaki, Handa, in the latter part of the fifteenth century. They brought with them the tradition of pulling carts decorated with cloth and bamboo branches, and this was the origin of the festival in the district, which is the oldest documented festival in the Chita Peninsula.[18] A scroll from 1755 depicts four floats being pulled in a festival in Okkawa, Handa.[19] In Kaminoma, Mihama, a float-festival started around 1700. Two early floats were destroyed by fire in the mid-nineteenth century.[20] A festival in Sakai, Tokoname, with a *dashibayashi ensemble* including flutes, *tsuzumi*, and drums, was documented in 1755.[21] In Fuki-Ichiba, Taketoyo, a festival including floats being pulled took place in the 1780s.[22] Historical records show that there were also festivals with floats at that time in several other places in the Chita Peninsula.

---

16 *Aichi-ken shōgai gakushū jōhō sisutemu: Manabi-netto Aichi* [Aichi prefecture lifelong learning information system: Learning-net Aichi] 2018 → *Owari Nishibiwajima matsuri: Yoritomo-sha no matsuribayashi* [The Nishibiwajima festival in Owari province: the music of the festival float, *Yoritomo-sha*] (Internet reference).

17 *Handa Dashimatsuri Hozonkai* [Handa Float-festival Preservation Society] → *Dashibayashi* [Festival float music] (Internet reference).

18 *Handa-shi shi* 1984, p. 10; Iga 1994, p. 46.

19 In *Handa-shi shi* 1984: 4 the scroll is called *Okkawa-mura sairei dashi ezu* (Illustrated handscroll of the Okkawa village float-festival). This scroll is analysed in McPherson 2007, pp. 118–122.

20 Iga 1994, pp. 133–134; Nakahashi 2011, p. 41.

21 *Sakai no ayumi to matsuri* [History and festival of Sakai] 2005, p. 158.

22 Iga 1994, pp. 26, 126, where *Chōshū zasshi* [Geographical notes on the Owari province] compiled in 1789 are summarized and a float from Fuki village is mentioned.

Float-festivals appear to have flourished in the Chita Peninsula around the mid-eighteenth century. This was a time when floats used at festivals began to be decorated in a variety of ways.[23] Later on, a local float variant developed in Handa. The float *Rikijinsha* of Nakagirigumi, built in 1826 and still in use in Kamezaki, Handa, was an early step in the development of the unlacquered *Chita-type* float with wood carvings, which represented a new sculptural aesthetic.[24] Many of the oldest floats have been exchanged for newer ones; but some still exist after being rebuilt, usually in a manner conforming to the *Chita type*. 'The oldest float still in use in Chita' is supposed to be the *Karakosha* of Ōno, built in 1741.[25]

In Nagao, Taketoyo, there was a castle, which no longer remains. The castle area included Takeo jinja and the neighbourhoods Age and Shitamo. The latter also had the Hachimansha shrine which is still in use. The Iwata clan that originally resided in the Nagao castle were succeeded by the Ōshima clan around the mid-seventeenth century. A *mikoshi* was dedicated to the shrine by the lord Ōshima Shirobē Hisanari, and a member of the Iwata clan, Iwata Shinhichirō, donated a float to Nagao village. It was called *Shinhichisha*, after the donor. A festival is said to have been held in the summer. On the festival eve, the float and a *mikoshi* were brought from Takeo jinja to Hachimansha, where the party stayed and returned on the morning of the festival day. It was described as 'an incomparably great festival in the area'. In the later years of the *Edo period*, late eighteenth to mid-nineteenth centuries, a float referred to as *Jijisha* was used.[26] It is unclear whether this was a new name for the same

---

23 *Handa dashimatsuri gaidobukku: oideya Handa, Chita-ji no sora ni Handa ga moeru* [Handa Float-festival guidebook: welcome to Handa, a fiery city under the sky of the Chita Peninsula] 1995, p. 49.

24 *Owari no dashimatsuri* [Float-festivals of the Owari province] → *Chōshū zakki: Kamezaki Nakagirigumi Rikijinsha, dashi chōkoku shūfuku fukugen* [Miscellaneous notes on Owari: Rikijinsha, the festival float of Nakagiri neighbourhood, Kamezaki district [Handa], restoration of the sculptures] (Internet reference); McPherson 2007, pp. 138–139; *Kamezaki Shiohimatsuri shashinshū: Shōwa no kioku, Heisei no fukko, sono saki e* [Kamezaki Shiohimatsuri in pictures: memory of Shōwa era, vitalization of Heisei era, and onwards] 2017.

25 Nakahashi 2011, p. 24.

26 This historical overview is built on Saitō and Saitō 2008, Chapter 4, pp. 1–2, *Takeo jinja: Nagaojō atochi, Tsukiyominomori* [Takeo shrine: the site of the Nagao castle, Tsukuyominomori] 2014 and its English version

float or a new float. There is also a 1757 description of a float which is, according to local tradition, considered to refer to the Age neighbourhood.[27] The festival gradually declined owing to orders to practise thrift, and it is unclear what happened to these floats.

By the first half of the nineteenth century merchants were becoming major sponsors for festivals, and the festivals were organized and carried out by young men's organizations, *wakamono-gumi*, on the village level. They performed certain protective police and firefighting duties, looked after the village common land, and took care of the shrine festivals. The festivals would sometimes express an element of opposition, and gradually the *wakamono-gumi* would be controlled by rules of conduct. Later replaced by youth groups that had a less formal position, they would still have a place in local festivals.[28]

At this time, the Chita Peninsula had developed non-agricultural production such as pottery, salt refining, and maritime trade. The production of rice wine, soy sauce, and vinegar created an economic base for a boom in float-building.[29] In the course of a few decades, more than half of the floats in the Chita Peninsula were constructed or traded. Higashi-Ōdaka obtained their float in the late *Edo period*, and there is a note saying that it was 'rebuilt' in 1834.[30] There are two different legends about its background: it was either bought from Yanabe in Handa or from Ōtani in the neighbouring township of Tokoname.[31] Ōashi's float is supposed

---

(Internet reference). Further information concerning Takeo jinja from Mr Iwata Takao, Chief Priest at Takeo jinja, personal communication 11 November 2021.

27 According to *Taketoyo-chō shi: shiryō-hen 2* [Handbook of Taketoyo: reference material 2] 1983, p. 320, it is 'unclear which neighbourhood the float concerned belonged to'. In *Bishū Nagao Komukaegumi Hōsha: sōken hyakugojisshūnen kinenshi* [The festival float Hōsha of the neighbourhood Komukae, Nagao district, Owari province: memorial magazine for the 150th anniversary of its construction] 2013, p. 8, it is said that the float described in the report *Biyō muramura saireishū* [Anthology of village festivals in Owari], published in 1757, can be thought of as the first float in the Age ward.

28 Fukutake 1967, pp. 103, 108, 111; Jensen 1989, pp. 79–84; McPherson 2007, pp. 141–146.

29 McPherson 2007, pp. 117–118.

30 *Taketoyo-chō shi: shiryō-hen 2* 1983, p. 227; Iga 1994, p. 123; Nakahashi 2011, p. 35.

31 Iga 1994, p. 123.

to have been made in 1796, and it was purchased from Ōtani in 1839.[32] In Nagao, Shitamo renovated their old float in 1859, a float was built in Komukae in 1863, and another was made in Age in 1867.[33] As a result of reforms in the early Meiji period which began in 1868, Takeo jinja became the village shrine; and during the Meiji period, the floats of Komukae and Age were offered there at the festival.[34] It was later moved to 15 April and thus became a spring festival.[35] While Higashi-Ōdaka had a float in 1834,[36] Fuki-Ichiba's dates from 1863,[37] and Honwakakai in Fuki built theirs in 1868[38].

Musical influences

By and large, the music played at festivals in the Chita Peninsula has spread there from Nagoya. Influences came from the music of the Atsuta jingū, generally referred to as *Atsuta kagura*, and from musicians in the Atsuta and Kasadera area. There was also important input from the major festivals in Nagoya, notably from the castle area.[39] The role of Ise jingū is less clear.

As early as the final decades of the *Edo period* there are documented contacts between priests or musicians, who were well acquainted with the rituals of Atsuta jingū, and the Kamezaki

32 *Taketoyo-chō shi: shiryō-hen* 2 1983, pp. 227, 287; Iga 1994, p. 122, Nakahashi 2011, p. 34.
33 Nakahashi 2011, p. 31. According to *Bishū Nagao Komukaegumi Hōōsha* 2013, p. 8, 'Shitamo renovated the old float in 1859, Komukae built the present float in 1863, and Age started building its present float in 1871' (translation by KL).
34 *Jingūsha sairei no ayumi: Ichiba-ku* [History of the Jingūsha float-festival: Ichiba ward] 2007, p. 3; Saitō and Saitō 2008, p. 4–2.
35 Mr Iwata Takao, Chief Priest at Takeo jinja, personal communication 11 July 2021.
36 *Taketoyo-chō shi: shiryō-hen* 2 1983, p. 227; Iga 1994, p. 123; Nakahashi 2011, p. 35.
37 Nakahashi 2011, p. 36.
38 Iga 1994, p. 125; Nakahashi 2011, p. 35.
39 According to Mr Hayakawa Masao, Yokosuka, personal communication 26 March 2002, the music had spread from Nagoya and developed variants in the Chita Peninsula, except in Taketoyo which he regarded as a separate case. Speaking about Nishinokuchi, Mr Fukaya Yoshihiro, personal communication 23 March 2002, was of the opinion that the *kagura music* probably came from Atsuta jingū and that the *dashibayashi music* went back to Fujita Rokurobyōe and the Nagoya castle area.

district in Handa. According to oral tradition, there were also direct contacts with Kamihanda.[40] Kamihanda seems to have had a central position in transmitting the repertoire further to other districts in Handa. After the Meiji restoration, those musicians whose services were no longer required in the revised rituals at Atsuta jingū moved to other places and functioned as teachers, thereby spreading the music called *Atsuta kagura* further. Their first concern was to add *kagura* to existing local *dashibayashi music*, and there are indications that they would arrange local festival tunes in the style of *Atsuta kagura*.[41] These Atsuta-shrine musicians were trained in *nō*, so *dashibayashi music* and *kagura music* were arranged in *nō* style.[42] It is quite likely that Nagao, Taketoyo, also learnt music from Handa – perhaps from Kamihanda, directly or indirectly, perhaps via Narawa. The music that is believed to have originated in *Atsuta kagura* then changed through oral transmission, so that each piece now exists in several variants.

Kamezaki represents *Atsuta kagura*, there called *Miyaryū kagura*, in which one player handles both the large drum (*ōdaiko*) and the smaller drum (*shimedaiko*). There are other *kagura* schools as well, and one of them, the *Asahiryū*, is considered to have originated in the village of Asahi in present-day Hekinan, located in West Mikawa just across the narrow strait to Handa. Several festivals in Handa evince influences from *Asahiryū*, two players handling these two drums.[43] In Nagao the term *kagura*, more specifically *futsū kagura*, is synonymous with *isami*, which is played on special occasions during the year.[44] The *ōdaiko* and the *shimedaiko* are handled by two players, which reflects the *Asashiryū* style. This is the case in Ōashi, too; but on one occasion the tune *Michiyuki* was performed during *isami* in the *Miyaryū* style, one player handling both drums.

The floats as historical evidence

The floats themselves are the most concrete evidence of historical relationships. There are several types of floats, which differ with

---

40 *Handa-shi shi* 1984, pp. 231, 234.
41 *Handa-shi shi* 1984, p. 246; *Shinshū Nagoya-shi shi* 2001, p. 711.
42 Hayakawa 2003a, pp. 16–17.
43 *Handa-shi shi* 1984, pp. 208–214; *Handa dashimatsuri gaidobukku* 1995, pp. 49–50.
44 *Bishū Nagao Komukaegumi Hōōsha* 2013, p. 42.

regard to size as well as in respect of construction details. Floats
spread from Nagoya to parts of the Chita Peninsula. The present-
day *Nagoya type* is rather wide and can house several musical
instruments. It is fairly common in the north-western part of Chita
Peninsula.

Many of the floats in the Chita Peninsula were built during the
years between the end of the *Edo* and *Taishō periods,* approximately from the 1840s to the 1920s. On these, the wheels do not
protrude; they are aligned with the sides of the float and protected
by a wooden board, so that the floats could pass easily through the
narrow roads of the villages in the peninsula. By the mid-nineteenth
century, Handa town had become the centre of this *Chita type.*[45]
The present floats of all six districts in Nagao, as well as most
places close to the city of Handa and to the south of that city, are
of this type. It spread to West Mikawa as well.

Among the older floats, that of Nakagumi in Kōwa originated in
Okkawa. According to an inscription, it was built by the carpenter
Kishimaku Zenbē of Yokomatsu in Agui in October 1755.[46] Its
shape is similar to today's *Chita type,* which may be taken to
suggest that the prototype of the *Chita type* was already nearly
complete by that time.[47] Floats with features similar to those in the
above-mentioned illustrated scroll from Okkawa in Handa city
dated 1755 are sometimes called *Hōreki type,* after the Hōreki
era 1751–1764.[48] They are partly lacquered, often in black, and
with nearly the same width of the upper and lower levels.[49] Black
lacquer combined with gold decorations resembles a Buddhist altar,
butsudan, and they are therefore sometimes called *butsudansha.*
In contrast to the *Chita type,* these older and often slightly smaller
floats are also referred to as 'old Chita form', 'early Chita form',
and similar designations.[50] They include the floats of Ōashi and
Higashi-Ōdaka in Taketoyo (see Figure 18), Hiratagumi in Futto,

---

45 *Bishū Handa: dashi emaki* [Owari province Handa: festival-float picture
   scroll] (Internet reference) 2017.
46 *Owari no dashimatsuri* [Float-festivals of the Owari province] → *Chita
   no dashikan B*: Kōwa Tenjinmatsuri, Nakagumi [Festival float museum of
   Chita: the festival float of the neighbourhood Nakagumi, Tenjinmatsuri,
   Kōwa district, Mihama town] (Internet reference); Iga 1994, p. 129.
47 Tatematsu 1994, p. 25.
48 *Handa-shi shi* 1984, pp. 78, 85–86.
49 *Taketoyo-chō shi* 1983, p. 227.
50 This type of float is sometimes called *Chita kogata* [Old Chita type].

Mihama town (see Figure 94), the Ōi district in Minamichita town, and Segi in Tokoname city.[51]

The tsuzumi drums

The smaller variant of the hourglass drum, the *kotsuzumi*, has a given place in the ensembles of *nō* and *kabuki*. The ensemble used for *Sanbasō* performance in *nō* employs three *kotsuzumi*. In the *Edo period*, before the introduction of *state Shintō*, *kotsuzumi* drums were used at Ise jingū for *daidai kagura*, which was the most elaborate form of *kagura* that pilgrims to Ise could offer to the deity.[52] *Daidai kagura* was not traditional at Atsuta jingū but was introduced in 1712. According to one source, it came from Edo; but there is also a detailed account about a small delegation from Nagoya that was permitted to travel to Kyoto in 1711 for the purpose of learning the dances and music of *daidai kagura*. The ensemble they learnt from included 'three *kotsuzumi*, flute, and drum'. *Daidai kagura* was performed at Atsuta jingū up to the early years of the *Meiji period*; it now survives in some other shrines.[53] In Chita and Mikawa, this kind of drum also has a presence in the folk performing arts of the *manzai* and in *Sanbasō* puppet traditions. In the case of *dashibayashi ensembles* it is used in several places, generally only for *michiyuki music* played when a float is paraded. But there are also places where *kotsuzumi* is not used in

---

51 This passage about some floats in the Chita Peninsula is based on *Aichi dashi zukan* [Picture-book of the festival floats in Aichi] 2017; *Aichi no dashimatsuri: Aichi-ken no dashimatsuri pōtarusaito* [Float-festivals in Aichi, portal website for float-festivals in Aichi prefecture] (Internet reference); *Owari no dashimatsuri → Chita no dashikan C: Mihama-chō, Futto Hirata-chiku* [Festival float museum of Chita: the festival float of the Hirata ward, Mihama town] (Internet reference); *Taketoyo-chō shi: shiryō-hen 2* [Handbook of Taketoyo: reference material 2] 1983, p. 227; *Handa-shi shi: sairei minzoku hen* [Handbook of Handa city: festival and folklore] 1984, pp. 78–90; Iga 1994; Nakahashi 2011.

52 *Uki-e Ise daijingū ryōsho daidai mi-kagura no zu* (Perspective picture of a most solemn *kagura* performance held at the two shrines in the Grand Shrine of Ise) and *Iconography of kagura performance at Ise 1* (Internet references).

53 *Shinshū Nagoya-shi shi* [A history of the city of Nagoya] 2001, pp. 708–709. Mr Kanō Yoshio has included documentation in the original and in a modern Japanese translation in *Atsuta kagura to Miyaryū kagura → Daidai kagura* (Internet reference).

the *dashibayashi ensembles* even if it exists there in connection with *manzai* or *Sanbasō*. This is the case in Handa and Agui, for instance.

The *kotsuzumi* is employed in some districts in Nagoya, not least around the castle area where the early festivals took place in Tokugawa times. In the northern part of the Chita Peninsula, it is used on the west side in Nishinokuchi, Yokosuka, and Ōta. Further south in the Chita Peninsula, it is used in an area stretching from Kosugaya in the west via Kaminoma to Futto and Taketoyo in the east. South of this area it is not common, though it can be found in Higashibata, Utsumi.

It is possible to think of different reasons for this geographical distribution. One view held by Hayakawa Masao, with his profound knowledge of *dashibayashi music* in Aichi, is that *kotsuzumi* were previously used everywhere but gradually fell into disuse.[54] This view is supported by the fact that the *kotsuzumi* drums seem to be dispensable, for instance in the case when there are not enough players for the ensembles; I have heard these explanations from, among others, Higashibata in Utsumi and Uemura in Futto.

It is still unclear, however, why the *kotsuzumi* should have fallen out of use only in the area to the southeast of Nagoya, including Agui and Handa, but not in several other places to the south and west. A possible explanation could be that *kotsuzumi* were not used in areas that were under direct influence of *Atsuta kagura*, in line with *Shintō* aesthetics, while those who were less directly influenced had greater freedom in their use of instruments. It is also possible that the older float-festivals in Handa – like Okkawa – had established their ensembles before the *kotsuzumi* became popular with *kabuki* influences in the 1700s. Other factors that may have affected the use of instruments might be certain legal limitations.[55]

The larger variant of hourglass drum, the *ōtsuzumi*, is used in an even more narrow area: a belt stretching from Kosugaya in the west via Kaminoma to Taketoyo, also including Tokoname town. North of that belt it is only found in Okada, Chita city. Its distribution thus partly overlaps with that of the *kotsuzumi*. *Ōtsuzumi* and

---

54 Mr Hayakawa Masao, Yokosuka, personal communication 26 March 2002.

55 Concerning the Tsushima area during the *Edo period*, 'it was decided that the only musical instrument which was allowed in the countryside was *taiko*. During the Bunka-Bunsei period [1804–1830], *tsuzumi/taiko/fue* were, however, allowed in the countryside as well, and also in the town area'. Kuroda and Yokoi 2013, p. 167 (translation by KL).

kotsuzumi are used together in Ōtani, Kosugaya, Kaminoma, Fuki, Higashi-Odaka, and in Ōashi and Nagao in Taketoyo. In Kosugaya and Kaminoma, the *kotsuzumi* and *ōtsuzumi* drums are played by one person, either held together, tied together, or with one drum held and the other placed on the floor. Similar ways of playing these two drums are common in accompaniment to *Sanbasō* performances. Both drums are needed for certain *dashibayashi* tunes, and especially the *three strokes rhythm* discussed in Chapter 9 demands that both drums be used.

The fact that the two *tsuzumi* drums are widely used together in Mikawa as well may be taken to indicate a historical relationship. It may well be the case that the *kotsuzumi* is more indispensable in places where the *kotsuzumi* and *ōtsuzumi* are used in combination. This could explain why it is used today in the area in the Chita Peninsula that has both these drums. If the combined *tsuzumi* drums spread from Mikawa, they might have spread further westward from the coastal area of Ōashi, Nagao, and Fuki facing the Mikawa Bay.

A characteristic trait of Nagao and Ōashi is the practice where three *kotsuzumi* players are seated beside one another in the far back of the float, facing backwards. There are examples of one or two *kotsuzumi* in several areas in the Chita Peninsula, but the players will often be seated inside the float, either on the floor or on a higher level. Sometimes two *kotsuzumi* players are seated in the rear of the float so that they face each other as in Yokosuka. In Nishinokuchi, 2–3 *kotsuzumi* players may be seated in the rear of the float, facing backwards. While there are districts in Nagoya where *kotsuzumi* is not used at all, three *kotsuzumi* beside one another – and sometimes more than three – occurs in some parts of the city, particularly in the castle area. Of these, Wakamiya had an influential festival with seven floats. It is just possible that the use of three *kotsuzumi* in the ensembles may stem from *Sanbasō* in *nō* or from *daidai kagura* of Atsuta jingū. Perhaps ensembles like that of Wakamiya in the Nagoya castle area served as a model for the three *kotsuzumi* in Nagao and Ōashi.

In the beginning of the 1950s, the three *kotsuzumi* employed in Nagao were played by three 'young seniors', who were around 20 years old and dressed in *kimono*.[56] As it seems to have been an

---

56 Mr Torii Shinkichi, Taketoyo, personal communication 26 October 2014, and *Jingūsha sairei no ayumi* 2007, p. 12.

established tradition by then, one may assume that it dates back
at least to the time before the Second World War. Banba bought
their float from Kamigō in Toyota in 1926 together with three
'*tsuzumi*' (*kotsuzumi*). A *hiradaiko* was bought in Narawa, Handa,
and different kinds of flutes were purchased in Atsuta and Nagoya.
This suggests that the use of three *kotsuzumi* in the *dashibayashi*
ensembles existed in Nagao by that time. There is no specific information about *shimedaiko* or *ōtsuzumi* in that source, though.[57]
Since the floats of the Age, Komukae, and Shitamo districts were
built around 1860, it is possible that the three *tsuzumi* drums
were introduced to the ensembles then, or between then and 1926.
There are no early sources concerning *tsuzumi* drums in Nagao, but
tsuzumi existed in Sakai in 1755.[58]

The repertoire

Several of the tunes played in Nagao can be traced to *Atsuta*
kagura. They probably reached Nagao primarily by way of districts
in Handa, particularly Kamezaki, Kamihanda, and Narawa. There
are also signs of relations with the Kaminoma area, as demonstrated
by the tune *Shinguruma* and its special drum pattern. On the other
hand, Nagao uses *Shagiri* for fast tempo, unlike the Kaminoma area
where the tunes *Seme* and *Hayabune* dominate. The origins of some
of the tunes in Nagao are unknown.

Nagao differs from many other places with regard to the relation
between *kagura music* – the music specifically offered to the *kami*
that includes the *isami*, *keigo*, and *hōnō* tunes in Nagao – and
michiyuki music, which is played when the float is paraded. In
Handa and Tokoname, the tunes employed for *michiyuki* are
different from those used for *kagura*. There are few crossovers
between the repertoires of *isami* or *kagura* on the one hand and
michiyuki on the other.[59] In Nagao, however, there are several such
crossovers; in the Komukae district, for instance, all the ten tunes
used in *isami* are also used for *michiyuki*.

In the notated documentation of the Komukae district, the
michiyuki repertoire consists of 13 tunes. Separately listed are

57 *Taketoyo-chō shi: shiryō-hen* 2 1983, pp. 301–304.
58 *Sakai no ayumi to matsuri* 2005, p. 158.
59 *Tokoname-shi shi: bunkazai hen* [Handbook of Tokoname city: cultural
   assets] 1983, pp. 560–573; *Handa-shi shi* 1984, pp. 217–230.

Shagiri, which is played while the float is turning, and two celebratory pieces played by the ensemble without *tsuzumi* drums (*Ochazuke* and *Okamesan*). The repertoire played while the float is paraded thus has 16 tunes. Ten of the *michiyuki* tunes are identical to the *isami* tunes. These are, however, differently performed: with few exceptions *michiyuki music* consists of medium-tempo pieces suitable for a walking speed, whereas *isami* performance tends to be faster. Furthermore, the *kotsuzumi* are only used for *michiyuki*.

The use of *isami* tunes for *michiyuki* may be unusual and characteristic of Nagao. As mentioned before (Chapter 4), *isami* is a musical practice that occurs on several occasions in the course of a year. The *isami* tunes probably existed before the first of the present floats were introduced. When new floats were bought or built around 1860, there had been a festival with a float in Nagao for nearly two hundred years. It is not known if there was continuity in the use of floats, or if there were periods without them. In either case, it is quite likely that *kagura* existed in the form of *isami*; and the *isami* tunes appear to have been arranged so as to fit with the tempo of *michiyuki* with the *three strokes rhythm*, so that they could be played by the *dashibayashi ensemble* when the float was paraded.[60] This would explain the similarities and differences between the respective repertoires of *isami* and *michiyuki* in today's practice. It also resonates with the still existing practice where the use of a float is preceded by *isami* performance.

Implications for *dashibayashi music*

In the early *Edo period*, the Tokugawa *daimyō* in Nagoya castle – starting with Ieyasu's ninth son – organized festivals in the castle area, the new festivals of the capital city serving as models. They favoured *nō* music, so *nō* musicians were involved in developing music for the festivals. The *satokagura* music of the large shrine Atsuta jingū also affected the festival music. Musicians of *satokagura* served as instructors, teachers, and performers of festival music in Atsuta and at other shrines. These two backgrounds give *dashibayashi music* its stylistic character.

It was particularly in mid-Edo times, around the middle of the eighteenth century, that float-festivals first spread into the Chita

---

60 *Jingūsha sairei no ayumi* 2007, p. 8; *Bishū Nagao Komukaegumi Hōōsha* 2013, p. 42.

Peninsula. Music and instruments are seldom mentioned in historical sources; but the earliest float in Nagao, Taketoyo, and the existence of the *kotsuzumi* drum in Sakai, Tokoname, are documented from that time.

There was an upswing in float construction in the 1830s–1860s, which probably meant more new festivals. This was when the *Chita-type float* became established. With the advent of *state Shintō* after the Meiji restoration, *satokagura* was abolished at Atsuta jingū, and still more performers became teachers or instructors in surrounding areas. The 1920s saw a new upward trend in float construction, float trading, and new festivals.

A common way of developing *dashibayashi music* in Nagao was to arrange tunes from the *isami* repertoire – which is a kind of *kagura music* – with the special *three strokes rhythm* so that it would function for the parading of the floats. At some point, the ensemble with three *kotsuzumi* and one *ōtsuzumi* became standard in Nagao. This suggests relations with other festivals in southern-central Chita Peninsula and with Mikawa.

One neighbourhood in Nagao, Banba, bought three *kotsuzumi* from a village in Mikawa in 1926. It is not clear why the number three became the norm in Nagao. Three *tsuzumi* drums are common in ensembles in Mikawa; but there are also several examples in Nagoya of three *kotsuzumi* seated in the back of the float. Three *kotsuzumi* are used in the accompaniment to *Sanbasō* in *nōgaku*; they also occurred in connection with the *daidai kagura* at Atsuta jingū. It seems that more than one influence operated in this context.

The results of the historical overview shed more light on the origin and dissemination of *dashibayashi music*, and they agree well with the outcome of the comparison of ensemble types and the review of *tune-complexes*. The fact that the style combines influences from *nōgaku* and *satokagura* is particularly significant, since this combination characterizes all the *dashibayashi music* in the area.

11
Change and continuity

The historical overview made it clear that the festival tradition and its music have been far from static. On the contrary, change appears to be an integrated ingredient in its development. Some periods have been dominated by stability and others by change, often determined by political or economic realities. Continuity is particularly evident in the manner that the spiritual contents of the matsuri and its rituals remain intact. The balance and tension between stability and change provides the basis for survival as well as for the revitalization and modernization of festivals.

This element has been recognized by McPherson, who called his dissertation on float-festivals in Chita 'A tradition of change'.[1] Schnell draws similar conclusions in his study of *Furukawa matsuri* in Gifu prefecture.[2] In his study of the social history of Kyoto's *Gion matsuri* Teeuwen writes: 'The festival came close to flopping at numerous junctions, but every time this happened, it has been reinvented by people whose agendas differed from those of their predecessors'.[3] Concerning the *matsuribayashi music* of Tokyo, Fujie argues that 'the study of traditional musics in Japan should be conducted in view of this process of survival and adaptation'.[4]

In recent times, it is obvious that changes in society in the post-war period up to the present day have affected all the festivals that have been studied here. The second half of the twentieth century, in particular, stands out as a period of change.

---

1 McPherson 2007.
2 Schnell 1999, pp. 290–291.
3 Teeuwen pp. 22, 221–225.
4 Fujie 1983, p. 43.

The floats and change

New float constructions are obvious evidence of change. When the float boom in the early twentieth century happened, shrine festivals were under the control of *state Shintō*, and it coincided with the growing nationalism that followed on Japan's victory in the Russo-Japanese War in 1905. Sean McPherson has shown how this trend can be seen in the sculptures of the floats from that period, and he has described how the festival in Tokoname started in 1905 as a celebration of the victory. The districts Segi and Ichiba already had floats at that time, while four other districts used the floats called *hanaguruma*, 'flower wagon'. The city then organized a festival for the war dead, *shōkonsai*, which developed into an annual shrine festival or *reisai*, today's *Tokoname-chiku sairei*.[5] McPherson describes pre-war cultural nationalism as present in the 'ritual, iconographic and architectural' aspects of the festivals:

> During the Taishō and early Shōwa periods, Chita festivals increasingly came to be imagined by participants and observers as markers of a national cultural identity rooted in notions of historical continuity, racial purity, and ethnocultural superiority.[6]

The ritual of paying respect to the war dead occurred at the time of the shrine mergers, when the policy was that there should be only one official shrine in a community. To many people, offerings were then to be performed at a different shrine and to new *kami*, as prescribed by the national ritual. Helen Hardacre comments on what these changes meant to people in general:

> It is doubtful that most people even noticed the change that took place when all the shrines were linked in a single hierarchy. Where people were aware of change, however, they were generally pleased to have the gods they worshiped locally recognized by the new government.[7]

The process of trading floats between neighbourhoods was very common. Thus, a float could pass through several owners. McPherson reports how one of Kamezaki's floats was traded:

---

5 McPherson 2012, 33–34; *Owari no dashimatsuri* [Float-festivals of the Owari province] → *Owari Chita chihō no dashimatsuri, Tokoname matsuri no tokushusei ni tsuite* [Dashimatsuri in the Chita area, Owari province, about special aspects of the Tokoname matsuri] (Internet reference).
6 McPherson 2012, p. 4.
7 Hardacre 1989, p. 84.

This process of adaptive reuse of dashi often extended through multiple owners. The 1815 Seiryūsha (Blue Dragon Vehicle), renamed Goōsha (August King Car) and used for a decade before its Shimohanda owners commissioned a new dashi in 1901, was then sold to Kyōwa District's Sunago-gumi, where it was renamed Hakusansha (White Mountain Car). When Sunago-gumi commissioned a new dashi in 1914, the Hakusansha lay disassembled in Sunago-gumi's storehouse until 1929, when it was sold to Ichihara-gumi of Taketoyo-chō and rechristened Agataguruma.[8]

In Taketoyo, the construction of a railway and the opening of new steamer-line routes in the latter part of the nineteenth century had led to an economic upswing. The new prosperity laid the foundations for a new float boom in the 1920s, not least since industrialists had become a new source of financing through their sponsorship.[9] Thus, it is said that Shitamo bought a new float from Kamihanda in Handa in 1923,[10] and three years later Ichiba had completed building its own float.[11] In 1926, Banba bought their float and musical instruments needed for an ensemble from the village of Kamigō in Mikawa, which is a part of today's Toyota.[12] This float from Mikawa was rebuilt to a *Chita-type* model and was first used at the local shrine Akiba jinja on 13 April 1926.[13] By this time there were five floats in Nagao, and from 1926 they all took part in the festival at Takeo jinja on the same date in April.[14] Not until 1947 did the district of Tamanuki buy a float from Narawa, Handa. Then there were six floats in Nagao, and

---

8 McPherson 2012, p. 20. Japanese characters have been excluded in the quotation.
9 McPherson 2012, p. 15.
10 According to oral tradition mentioned in *Taketoyo-chō shi: shiryō-hen 2* [Handbook of Taketoyo: reference material 2] 1983, p. 323 and *Bishū Nagao Komukaegumi Hōōsha: sōken hyakugojisshūnen kinenshi* [The festival float Hōōsha of the neighbourhood Komukae, Nagao district, Owari province: memorial magazine for the 150th anniversary of its construction] 2013, p. 8.
11 Iga 1994, p. 118; *Jingūsha sairei no ayumi: Ichiba-ku* [History of the Jingūsha float-festival: Ichiba ward] 2007, p. 1; Nakahashi 2011, p. 32; *Bishū Nagao Komukaegumi Hōōsha* 2013, p. 8.
12 Iga 1994, p. 116; *Taketoyo-chō shi: shiryō-hen 2* 1983, pp. 298–304; *Bishū Nagao Komukaegumi Hōōsha* 2013, p. 8. According to some references the float was bought in 1925.
13 *Taketoyo-chō shi: shiryō-hen 2* 1983, pp. 301, 304.
14 *Jingūsha sairei no ayumi* 2007, p. 13; Saitō and Saitō 2008, Chapter 4, pp. 6–7.

they all performed as an offering to the deities at Takeo jinja from 1950. After the devastating Isewan typhoon in 1959, however, floats were not used again until the practice could be gradually resumed, starting in 1968 with Komukae and Age, followed the next year by Shitamo and Ichiba. The *Nagao no harumatsuri* was thereby revived, although the two wards Banba and Tamanuki were missing. They joined again in 1980 and 1981 respectively.[15]

Tamanuki, Nagao, is a good example of change.[16] A fairly recent settlement within Nagao and Taketoyo town, it includes an area called Rokkanyama.[17] This area was, at one time, used by the Morita family in Kosugaya – producers of *sake*, *miso*, and soy sauce – with the intention of growing grapes for producing wine. This project did not turn out well owing to devastating insects that destroyed the plants, but a shrine was built there called Taga jinja, referred to here as Taketoyo Taga jinja.[18] This is where the people in the area made offerings to their tutelary *kami*, and theatre and *kagura* were performed there as well. In the late 1920s, *isamidaiko* began to be offered at Takeo jinja, the drum being transported on an ordinary cart.[19] *Isami* music had been taught by Torii Kichitarō, who had moved there from the Shitamo ward in 1921. The move to Takeo jinja occurred during the time of shrine mergers, when the state policy was that only one shrine per village would be recognized as legitimate.[20]

---

15 *Jingūsha sairei no ayumi* 2007, pp. 9–10, 13–15; Saitō and Saitō 2008, Chapter 2, p. 3, Chapter 4, pp. 5 and 7; *Gyokushinsha: dashi kenzō 70-shūnen kinenshi* [The festival float *Gyokushinsha*: memorial magazine for the 70th anniversary of its construction] 2018, pp. 4, 6, 9. Some other sources have 1949 for the purchase of Tamanuki's float.

16 The information concerning Tamanuki basically stems from Saitō and Saitō 2008, and *Otaga kōin ni yoru ohayashi* [Festival music played by Taketoyo Taga shrine parishoners] Saitō 2006; *Gyokushinsha* 2018.

17 This area had six low hills in a row and was therefore called Rokkoyama (six hills), which may have changed to Rokkanyama (six *kan* hills). It is also said that Mr Morita bought the area for six *kan* (a currency) in order to open a farm, and this may have led to the name Rokkanyama; *Taketoyo-chō shi: honbun-hen* [Handbook of Taketoyo town: main text] 1984, p. 364.

18 *Otaga kōin ni yoru ohayashi.* According to the Grand Taga Taisha shrine, in Shiga prefecture, there are more than two hundred branch shrines (personal communication 19 October 2023). The Taga jinja in Taketoyo town will therefore be referred to as 'Taketoyo Taga jinja'.

19 Saitō and Saitō 2008, Chapter 2, pp. 1–2 and *Gyokushinsha* 2018, p. 3.

20 Hardacre 1989, pp. 29, 98–99.

By 1947, the population of Tamanuki had increased as more people had moved into the area to find their livelihood there. A large proportion of land remained to be developed, and there was some industry as well. At that time, they bought the festival float from Narawa, Handa.[21] This newly acquired float was repaired, and at its completion a ceremony was held at Taketoyo Taga jinja in March 1948. From the same year onwards, it also took part in the major *Nagao no harumatsuri* at Takeo jinja, and it was formally included in 1950. Music was taught by teachers from the Komukae ward. The float was damaged by the Isewan typhoon in 1959, as were the *sayagura* and *kōminkan*. The highest priority then was to restore the city and rebuild the living-houses, which was a time-consuming and costly project. That being so, the float was sold to the film-making company *Daiei* in September one year later; but in 1978, after nearly two decades, it was bought back. The following year, players for the ensemble began their training, and for two years the float was pulled in the Tamanuki area only. It was named *Gyokushinsha*, and that was when Tamanuki was again accepted at the festival at Takeo jinja in 1981.

When Tamanuki's float was first acquired, it only consisted of the bare frame and wheels. Little by little, cloth was bought to cover it, carved sculptures were added, and from the 1990s onwards, money could be raised to buy embroideries. A new *sayagura* was built in 2002. The next project was then to repair the wooden figurines. Since the year 2000, Tamanuki has also resumed the practice of offering at Taketoyo Taga jinja before going to Takeo jinja during the *Nagao no harumatsuri*.[22] The development in Tamanuki exemplifies how change proceeds continuously, and how 'new' neighbourhoods strive to become established and integrated in a city.

A similar development had occurred in Banba in Nagao, where theatre (*kabuki*) had been performed as part of the festival since the beginning of the 1800s. After Meiji, the theatre was replaced by *isami* in daytime and fireworks in the evening. The *isamidaiko* drum itself still exists.[23] This practice continued until a float was purchased. Similarly, Ichiba had practised *isami* even before their first float was built. These *isami* tunes were remade into

---

21 According to *Gyokushinsha* 2018, p. 4. Some other sources have 1949.
22 *Otaga kōin ni yoru ohayashi* [Festival music played by Taketoyo Taga shrine parishoners] Saitō 2006.
23 *Taketoyo-chō shi: shiryō-hen 2* 1983, pp. 298–301.

mitsuboshi – the *three strokes rhythm* – and used for *michiyuki* together with tunes learnt from Komukae and Age.[24] In its main outline, the process of moving from *isami* to float with an ensemble appears to have been a common pattern, and even today similar processes seem to be going on in the Chita Peninsula.

The five floats of Morozaki on the southern tip of the Chita Peninsula are a special case. As late as 2014, four of them differed from the average in the Chita Peninsula by being lower, having no roof section on top.[25] The fifth, *Arai*, had recently been rebuilt so that it had a roof on the *uwayama*, with the spires called *bonden*. In connection with the repair work that had started in 2013, it was discovered that all the floats had been built between the 1860s and the years around 1940. They all had a solid wooden frame, and some were connected to craftsmen in the Kamezaki district in Handa. *Arai* and three of the others were constructed as if a roof section had originally been intended. They were therefore restored, and these four floats now have the same general shape as most floats in the Chita Peninsula.[26]

Nowadays, it is rare for a float to be traded. Attitudes towards festivals have changed, and since around 1950 the floats have increasingly come to be seen as significant cultural heritage. The displaying of actively used floats in museums that occurs in Handa, Chiryū, and Takayama is a sign of this development. Those areas that have floats which were on some occasion purchased from other neighbourhoods are now proud of having floats that are old, and they are repaired, restored, and developed in various ways. As a result, perhaps, very few floats are built these days – less than ten in the Chita Peninsula since 1950.

The formation of *Dashi hozonkai*, 'festival-float-preserving associations', is a further sign of this change in attitude.[27] Preservation societies, *hozonkai*, had existed since around 1897, when several temple and shrine *hozonkai* were formed, and folk-song *hozonkai* are known since around 1911.[28] The 1950s saw a growth of rural

---

24 *Jingūsha sairei no ayumi* 2007, p. 8.

25 Kitō 2021, pp. 121–123.

26 Mr Mori Takashi, Minamichita town, Board of Education, Education Department, Social Education Section, personal communication 7 June 2022.

27 Thornbury 1994; Hashimoto 1998.

28 Hughes 2008, pp. 212–215.

associations, which was linked to social and economic changes. Many of the large kinship-based groups had lost much of their importance, and associations took over their role in interpersonal relations.[29] Their main function is to preserve, but they should also revive practices or introduce changes when that is felt to be necessary. In many respects, they carry on the responsibilities of the earlier youth groups and other community organizations.

Recruitment to the ensembles

The recruitment of new members to player ensembles is crucial for the survival of music at float-festivals. Urbanization has often led to less interest in festival participation, since many newcomers to urban areas do not have a close connection to a shrine.[30] There are different reasons for this development. Ian Reader has pointed out that with the passage of time, more people have been born in cities and grown up there:

> The move from a rural and agricultural economy to an urban, industrial one has also obviously diminished the importance of community and calendrical festivals centred on the relationship between the kami and the seasonal agricultural cycle of production.[31]

In villages and towns, many young people move out to study or to work elsewhere. There are also natural fluctuations in birth rates. Such changes have made the issue of recruitment all the more important. In Nagoya some festivals, including *Wakamiya matsuri*, recruit both residents and children outside the festival area. In Tsutsui, with its *Tennōsai*, children are recruited by application circulated in chosen elementary schools.[32]

As late as the 1950s, the three young male adults who played the *kotsuzumi* seated in the back of the floats of Nagao were dressed in male *kimonos*, but by the end of the decade, the short jackets called

29 Norbeck 1971, p. 186.
30 Kawano 2005, pp. 106–111, has a detailed description concerning the Sakae neighbourhood in Kamakura.
31 Reader 1991, p. 58.
32 *Nagoya jōka no dashi gyōji chōsa hōkokusho: Nagoya no dashi gyōji sōgō chōsa* [Survey report of festival float events in the castle town Nagoya: a comprehensive survey of Nagoya festival float events] 2018, pp. 414, 418.

Figure 96 Young children in the ensemble of Fuki-Ichiba, Taketoyo
(2 April 2005).

happi had become common.[33] The *Hayashi hozonkai*, 'Festival
Music Preservation Society', formed in the Komukae ward in
October 1976, decided that younger children should be taught the
instruments, whereupon children aged 9 to 15 years were recruited
(from 3rd grade in primary school to the end of junior high
school).[34] In Ichiba, schoolboys from 7 to 12 years old (1st–6th
grade) began their training in the same year.[35] In Ōashi, too, boys
from grades 3–6 start practising the *kotsuzumi*.[36] This adaptation
of the traditional age-group system to fit the school ages increased
the recruitment base for players to the ensembles and became
standard (Figure 96). Since players of other music instruments are
recruited as well as those who start by learning the *kotsuzumi*, this
organization has had a stabilizing effect on the ensembles.

Other activities in the Chita Peninsula that have had an effect
on the recruitment and stability of the ensembles include fairly

---

33 Mr Torii Shinkichi, Taketoyo, personal communication 16 October 2014;
   Saitō and Saitō 2008, pp. 2–5.
34 *Bishū Nagao Komukaegumi Hōōsha* 2013, p. 42.
35 *Jingūsha sairei no ayumi* 2007, p. 9.
36 Personal communication, Ōashi, July 1997.

Figure 97 Children in yellow caps and some mothers helping to pull
the float at the front end of the ropes. Tamanuki in Nagao
(13 April 2007).

regularly organized concerts of *dashibayashi music*, like those in
Handa and Tokoname. Several ensembles from individual districts
participate in those events. In this way, the ensembles and their
players become more visible, not least among the players themselves since those from different districts can hear and inspire
one another. Similarly, the child ensembles, *kodomobayashi*, that
perform at several local festivals encourage the youngest players
and increase their motivation to engage with *dashibayashi*. Another
way of increasing recruitment is to permit female participation.
Increased participation of young children also attracts more parents
as viewers of the festivals (Figure 97).

Gender

Another tension that has to do with modernization and secularization concerns gender. Traditionally, there are many taboos
in *Shintō* which limit the contact of females with the float and
its musical instruments, as well as with the ritual elements of the
festival. In fact, though, females play an important and indeed

leading role in Japanese mythology and early religious practice; but
this changed so that in *Shintō* females are now considered ritually
impure and therefore kept away from rituals, with the exception of
miko dancers, 'shrine maidens'.

It was not until the mid-*Edo period* that females were banned
from the *Gion matsuri* of Kyoto. Since the end of the Second World
War, females have occasionally taken part unofficially. In 2001, it
became officially known that two floats had included females for a
decade. Although this started a debate, and 30 out of a total of 32
floats were against it, the participation of girls and women could
continue unofficially. In 1996, an association that came to be called
Heisei Onnaboko Sayanekai was formed for females who practise
and perform *matsuribayashi music*. Anybody who was interested
could join the association. The association's applications to participate in the parade with their own *hoko* (float) have been turned
down, though.[37] Even though there are places where females may
be *mikoshi* bearers, Helen Hardacre finds that traditional values
still dominate.[38]

> These gendered dynamics of *matsuri* make festivals into occasions
> for displays of masculinity and a traditional pattern of gender
> relations in which men hold the roles of dealing with the public or
> 'outside,' while women take charge of the private, or 'inside.'

Even so, a national survey conducted by Helga Janse shows that
processes of change are going on in many festivals:

> approximately half of the festivals [from where a reply was received]
> have undergone changes in terms of gender roles. The primary
> direction of change was towards increased gender inclusion. The
> primary reason for the change to allow women to participate in
> roles that had earlier been limited to men was reportedly a shortage
> of people to participate in the festivals, while a change in attitude/
> consciousness towards female participation was mentioned in a few
> cases.[39]

Some of the responses expressed a change in the perception of religiosity and gender. The festivals in the Chūbu area, which includes
Owari with the Chita Peninsula, proved to have the greatest

---

37 Summarized after McLaren 2001 and *Heisei Onnaboko Sayanekai web*
[Heisei female festival float association web] (Internet reference).
38 Hardacre 2016, p. 479. For female roles in festivals, see also Schnell 1999,
pp. 111–112, concerning Furukawa, Gifu prefecture.
39 Janse 2019, p. 2099.

variation with regard to gender rules. Some did not have any gender rules at all, while only males were allowed in others. According to Janse, '[m]ore than half of the festivals had undergone changes in the gender roles/rules, opening up for female participation in roles that had previously been restricted to men'.[40] The leading formal functions were still handled by males only. In Nagoya, Tsutsui allowed females to mount the float around 1984, and Wakamiya did the same in 1993.[41]

During my fieldwork period, increased female participation has taken place in many festivals. These days it is more common for girls to join the ensembles, initially mainly for playing the flute or *kotsuzumi*, but later also for playing on *ōtsuzumi*, *shimedaiko*, and *hiradaiko* or *ōdaiko*. Similarly, girls could first join pulling the float dressed in *happi* in the front part of the ropes; but now there are places where they may also join in pulling the float placed between the front shafts, being lead singers of the *Ise ondo* as in front of the shrine's *torii* in Yamakata, Tokoname town, or leading the cheering, standing on the front of the float as in Fuki-Ichiba (Figure 98). This development suggests that the social meaning of festivals tends to dominate over the ritual meaning. In some cases, it is also a practical necessity to include girls when there are not enough boys in the local community. This was mentioned as an important factor in Nishinokuchi in Tokoname.[42] In Taketoyo, some neighbourhoods accept female participation while others are opposed to this development. In the Ichiba ward, girls were first recruited to the ensemble in 1994 because of a declining birth rate.[43] At the *Taketoyo fureai dashimatsuri* in October 2019, there were several ensembles with mixed male and female participation, including the wards Ichiba and Shitamo of Nagao, Ōashi, Higashi-Ōdaka, and Fuki.

City float-festivals

A traditional float-festival is centred around a shrine and organized by priests, laymen, and residents. In modern times, city offices have become important co-organizers. In Taketoyo, care has been

---

40 Janse 2019, p. 2098.
41 *Nagoya jōka no dashi gyōji chōsa hōkokusho*, pp. 414, 418.
42 Mr Fukaya Yoshihiro, Nishinokuchi, personal communication 23 March 2002.
43 *Jingūsha sairei no ayumi* 2007, pp. 9, 14.

Figure 98 A female leading the cheering and singing on the front of
the float. Fuki-Ichiba, Taketoyo (2 April 2016).

taken to adjust the *Nagao no harumatsuri* to modern circumstances without damaging its essence. The practical carrying out
of the festival has been fitted into modern traffic regulations and
rules concerning safety, and responsibility for conduct has been
delegated to local festival generals.

In the *Shintō directive* of 1945, *Shintō* was separated from the
state.[44] This separation had immediate effects on shrine rituals, and
it changed the practical circumstances of the festivals that were
gradually revived. The Law on the protection of cultural properties, *bunkazai hogohō*, from 1950 had a category for tangible
folk cultural properties, *yūkei minzoku bunkazai*, which covered,
for instance, festival floats and puppets, whereas intangible folk
cultural properties, *mukei minzoku bunkazai*, might include folk
performing arts at festivals.[45] This law led to an increase of civic
pageants that were not based on shrine rites.[46] The so-called

---

44 Hardacre 1989, pp. 40, 167.
45 Thornbury 1994; Hashimoto 1998; Lancashire 2011; Alaszewska 2012,
   pp. 198–199; Arisawa 2012.
46 Hardacre 2016, p. 479.

'festival law', *omatsuri hōan*, from 1992, encouraged city councils to develop festivals as cultural activities for their citizens and also in order to market the city and attract tourists.[47] In 2016, as many as 33 local festivals attained UNESCO Intangible Cultural Heritage status, including *Shiohimatsuri* in Kamezaki, Handa, and those of Tsushima Aisai, Chiryū, Inuyama, and Kanie.

The political engagement that spurred festival activities in Japan and the Chita Peninsula was no exception. A city float-festival was organized in Nagoya in 1955. With nine floats it was modelled on the old *Tōshōgū sairei* that had been discontinued during the Second World War. Due to the law that separated government and *Shintō*, the religious aspects were toned down.[48] Handa with its 31 floats followed in 1979.[49] Since 1994, the *Taketoyo fureai dashimatsuri* has been organized every five years. Nagao, Ōashi, and Fuki all join in, so that all 11 floats of the town take part. However, there was an element of tension between the spiritual and the commercial contents of the festival.

City float-festivals differ from the shrine festivals in that they are organized by the town government and that the religious components are overshadowed by promotional, commercial, and social ones. This development reflects the effects of urbanization and modernization.[50] During a city float-festival, the floats will be paraded on their individual routes to the area where the festival is. If religious rituals are performed, they may occur in a different place than the main festival event and not be visible to onlookers.[51]

The use of festival floats always has a spiritual aspect. When the first *Taketoyo fureai dashimatsuri* took place in 1994, this matter was solved by performing the ritual of the descent of the deity for

---

47 Thornbury 1994; Hashimoto 1998; Alaszewska 2012, pp. 199–201. The formal name in English is 'Act on the Promotion of Tourism and Specific Regional Industries through Traditional Festival and Events'.
48 *Nagoya jōka no dashi gyōji chōsa hōkokusho* p. 295.
49 *Bishū Handa: dashi emaki* [Owari province Handa: festival-float picture scroll] (Internet reference) 2017; Yoneyama 2000, p. 36.
50 In this text 'a festival performed in a shrine, *jinja*' is called '*jinja sairei*' following the term '*toshi sairei*', 'city float-festival', as an established concept. For the effects of urbanization on *matsuribayashi* in Tokyo, see Fujie 1983.
51 In *Gion matsuri* in Kyoto a secular shop is turned into an *o-tabisho* or temporary shrine for the *kami* and during the main palinees, Porcu 2020, pp. 60–65.

one of the floats – that of the Age ward – as a representative of all the floats relating to the shrine, Takeo jinja. About the time of the fifth *dashimatsuri* the practice was altered and since then the ritual is performed by the priest for each individual float, when it is taken out to be used at the festival, and the ritual of the ascent of the deity is done when they have finished.[52]

Even though city festivals are often seen as secular there is thus no clear distinction between the secular and the religious. The city float-festivals do have spiritual meaning, at least to those closely involved in the preparation and handling on the floats, but it does not permeate the main public event as it does in a shrine festival. On the other hand, increased domestic tourism – not least locally, within Aichi prefecture – with brochures and festival information in online tourist guides has led to an 'eventization' of the shrine festivals, so that they contribute to the marketing of towns.[53]

The local festival districts gain the support of the town hall while still being able to carry out their shrine festival without giving up its religious and social contents. Their participation in the city float-festivals is important for the hometown's publicity and commercial promotion. Ultimately, this is hence a combination of the different interests of the town and of the local festival districts.[54]

The music and change

With regard to the music itself, one obvious element of change has been the borrowing of tunes from other places. That this has been normal practice is evident from the names of individual pieces. For instance, Komukae in Nagao has a tune called *Ōashibayashi* (refers to Ōashi in Taketoyo), Banba has one called *Tsushima kuzushi* (Tsushima has famous festivals in late July and in October; *kuzushi* means 'variation'), and in Fuki there are pieces called *Ōashishagiri* (after Ōashi in Taketoyo) and *Kōwabayashi* (after Kōwa south of Fuki). Some tunes are widespread, for instance *Okazakibayashi* or *Okazaki* (after the castle-town of Okazaki in Mikawa), which is found in Handa, Nagao, Kosugaya, Kōwa, and

---

52 Mr Iwata Takao, Chief Priest at Takeo jinja, personal communication 1 October 2024.
53 McPherson 2007, pp. 189–190.
54 For a documentation of a city float-festival, see *Tokoname dashi matsuri* (AV reference).

Utsumi. Names like these indicate that tunes have been taken over from other places, either directly or via intermediary festivals.

Periods of decline and periods of revival have succeeded one another, and there have been attempts to restore what was conceived as the traditionally correct music at a specific point in time. The emergence of a historicizing attitude after the Second World War reflects government policies. It has increased the ambition to restore festival tunes to what is considered their original form. In Kamezaki in Handa, for instance, this ambition led to experimentation with Western notation.[55]

The recordings made by Komukae (1953 and 1959) and preserved in graphic notation (from 1987 to 1990) also mark an interest in documenting the music relating to the festival.[56] The recordings from 1959 include spoken comments about the use of individual tunes during the festival. Many of the tunes have survived or been restored, and they are still used in similar ways. This documentation certainly played a role not only for Komukae, but also for other districts in Nagao when the festival was re-instated after a lapse of several years due to the Isewan typhoon.

In 1965 the musicians of Tamanuki, Nagao, reunited after a lapse from 1960, to record a tape in order to ensure that the manner of their playing would be remembered. These recordings involve more variation and improvisation. The flute playing has many embellishments, and the drum playing is freer. There is also much room for individual styles, and the tempo is generally faster.[57] In the case of Tamanuki, the interruption of the festival lasted till 1981. Then the restored ensemble was taught the Komukae versions of the tunes. While this 'restored' repertoire has limited the degree of variation, it is well adjusted to young players and conducive to the stability of the repertoire.

---

55 *Handa-shi shi: sairei minzoku hen* [Handbook of Handa city: festival and folklore] 1984, p. 212.
56 *Taketoyo-chō Komukae-ku: Matsuribayashi 1–4* [Taketoyo town, Komukae ward: festival music 1–4] 1987–1990 and *Komukae-ku Hōōsha: matsuribayashi* (AV reference);
57 *Tagakō kagura* [Kagura of the Taga shrine parish] and *Otaga kōin ni yoru ohayashi* [Festival music played by Taketoyo Taga shrine parishoners]. These tape recordings were kindly made available to me by Mr Saitō Kiyotaka. The nature of variation in *matsuribayashi* music is described in Malm 1975 and Fujie 1986a, 145–157.

Consequently, the ambitions to preserve and restore the music have no doubt led to a certain standardization of the way it is performed. The Komukae recordings from 1959 and the notation appear to present the tunes in a basic pedagogic form which is fairly easy to learn and suitable for young players recruited among school-children. When practising before the festival every year, they are taught the manner of playing found in the notation and the record-ings. During the festival, however, the ensemble will be exchanged several times. The most experienced musicians are chosen to play at the most crucial moments, for instance when the float enters the shrine yard to perform there. In addition, when *hōnō* pieces are played in celebration of individual persons during the route through the city, the players have an opportunity to display some virtuosity.

Since the music is deeply embedded in the festival, it is affected by the same changes as the festival at large. The present-day histori-cizing view of the festival may thus be seen in the music as well, and the effects of modernization create new situations for the musicians. For instance, in the city float-festivals *dashibayashi music* is often staged and large ensembles created by putting together several of a neighbourhood's *dashibayashi ensembles* (Figure 99). In compari-son to performance inside a float, staging changes the relationship between performers and audience.

As shown by the development in Chichibu night festival, Saitama, which introduced the designation of their festival music as National Intangible Cultural Property in the late 1990s, such changes may, in the long run, include clothing and physical movements in addition to the repertoire.[58]

Negotiating past, present, and future

In line with history research in general, the study of festivals in the twenty-first century has focused on ongoing processes rather than on ancient historical origins.[59] The understanding of tradition itself has received much attention, not least under the influence of Eric Hobsbawm's study of the invention of tradition.[60] This approach has been used for research on major historical and social develop-ments, but it has also been applied to studies aimed at revising

---

58 Alaszewska 2012, pp. 204–212.
59 Gerow 2005, p. 400.
60 Hobsbawm 1983.

Figure 99 *Matsuribayashi ensemble* players of Tamanuki ward on stage and TV screen at the city float-festival *Taketoyo fureai dashimatsuri* (14 October 2019).

or extending a practice.[61] John Breen's comment concerning the changed circumstances for festivals after the introduction of *state Shintō* with nationally prescribed state rites for shrines represents this view:

> This study of the Sannō Festival at Hiyoshi Taisha in Shiga Prefecture starts from the premise that all festivals reproduce and reinvent themselves over time, obfuscating their origins, typically claiming specious roots in the ancient or mythical past.[62]

The radical changes that occurred in the post-war era after the separation of state and *Shintō* had considerable effects on festivals in general, and consequently on float-festivals and their music as well. In his history of float-festivals in the Chita Peninsula, McPherson refers to this period as 'cultural amnesia, commodified nostalgia and the reinvention of dashimatsuri, 1945–2005'.[63] The post-war

---

61 Vlastos 1998, p. 9.
62 Breen 2020, p. 78.
63 McPherson 2007, pp. 189–213.

evolution of float-festivals is not nationalistic even though symbols might live on, for instance in the iconography of floats.[64] It is certainly national, though, forming part of a national ambition to revive and reactivate folk performing arts in general.

The main objective with the protection law was to recognize and preserve Japan's cultural heritage. While the law certainly led to increased efforts to preserve many folk performing arts, it was also criticized for turning them into cultural icons with limited possibilities of renewal and development.[65]

Domestic tourism evolved and expanded in the post-war era and influenced folk performing arts, particularly after the festival law of 1992. Hashimoto Hiroyuki argues that folk performing arts have been objectified by tourism:

> The purpose of the Law is thus to use folk performing arts to revitalize local communities. As a result, we can observe various contemporary cultural phenomena in which folk performing arts are transformed into tourist resources.[66]

The changes affect the work of the preserving associations, *hozonkai*, which see to it that the performance is carried out regularly and that it is passed along to future generations. They and others who are active in performances must react to the effects of tourism and other aspects of modernization. Helen Hardacre notes important effects on local practitioners: 'increasing domestic tourism, and growing acceptance of outsiders coming as spectators to the festivals of shrines to which they have no personal or traditional relation'.[67] These circumstances – nowadays taken for granted by people who travel to see particular festivals or performances – were not always present, and they presuppose changes in attitude among practitioners. The latter have devised two strategies which they apply in two different contexts: preservation and tourism.[68] The coexistence of shrine festivals and city float-festivals in Handa, Taketoyo, and Tokoname illustrates this strategy.

In a study of *kagura* in Tōkamachi City, Niigata Prefecture, based on participant observation, practitioners' relation to changes

64 McPherson 2012, p. 16.
65 Thornbury 1994, p. 222.
66 Hashimoto 2003, p. 226.
67 Hardacre 2016, p. 481.
68 Hashimoto 2003, p. 234.

resulting from depopulation and tourism was characterized as follows by Susanne Klien:

> on the one hand, group members often claim that the tradition they engage in has not changed over time. At the same time, however, participant observation and follow-up interviews reveal that considerable change has occurred, sometimes as a conscious decision by practitioners.

With reference to Hizky Shoham, who views tradition as 'an assigned temporal meaning, i.e., a symbolic activity in which various social groups attribute traditional qualities to certain sectors of life that are understood as binding together different times', Klien goes on to conclude that preservation is characterized by ongoing adaptation to constantly changing environments and circumstances:[69]

> The tension between the dynamic practices that comprise traditions, and the perceptions of traditions as antimodern values, illustrates the pressures that practitioners face in revitalizing such traditions. Adjusting previous iterations of a particular tradition and shaping it so that it transcends time and space is no easy task... Reproducing the past and connecting the past to the present and future may be a key incentive for members to continue.[70]

Even though continuous reinvention and ongoing adaptation may be different words for the same thing, the latter appears more relevant to the festivals and festival music of the Chita Peninsula, since they develop in continuity rather than in distinct steps. This is particularly true of *dashibayashi music*. Experiences from my fieldwork have rendered the links to the past, present, and future evident. This is what makes it possible for people who take active part in festivals and music to express pride in keeping a tradition and passing it on, while they are simultaneously able to express similar pride in the necessary modernization that is accepted for keeping the tradition alive and adapting to new developments in society.

---

69 Shoham 2011, 313–315; Klien 2020, 250.
70 Klien 2020, 253, 258.

12

The wider perspective

Parades or processions common in float-festivals seem to be universal, and they have been documented in Mesopotamia since ancient times.[1] Participants in processions often transport symbolic or sacred objects. In Catholic festivals figures of saints are carried, like the *Virgin of El Rocío* in Andalusia, Spain.[2] Sometimes such objects are carried in some form of palanquin or transported on a chariot, as in western Indian Himalayas and South Asia.[3] In the *Kumari* cult of Nepal, the living goddess is carried to the ornamented festival float where she is enshrined.[4]

Parallels in Japan are the *chigo*, or sacred child, of the *Gion matsuri* in Kyoto as well as the child *Sanbasō* dancers in the Chita Peninsula, whose feet may not touch the ground while they are representing the divine power.[5] Some Japanese festivals, like *Gion matsuri* in Kyoto and *Takayama matsuri* in Gifu prefecture, attract many international tourists.

Elisabetta Porcu has studied the *Gion matsuri* as a combination of glocalization and the production of locality.[6] The World Exposition in Osaka in 1970 included festival groups from all over the country at a time when they were not commonly seen detached from shrines, and festival groups were invited to make appearances abroad.[7] Similarly, at the World Exposition in Aichi in 2005, over one hundred festival floats from Aichi prefecture were displayed,

---

1 Roy 2005, p. 5.
2 Molinié 2013.
3 Halperin 2016; Bloomer 2017.
4 Anderson 1977, p. 134; Allen 1996.
5 Shimada 2006, p. 150.
6 Porcu 2022, p. 2.
7 Hardacre 2016, pp. 480–481.

much like a giant city float-festival.⁸ Consequently, the festivals of Chita Peninsula – including their music – are also part of the global process.

This resemblance raises the question whether there are also parallels in the music that accompanies parades or processions of festival floats, palanquins, or similar objects. Is it meaningful to speak of such festival music and, if so, what characterizes it? Are there similarities in the musical structures themselves? What are the functions of this music? What could be learnt on these matters from my research on the music of Japanese festival floats, or the other way around?

The present chapter discusses *dashibayashi music* on a more general level, in relation to music at religious festivals elsewhere in the world. This comparative perspective serves two ends. The first is to better describe the actual *dashibayashi music* while contrasting it to other similar musical traditions. The second is to add to the knowledge of festival music at large.

There appears to be surprisingly little research on Japanese festivals in a comparative perspective. One exception is Michael Ashkenazi's 1993 study of festivals in Yuzawa, Niigata, which has a section called 'Festivals outside Japan' in the final chapter of the book.⁹ No comparative study of Japanese festival music has been found. There are, however, studies on the principal level dealing with such concepts as 'tradition', 'ritual', and 'festival' as overarching human phenomena.

The following comparison is grouped under subheadings found in the existing literature. Many are expressed as opposites. Roberto DaMatta ascertains that it is not always possible to use dichotomies like sacred or profane, formal or informal, and loose or structured, as all such aspects may be present in the same religious festival.¹⁰ While certainly problematic, such opposites are nevertheless practical. They were used here on the basic understanding that each one is seen as a continuum rather than a clear divider.

The structural function

Many religious festivals in the world have a similar basic form with a starting point, symbolic objects carried or pulled on carts in the

---

8 McPherson 2007, p. 210.
9 Ashkenazi 1993, pp. 149–152.
10 DaMatta 1991, pp. 42–49.

community (parading in single units or in organized procession), a gathering in a sacred place (shrine, temple, or church) where a specialist conducts a ritual, a return to a starting point, and a final point often followed by a feast. A festival will last for a few days or even longer, and there will be music at all or most stages of it. Music in festivals often serves the purpose of articulating the ritual order. The *Devr*, 'god ceremony', of the Kotas in the Nilgiri hills of southern India lasts for up to twelve days. The music consists of 'rather context-free' to ritually-specific pieces.

> Special music pieces, forms of significant sound, and silences of various lengths qualitatively highlight the ceremony's structural sections, which are both spatiotemporal and social.[11]

During a temple fair in northern China, several rituals are performed, each one with its special music.[12] Zhao describes in detail how music and stages of the ritual are coordinated in the *Jiacun Double-Fourth temple festival* in northern China:

> No sooner had he finished the opening declaration than came three beats of a big gong and then another three beats of a big drum, followed by 'Open the Door Wide' (*Dakaimen*), a piece of suona or shawm music performed by the Entertainers under the direction of Master Bamboo Staff. When the procession arrived at the Earth God Temple, Du Tonghai took a step forward and made a deep bow... He then went a few steps up to the door and knocked on it to the suona music of 'Open the Door Wide'. The door opened inward, and the ritual of offering incense, singing prayers, pouring wine, kneeling and kowtowing was performed to the accompaniment of 'Drumming for Offering Incense' (*Shangxiang*)... The procession then returned to the Bixia Temple, retracing the earlier route through the village.[13]

Concerning the *Lingsar temple festival* in Lombok, Bali, David Harnish summarizes the structural function of the music as follows:

> The music and dance performances drive the festival from its initiation, through its various stages, to its conclusion, and they order the sequences of rites and events as well as the subjective experiences of the participants.[14]

---

11 Wolf 2006, p. 198, with a full description of the ceremony and its music on pp. 186–199.
12 Jones 2007, pp. 78–82.
13 Zhao 2021, p. 30.
14 Harnish 1997, 92, 98.

A similar structural function is present in *dashibayashi music*. The floats are large and heavy vehicles, and participants in the festivals stress how important the music is for handling them. The music accompanies every movement of the float. There are certain tunes, or certain ways of performing tunes, for the major activities during the parade from the starting point to the shrine, at the shrine, and on the way back. The beginning of a tune is signalled by high-pitched solo tones from the leading flute player in the float. These signals differ with different kind of tunes. They inform the rest of the ensemble that it is time to start and what tune will be played. The signals also prepare the other participants for the next movement, which will be started by further signals from the *hyōshigi* clappers and by lifted handheld lanterns. In this manner, the ensemble and the music they play lead the procession as well as guiding the actual activities of a float, as exemplified in Table 6.

The special–general continuum

Processions in religious festivals in Portugal are accompanied by non-professional civil wind bands modelled on military bands in the early 1800s. Together with other kinds of groups and artists, these wind bands also take part in the secular festivities that finish off the festival.[15] The wind bands have similar functions in the former Portuguese colonies and in the Portuguese diaspora.[16]

The musicians in shawm bands at temple festivals in northern China are not usually professionals, but they receive money for their playing.[17] The *pāncai bāyā* ensemble of Nepal consists of wind instruments, drums, and cymbals. The ensemble is also called *damāi bāyā* after the musicians, *damāi*, who are professional in the sense that they are paid, while their 'supplementary caste occupation' is tailoring. The *pāncai bāyā* perform in a calendrical cycle of festivals and in all sorts of processions.[18] In the case of the *pāncai bāyā* ensemble of Nepal, the music at the festivals has both special and general parts. Carol Tingey recognizes three types of repertoires:

---

15 Castelo-Branco 2000, p. 579.
16 Brucher 2013.
17 Jones 2007, pp. 3, 5, 71–84.
18 Tingey 1995, 11–12; Moisala 2000, pp. 699–700.

Table 6 Condensed example of float movement and music.

Float	Music
Before starting	Celebratory
Starting	Fast
Parading on level ground	Medium
Turning	Fast
Uphill	Slow
Downhill	Slow
Honouring persons or places	Celebratory
Entering the shrine	Fast
At shrine building	Celebratory
Leaving the shrine	Fast
Arriving at storing house	Fast
In storing house	Celebratory

- a popular repertoire that is not ritually significant but may be used in ritual settings such as processions;
- context-related pieces that are or were associated with rituals or seasonal activities, but are only loosely connected with these activities in their actual performance today; and
- a ritual repertoire which is indispensable for specific ritual activities, and which cannot be played elsewhere.[19]

The best-known Brazilian festival is no doubt the *Carnival of Rio de Janeiro*, but there are several kinds of carnivals. Pinto compared the carnivals of Rio de Janeiro, Salvador, and Pernambuco and found three types of carnival performance, *música carnavalesca*: parade and spectators separated; free participation in the parade; and formally organized spontaneous processions that combine these two.

> [P]opular notions during the late 1920s singled out the *marchinhas de carnaval* (carnival marches) as the main carnival repertoire, to which was later added the *sambas de enredo* of the *escolas de samba*.[20]

A festival ensemble of *Festa do Divino* – the festival of the Divine Holy Spirit – in the town São Luís do Paraitinga in south-eastern Brazil is called *folia do Divino*. It consists of four professional musicians, all of whom sing and play two *violas* (double-coursed

---

19 Tingey 1994 quoted in Wolf 2000, p. 284 (the bullet points are mine).
20 Pinto 1994, p. 21.

lutes with ten strings), snare drum, and triangle. The *viola* is considered a sacred instrument in south-eastern Brazil. In the *Festa do Divino* in Mossâmedes, Goiás, there are also other kinds of music in the festival, and there is music for most of the ritual events.

> Some styles, such as the music of the *folia do Divino*, the town band, the church choir and other groups, are associated locally with specific moments of the festival, such that one can speak of a festival repertoire, even though many of these genres are also performed for other religious occasions. Other musical styles... may also be heard during the festival, but they are not considered part of this repertoire, nor are they integrated into the ritual sequence of the celebration.[21]

It is apparently common for festivals to have music and music ensembles that are specific to the festival and thus form part of the festival soundscape. What differs is to what degree the music is also used in situations other than the festival processions. *Dashibayashi music* tends to be played at festivals only, but a change takes place when it is used in staged concerts outside the ritual context.

Dashibayashi music consists of special tunes that are traditionally played at the festival and nowhere else. Music played as accompaniment to puppet performances uses different tunes, in many cases stemming from the music of *nō* drama.[22] This music is also performed inside the float or just behind it, with additional or different players and instruments. It happens that players from the ensembles perform what is called *isamibayashi* on certain occasions during the year. With the exception of a few tunes that have crossed over to the *michiyuki* repertoire and are differently played, this is considered a separate repertoire.

Dashibayashi ensembles consist of amateurs recruited from the neighbourhood and trained during special sessions in advance of the festival. *Kagura* dance and music is often performed at festivals, but usually on a special stage and by different musicians. Ensembles are organized in a similar manner at float-festivals in other parts of Japan, but there are differences too. In Tokyo, for instance, festival music is not only performed by amateurs; since the end of the Second World War, it has also been played by professional players organized in guilds.[23]

---

21 Reily 1994, 12–13.
22 Hayakawa 2003a, p. 17.
23 Fujie 1986a, pp. 89 ff.

The sacred–secular continuum

A festival with interesting parallels to the float-festivals exists in the Kullu Valley, Western Indian Himalayas. Here several palanquins, called *rath*, are carried around in processions.[24] These *raths* are richly decorated, and each of them bears an image of the local deity. The accompanying ensemble consists of drums, wind instruments, and cymbals. The *raths* criss-cross the lanes of the village. At the climax of the procession, they gather at the top of the hill where the village is located, and finally the procession encircles the village, all the time accompanied by the music. The *raths* are kept in a temple where they are disassembled and then reassembled for the next event. They 'must be assembled and reconstructed in order to ritually exist'.[25] The reconstruction is carried out by the head musician – the player of the small barrel-drum called *dhauns* – and an oracle.

> Indian deities in general, and those of the Indian Himalayas in particular, emerge as complex agents whose cognition is distributed among community members and whose agency is articulated and enacted in public rituals... During this festival, explains a middle-aged devotee from Old Manali, '[t]he god Manu circumambulates the village. He marks his territory. He draws the boundaries that the external ghosts and demons *(bhut prêt)* are not allowed to cross'.[26]

Temple fairs in northern China include ritual music directed to gods, as well as entertainment music.[27] In South Asia, music is used to invite deities into occasions of worship or healing.[28] There are examples of music believed to be divine among the Kotas in the Nilgiri hills of southern India:

> there is also a special time set aside on a few of the evenings when twelve special melodies (*devr kol* literally 'god tunes') are played, more or less in a fixed order... [T]here are no words to these melodies, and no other activities occur at this time. The Kotas believe their gods appreciate these melodies, which are said to be of divine origin...[29]

---

24 Halperin 2016.
25 Halperin 2016, p. 311.
26 Halperin 2016, pp. 305, 315.
27 Jones 2007, p. 76.
28 Wolf 2000, p. 278.
29 Wolf 2000, p. 281.

In Spain, *romerías* – both sacred and secular songs – accompany pilgrimages to local shrines.[30] For the population of São Luís do Paraitinga in south-eastern Brazil, the musical performance at the *Festa do Divino* – the festival of the Divine Holy Spirit – is viewed as a donation to the Holy Spirit:[31]

> To devout community members... the presence of the *folia* [ensemble] in their homes is tantamount to the presence of the Divine Holy Spirit himself, blessing in return for their donations.[32]

That the music at pilgrimages and saints' festivals may be both sacred and secular is further stressed in connection with the rituals of the *Virgen del Rosario fiesta* in Iruya, Argentina:

> The musical spectrum ranges from Catholic religious songs and the music of the *cachis* adoration (*quena, caja, corneta*) to *cumbia*, Argentine patriotic anthems, and local, Andean, and national folkloric music (*copla, huayno, zamba*, among others).[33]

In Bali, gamelan music is performed in a wide variety of contexts, from the secular to the highly sacred.[34] Speaking about the Lingsar temple festival in Lombok, Harnish describes how the spiritual dimension permeates both objects and music:

> The very act of performance necessarily represents or signifies something beyond the music itself. Religious festivals are so charged with socioreligious energy that every act – such as the playing of music – and every object – such as the music itself – [comes] to symbolize and represent other realms of experience and meaning.[35]

In nearly all the examples, it appears that the music is thought to please the deities, to be divine, or even to have a divine origin. Some music is performed with the intention of attracting the deities, sacrificing to them, entertaining them, or communicating with them. This is, of course, particularly obvious in respect of the music used by specialists, such as priests, in their formalized rituals, but it also applies to much of the music played during processions.

In the general classification of folk performing arts in Japan, the festival float is placed in the category called *furyū*, which

---

30 Keller et al. 2000, p. 591.
31 Reily 1994, p. 33.
32 Reily 1994, p. 16.
33 Avenburg 2012, p. 135.
34 Downing 2010, p. 54.
35 Harnish 1997, 98.

means 'ornamental'.[36] It includes 'performances for warding off
evil or disease'[37] and 'images of splendid innovation'.[38] Yanagita
Kunio held the opinion that urban *matsuri* became more extrava-
gant in the early *Gion matsuri* in Kyoto, basing that view on
the development of festival floats with increased decorations
and increased performing arts. These features attracted spectators and made the *matsuri* lose much of its religious character.
Therefore, according to this view, floats and *dashibayashi music*
are predominantly ornamental or decorative.[39] Today, the processions of *Gion matsuri* in Kyoto include both *mikoshi* palanquins
and floats called *yamahoko*. The *mikoshi* procession is seen as
the religious part and the *yamahoko* procession as an entertaining part. But the *yamahoko* also have the function of '[purifying]
and [preparing] the path for the *mikoshi* to Yasaka Shrine', and
a *Shintō* priest purifies the members of the floats.[40] With regard
to the festival of the Sakae neighbourhood in Kamakura, Satsuki
Kawano actually mentions how the priest transfers the *kami* into
four *mikoshi* and also purifies the bearers.[41] When the festival is
over, he 'removes the kami... and returns them to the altar in the
main shrine building'.[42]

Key ritual actions at the *Nagao no harumatsuri* in Taketoyo
include summoning the deities, *kami*, to the respective floats by the
priest's invocation, *norito*, by offerings, and by music. From that
moment on, the float is considered divine. The priest then purifies
all those who participate in performing the festival. Along the route
of the floats one or more participants will spread out salt, which is
an agent of purification.[43]

Not only the priest but also those who handle the float, the
musicians, and other people that take active part are considered
to be charged with divine power for as long as the festival goes
on. This also applies to the *dashibayashi music* that is intended
to entertain and please the deities. That is particularly true of

36 Lancashire 2011, pp. 6–7, 73.
37 Groemer 2002, p. 605.
38 Thornbury 1997, p. 17, based on the classification of Honda Yasuji (quoted
   in Lancashire 2011, pp. 6 ff.).
39 Yanagita 1993, pp. 179–182.
40 Porcu 2020, p. 43.
41 Kawano 2005, p. 98.
42 Kawano 2005, p. 100.
43 Reader 1991, p. 67.

the celebratory music called *hōnō* or 'offertory', played when the deities are summoned to the float at the start of the festival and when the float is standing still in front of the shrine building. Herbert Plutschow comments on this phenomenon, referring to symbolic objects such as *mikoshi* palanquins or floats:

> Japanese religion may not be unique in considering these 'objects' not only as deities but also those who carry them... Priests are often seen not only as 'servants' of deities, but, by virtue of serving them, as the deities themselves.[44]

This view among active festival people was clearly expressed to me in discussions during two lectures I gave in 2015. A lecture in Takeo jinja was attended by the priest and by experienced leaders of the festival. At another lecture in the community house of the Komukae neighbourhood, younger people also took part. It became clear that the leaders and the most experienced participants in the festival regard the festival float and the music as sacred. The younger participants, including those who play an instrument, all learn by being part of the festival. They learn proper behaviour regarding rituals and sacred objects, and they acquire an under-standing of the religious intention behind the ritual actions. Those who participate as spectators at the climax of the festival will go to the shrine, where those who so desire, and who have the oppor-tunity to do so in the crowded area, will conduct the common religious rituals to clean their hands and mouths with water and to pray to the deities.[45] Perhaps one might think in terms of 'degrees of sacredness', with the priest or specialists at one extreme and the casual spectator at the other.[46] The spiritual power that is attracted by the ritual actions more or less permeates all the people and objects involved.

The change–continuity continuum

Most of the reports on change in festivals that are contained in the international literature deal with fairly contemporary changes. With regard to the popular Brazilian Catholic Holy Divine Spirit

---

44 Plutschow 1996, p. 118.
45 See Reader 1991, pp. 15–20 concerning 'primacy of action' in Japanese religiosity and Kawano 2005, pp. 4–6, about the relation between non-specialists and rituals.
46 Cf. Plutschow 1996, p. 118.

Festival (*Festa do Divino*), Siuda-Ambroziak and Mariano observed how 'these festivities, characterized by the fluidity between sacred and profane rituals, have been constantly shaped to fit best in the new social and cultural characteristics and changing needs of local communities'.[47] This observation is germane to the discussion of change in Japanese festivals. Since *dashibayashi music* is itself subject to change as well as the festival to which it belongs, the two are best considered together. Frequently mentioned changes in the international literature are listed below. They come from studies of festivals that have survived by adapting to new situations, so most of these changes are actions implemented with a view to achieving continuity.[48] They will be commented on from the Japanese perspective as present in the material of this study, particularly that of the *dashibayashi music* in the shrine festivals of Owari (with Nagoya and Chita Peninsula).

- *Loss of traditional customs and an accelerated trend toward secularization.*
  There are several examples of loss of tunes in the musical repertoire at float-festivals. In some places, too, certain musical instruments have fallen out of use, for instance the *kotsuzumi* drum and the so-called *furedaiko* or 'warning drum' that sometimes preceded the float parade.
- *A general liberalization of the rules of behaviour.*
  Recent examples are the fashion among participants of dyeing their hair green or orange and of making noise with plastic megaphones of the kind used at baseball games. These have now been banned from most festivals, though. Rather, the trend is now towards stricter control of behaviour, not least concerning the consumption of alcohol (*sake*).
- *Decrease of public participation in purely religious ceremonies.*
  This is hardly noticeable, particularly since religious ceremonies are not collective.
- *Lower level of participation among young people.*
  There are examples of this phenomenon, and the tendency towards a decrease in participation among young people is a reality that has been met by organized recruitment to ensembles and by the inclusion of female participants.

---

47 Siuda-Ambroziak and Mariano 2021, p. 242.
48 The list is compiled from Davis 1972, pp. 39, 49, 53; Downing 2010, p. 55; Siuda-Ambroziak and Mariano 2021, pp. 226, 239, 243, 244.

– *An increased role for the municipality in the organization of the festival.*
    As early as the decades around 1900, city councils and police tried to control order and to avoid accidents or traffic incidents.[49] These days, the municipality, with its different administrative units, is involved in the planning, marketing, and implementation of festivals in towns and cities, so there are now many interest groups that collaborate in organizing festivals.[50]
– *More stress on secular activities that attract crowds.*
    Stage shows of *dashibayashi music, kagura,* and puppets have become common. In some cases, puppet performances on floats are directed to the audience rather than the shrine. There are innumerable examples of new features being added to festivals. One instance is the evening parade of floats with lanterns from the shrine in Nagao, Taketoyo, to an area where they and onlookers gather, which was introduced in 1993.
– *New role as a symbol of local and national identity folklore.*
    Since *dashibayashi music* is local in style in the villages and towns, as well as in the larger part of Aichi, it has a potential of becoming such a symbol; but that has not really happened. Rather, it is the festival floats and the puppets that have become symbols of folk-art in Aichi prefecture.
– *More differentiated and specialized roles for musicians.*
    Concerts of *dashibayashi music* and *kodomobayashi,* 'children ensemble', performances on stage are fairly recent new roles for *dashibayashi* musicians. This development is even more pronounced in urban float-festivals.
– *Increase of professional musicians.*
    In Aichi prefecture, the musicians in the *dashibayashi ensembles* are not professional musicians.
– *Female participation in ensembles.*
    Female participation is a relatively recent phenomenon. The first time I saw female participants was in Yata, Tokoname, in 2001, but now it is not uncommon. One reason is the need to recruit more musicians; another is the changing gender roles in society.

In the 1970s Herbert Plutschow commented on change and continuity in Japanese festivals in the following manner:

[U]nder the influence of the state, many Japanese *matsuri* developed into stable, codified traditions, which... have been reduced to calendrical customs from which people extract, at best, their cultural, national and local identity... On the other hand, one can detect

---

49 Ellefson 2011, pp. 128–129.
50 See Akaike 1976 and Littleton 1986.

ts of Japan

conservative forces in *matsuri*. Unless they have to adapt themselves
to new outside, or, in some cases, to crisis situations, *matsuri* tend to
be imitated and performed according to tradition.[51]

Plutschow also says that local festivals were poorly documented
at the time when this was written, so his discussion was probably
based on some of the major city float-festivals. With the possible
exception of those big city float-festivals that take place on an
annual basis, the shrine festivals in Owari have not been reduced
to calendrical customs to that degree. The conservative forces he
mentions are what results in continuity: 'the intrinsic adaptability
of *matsuri* emerges in contrast and complement to the weight of
tradition'.[52] It can be concluded that the changes the Japanese float-
festivals and their music have undergone, and the measures that
have been taken for the sake of continuity, are not unique to Japan
but have very similar international counterparts.

Modernization and festivalization

James Peacock applied trends in modernization presented by
Marion Levy Jr. to the Indonesian drama *Ludruk*.[53] His summary of
dimensions of the modernization process was, with some additions,
used by Martha Ellen Davis in her analysis of the *Fiesta de Cruz* in
San Juan, Puerto Rico: increasing centralization, bureaucratization,
specialization of units, monetization, secularization, and rationali-
zation.[54] Davis found the revived version of the *fiesta* substantially
different from the traditional one. New functions were related to a
new role as a 'symbol of local and national identity-folklore'. The
role of the musician had become differentiated and specialized, and
there had been changes in the organization:

> The organizer may be an individual, groups of individuals, community
> action committees, or the city government. The organizer's role is
> much more complex than in the traditional presentation. Since the
> *Fiesta de Cruz* is now a public celebration, the organizer must secure
> from branches of the city government permission to use a public
> place.[55]

---

51 Plutschow 1996, pp. 1–2.
52 Porcu 2020, p. 2.
53 Levy 1966; Peacock 1968, pp. 217–233.
54 Davis 1972.
55 Davis 1972, p. 48.

Renata Siuda-Ambroziak and Fabiene Passamani Mariano found similar developments in a study of contemporary transformations in the Brazilian *Festa do Divino*:

> decrease of [the] public participating in purely religious ceremonies, mainly during processions and masses, which made it necessary, for instance, to shorten the time of the Festa by means of resigning from traditional novenas and some other, more time-consuming, traditional activities of social and popular religiosity character (folias); competition between religious and profane parts of the Festa, with much more stress put recently on secular activities that attract crowds (dinners, auctions, dances, concerts).[56]

In their sociological study of urban development, Hartmut Häussermann and Walter Siebel introduced the concept 'festivalization'.[57] Their concern was big modern festivals or events in which the marketing of a city was an important aim. Such events are organized by special associations or project groups, rather than by the ordinary communal institutions. They often collaborate with the tourist industry, which has been characterized by Tommy Andersson and Donald Getz as a 'mixed industry' where 'private firms, public agencies and not-for-profit associations – all of which co-exist in most societies – both compete and collaborate'.[58]

Speaking about the *Carnival of Santa Cruz*, Tenerife, Waldemar Kuligowski 'perceived tradition as an important part of the festivalization process', and he recognizes 'the process of the festivalization of traditions as an emerging cultural trend:'[59]

> Furthermore, we can observe a deep connection between two types of industries: the festival industry and the tourism industry. The logic of cooperation between them is simply this: the festival industry provides the experience, and the tourist industry provides the audience.[60]

The changes that festivals have undergone from the late twentieth century onwards result from the effects of modernization in society. The trends that Sonoda Minoru found in a study of an urban festival – *Kanda matsuri* in Tokyo – pointed in that direction as early as the 1970s:

---

56 Siuda-Ambroziak and Mariano 2021, p. 243.
57 Häussermann and Siebel 1993.
58 Andersson and Getz 2009, p. 847.
59 Kuligowski 2016, p. 35.
60 Kuligowski 2016, p. 36.

thriving urban *matsuri* do not necessarily express their original religious symbolization. On the contrary, at least some *matsuri* thrive only because their mobilization relies on other values, social, economic, or political.[61]

Consequently, research on current traditional religious festivals and their music has common ground with modern festival and event research. It is not difficult to find parallels in the modern development of Japanese float-festivals, particularly regarding city float-festivals which have increased in number since the 1950s. City float-festivals tend to be more like general events than religious festivals. In a recent study of *Gion matsuri* in Kyoto, it is described as a multi-layered event in which religion interplays with 'different arenas of contemporary society, including local communities and government, tourism, the economy, and cultural policies', and where 'issues of globalization can be seen at play at the local level'.[62]

The city float-festivals in the Chita Peninsula that take place every five years are smaller and more local, but like the *Handa dashimatsuri*, they have the potential to attract many visitors. While a shrine festival usually lasts for two or three days, a city float-festival is often a one-day event. At shrine festivals there are sometimes stalls for 'street food', sweets, and children's toys. At a city float-festival, the stalls also display and sell local products. In a shrine festival, the neighbourhood or neighbourhoods connected to a shrine participate together. In city float-festivals, all floats from the relevant city – or a representative selection of them – participate, regardless of which shrine they are connected to, and the floats gather in a 'neutral' place chosen for the show. The religious contents are overshadowed by marketing and commercial interests and by entertainment. For the musicians, this normally means that they also perform outside the float, usually on a stage. Special music relating to the puppets of the floats may be featured, too, as well as other representatives of the neighbourhoods' music or dance traditions. Financing is mixed: members of the neighbourhoods participate as volunteers, people in the neighbourhood donate money to support participation in the festival, and the city council funds the marketing and their part of the organization and planning.

As we have seen, some of these effects of modernization are also, to some extent, present in the shrine festivals that go on as usual at

---

61 Sonoda 1975, p. 135.
62 Porcu 2020, p. 40, and 2022, p. 1.

another time of the year; but the religious content still dominates there. City councils tend to become increasingly active in marketing both the city's shrine festivals and the city float-festival; but still, city float-festivals have not replaced the shrine festivals. Those that take place only every five years are more of a complement to the yearly shrine festivals. The shrine festivals in Owari and the Chita Peninsula maintain their religious focus, and even though they continuously adapt to new circumstances, the activities contained in the festivals survive. This is evident in the continuity of the *dashiba-yashi music* as well.

Festival music research

Festival music is a large field, and there is as yet no clear definition of it. While the functions of festival music are often similar, the music of processions at religious festivals internationally appears to be very diverse and largely dependent on the music in the festival's cultural context. With few exceptions, however, such music has one characteristic in common, namely loudness. This circumstance, in turn, makes the choice of musical instruments similar. Most ensembles are dominated by percussion instruments like drums, gongs, and cymbals. Melodically, the shrill and penetrating sounds of reed instruments, high-pitched flutes, or horns are common. It is equally important for the instruments used for the procession to be portable. Concerning African processions in general, Nketia says:

> Some go in procession with just one or two small drums and leave the rest of the instruments behind; others move to the accompaniment of a few rattles and bells or percussion sticks.[63]

Large instruments can be made portable by the use of slings. Alternatively, 'heavy drums are carried on the heads of non-drummers, while the drummers stroll behind and play them'.[64] At Japanese float-festivals, the whole ensemble is made portable by means of having it placed in a float. In this process the flat *hiradaiko* drum is preferred, since it needs less space than the large *ōdaiko*. At other processions that take place in connection with a festival, an *ōdaiko* may be placed on a stand or carried on a small wagon (cf. Figures 33 and 34).

---

63 Nketia 1974, p. 233.
64 Nketia 1974, p. 233.

The loudness is related to a function that *dashibayashi music* shares with many others, namely that of signalling the start of a festival and of informing the community that a festival is going on, or even what kind of festival it is.[65] Another common trait is that festival music, just like traditional religious festivals, is affected by changes in society that are the result of global trends in modernization.

In this case, the focus has been on music at processions that form part of seasonal religious festivals. In the case of Japan, such festivals also include music related to the more strictly liturgical ceremonies carried out by *Shintō* priests and by music and dance performances besides the processions. These would also have parallels in, for instance, Catholic or Hindu festivals.

The delimitations chosen for this study mean that it deals with one particular kind of music in one special variety among a multitude of seasonal festivals in Japan. In addition, the comparative perspective is focused on music played during processions in seasonal festivals, leaving out other music as well as similar music belonging to life-cycle festivals or rituals.

With these delimitations, it has been useful to see Japanese *dashibayashi music* as one component in a wide spectrum of musical activities in festivals. As there is a disturbing lack of overview in respect of festival music, such information as can be consulted is often scattered 'by-products' of festival studies by non-music specialists. Considering that festival music plays important roles in people's lives, further study might increase our knowledge of the use of music in human communities in a more general sense.

The inter-cultural perspective has made it possible and relevant to develop insights into *dashibayashi music* further, and to express them in a form that may be useful in future comparative studies: the music has strongly structural functions in the carrying-out of the festival; the music ensembles consist of amateurs (or perhaps 'volunteers' would be more exact); the ensembles only exist in this particular situation; the music is sacred in the sense that it is directed to deities and seen as an offering; the music is nevertheless entertaining for humans as well; the music is continuously adapted to new circumstances; and the music is subject to global trends of modernization.

---

65 Harnish 1997, p. 87; Castelo-Branco 2000, p. 579; Wolf 2000 p. 281; Zhao 2021, p. 31.

13
Conclusions

This study started out with two seemingly simple questions concerning the festival-float music – the *dashibayashi music* – of Nagao, Taketoyo: *why the festival music in Taketoyo is constructed the way it is* and *why the hourglass drums are so prominent*. These questions turned out to be rather more complex than one might have expected. Perhaps it was bad luck – or maybe good luck – to come across this festival music that turned out to be somewhat a-typical. As Hayakawa Masao, the *dashibayashi music* scholar in Aichi, put it: 'They have a music of their own there'.[1] This is true; but during my study it has also become clear that the festival-float music of Nagao has several ties to the music of other places.

This circumstance made it necessary to carry out a comparative study of festival-float music in the whole area of Owari (including Nagoya and the Chita Peninsula) and Mikawa. The shrine festivals are religious festivals and may be regarded as intrinsically religious rituals. That also applies to the festival-float music, which is an integral part of the festivals. Festival-float music is designed to facilitate the movements of the festival floats, and it marks different stages of the festivals: the start, the float parade, turns or stops on the way, entrance into the shrine area, the offering of music to the deities in front of the shrine building, departure from the shrine area, parading, the return to the starting point, and the ending. There are more or less elaborate repertoires – sometimes sets of tunes – for those different stages. These features are held in common with processional music of many religious festivals, not only in Japan but also internationally.

One strong stylistic characteristic is the influence of *nōgaku* – the music of *nō* drama – which probably dates back to the samurai

---

1 Hayakawa Masao, Yokosuka, personal communication 26 March 2002.

lords' promotion of *nō* at the time of the festivals in Nagoya in the early seventeenth century. This background is evident in the instrumentation, with flutes, the laced *shimedaiko* drum, and the hourglass drums *ōtsuzumi* and *kotsuzumi*. There are also individual tunes that can be traced to the repertoire of *nōgaku*.[2] An obvious example is the music that accompanies *Sanbasō* performances, which are particularly common in central Chita Peninsula. Like the dance itself, it is basically the same as the music used in *Sanbasō* performance in *nōgaku*. Influences from *kabuki* theatre have come later and might be present in such tune names as *Shagiri*. Perhaps the use of the three-stringed *shamisen* lute in Mikawa may also be accounted for along the same lines. Some musical instruments used in the offstage *geza ongaku* occur in festival music, but it is sometimes unclear whether they spread from *kabuki* or were imported to *kabuki* in order to represent the sounds of society.[3]

In addition, there are parallels between *dashibayashi ensembles* and other folk art performances. The simultaneous use of *kotsuzumi* and *ōtsuzumi* in the accompaniment to *Sanbasō* performances constitutes a possible link to the combination of these two drums in many *dashibayashi ensembles*. The typical way in which *manzai* performers hold the *kotsuzumi* in front of them has parallels in *dashibayashi ensembles* and might be seen as a folk performing style of *kotsuzumi*.

Another powerful characteristic of festival-float music is rooted in *kagura music* at shrines, particularly the Atsuta jingū in Nagoya. This so-called *satokagura* were dances and music on flute and drums. That may be the reason why the *dashibayashi ensembles* in the area differ from the ensemble of *nōgaku* by having a large drum, an *ōdaiko*, or – more commonly – the large suspended flat *hiradaiko*, which demands less space inside the float. The *Atsuta kagura* probably began to spread to surrounding localities in mid-Edo times, perhaps during the eighteenth century when several local float-festivals were started in the Chita Peninsula. This process continued into the early *Meiji period*, when state *Shintō* abolished *satokagura* from shrines and many performers functioned as instructors and teachers. Many of the tunes in *dashibayashi music*

---

2 Hayakawa 2003a, pp. 16–17.
3 Hayakawa 2003a, p. 16; *Kabuki A to Z: the Japan Arts Council's Culture Digital Library* 2018; *Invitation to Kabuki: Guidance for Japanese traditional performing arts Kabuki* 2019 (Internet sources).

can be traced to Atsuta. Thus, the *dashibayashi music* in Owari and Mikawa has a common background and is characterized by its roots in *nōgaku* and *satokagura*. This is not only seen in the instrumentation of the ensembles, but also in the musical structure with melody lines combined with percussive patterns of varying lengths.

Some tunes – such as *Shagiri*, which is particularly often used when a float is being turned – are spread over most of the area and are usually easy to recognize. Other tunes have changed in different localities to an extent that sometimes makes them difficult to recognize. Phrases and names change and appear in new combinations. By looking at them grouped in *tune-complexes*, some relationships may be observed. Thus, the tune *Shinguruma* (meaning 'new float') played in Nagao, Taketoyo, may on fairly safe grounds be traced back to Atsuta in Nagoya. Related local versions of this tune are found in southern-central Chita Peninsula.

While having tunes with roots in Atsuta, several localities in a 'belt' stretching across southern-central Chita share certain traits that differ from other places, notably the *three strokes rhythm (mitsubyōshi)* and floats with two or three interior levels. Furthermore, the combination of *kotsuzumi* and *ōtsuzumi* drums, so typical of the music heard during *Nagao no harumatsuri*, only occurs in this area. Additionally, the simultaneous use of *kotsuzumi* and *ōtsuzumi* drums is very common in Mikawa, as are floats with interior levels. These practices may well have been taken over from Mikawa by way of traditional waterways between Mikawa and the east coast of the Chita Peninsula. For instance, the Banba neighbourhood in Nagao bought a float and three *tsuzumi* drums from a village in Mikawa in the 1920s, and several neighbourhoods in Mikawa have purchased floats from the Chita Peninsula.

Mitsubyōshi, the *three strokes rhythm*, appears to be used in southern-central Chita Peninsula only. It is of great importance for *dashibayashi music* in Nagao, where it is used in the majority of the *michiyuki* tunes when parading the floats. There are accounts of how *dashibayashi music* was created by arranging *isami* tunes – a kind of *kagura music* – in *mitsubyōshi* style. The *kotsuzumi* and *ōtsuzumi* drums are crucial for playing this rhythm, and this circumstance may explain why those two drums are always employed whenever *mitsubyōshi* occurs. There are thus important parallels between Nagao and the other festivals in southern-central Chita Peninsula, but there are differences too. In certain respects, Nagao is similar to Handa, for instance in the use of the tune *Shagiri* for uptempo movement. In many cases, influences from Atsuta came to Nagao via districts in Handa. However, direct contact cannot be excluded, particularly in the case of the placement of three *kotsuzumi* players in the back of the float, which is reminiscent of some floats in Nagoya, including that of *Wakamiya matsuri*.

The *dashibayashi music of* Nagao may be characterized as a distinct mixture of influences from Atsuta/Nagoya and Handa on the one hand and from West Mikawa on the other, in combination with traits specific to southern-central Chita Peninsula. Its most prominent feature is that all *michiyuki* tunes (*Shagiri* excepted) are played with a strong *mitsubyōshi* rhythm performed by an ensemble with one *ōtsuzumi* and three *kotsuzumi*.

What has been said so far concerns *dashibayashi music* at traditional shrine festivals. Changes in the celebration of the festivals, particularly since the post-war years, have led to changes in the music. Recruiting quite young boys to the ensembles increased the number of players and made the ensembles more stable. Revisions of the music created more standardized repertoires than before. In many cases they were simplified, too, becoming more easily available to young learners. In fact, when comparing present performances of the Tamanuki neighbourhood in Nagao with recordings made in the mid-1960s, one has the impression that the latter comes from a different village. The more recent tendency to include girls as well as boys in the ensembles means both an increased recruitment base and an adaptation to changing gender roles in society.

Many shrine festivals have become more like events marketed to attract not only residents of the town itself, but also people who travel to watch festivals. The music is altered in a different way when the same tunes are played in the same manner, but in a context without a religious ritual, by musicians in new constellations. These developments are in line with changes in religious festival music internationally. For more than half a century, the Japanese float-festivals and their music have been undergoing the same modernization processes as other religious festivals in the world; and they, too, form part of the global trend of festivalization.

Epilogue

The first Japanese festival I ever saw was that of Kawahara jinja in Nagoya, where there are no festival floats. This was in July 1990. My first festival in the Chita Peninsula was the *Nagao no haru-matsuri* in 1992. My last visit to a festival in Taketoyo was the *Taketoyo fureai dashimatsuri* in 2019, and the very last of all was *Miyoshi Hachimansha aki no taisai* in Mikawa in October the same year. After that, the Covid pandemic put a stop both to the festivals and to my journeys.

My period of research coincides almost exactly with the *Heisei period* (1989–2019). The start of the new *Reiwa period* on 1 May 2019 was celebrated by festival activities in many places. In Nagao, Taketoyo, the two floats of Age and Komukae were offered in celebration at Takeo jinja. In the following spring there would be no *harumatsuri*. Like most festivals all over the country, those in the Chita Peninsula were cancelled because of the pandemic, and only minimal *Shintō* rituals were carried out. The cancellations continued in 2021.

Even a short break in festival activities could cause much damage, particularly in the type of festival that involves large numbers of people in the planning process and festivals located in areas of depopulation. One reason for this is, of course, financing, which depends on donations by residents in connection with the carrying-out of a festival. Furthermore, having a festival is important for keeping contacts with participants and spectators. Many of the activities that are performed by the participants are in fact transmitted and learnt through participation.

The Agency for Cultural Affairs had already supported those festivals that had been designated National Intangible Cultural Property. With the intention of minimizing the effects of the pandemic, this support was now extended and became available to all festivals. The Agency's support included the maintenance of floats and other equipment as well as the training of successors to participants. Digital support would be available for documentation and even for the online streaming of festivals.

The *Nagao no harumatsuri* with floats was partly resumed in April 2022, when five of the six wards pulled their floats to Takeo jinja. This was, however, performed under the observation of several restrictions. For example, the instructions pertaining to the Tamanuki neighbourhood demanded that those participants who had to be close to one another, as was the case with the musicians, had to take a Covid test each morning. A plastic screen was used to shield off the flute players from the others. The floats were pulled at walking speed only and along the shortest route to the shrine. No running or shouting was permitted, and the tune *Shagiri* was not to be used when a float had to be turned. No audience was allowed to accompany the floats on their way.[1]

In this manner the festival could be carried out in a safe albeit limited way. The float-festivals were resumed along similar lines in other parts of the Chita Peninsula, too. Once again, the festivals and *dashibayashi music* had demonstrated their ability to adapt to serious and unpredictable conditions. The tradition of change again became evident in the spring of 2025 when the name *Nagao harumatsuri* was changed to *Shagiri matsuri*, thus emphasizing the exciting custom of *shagiri* when festival floats are turned ninety degrees.

---

1 *Kairan: Tamanuki san kumin no minasama e* [Circular: to the residents in the three sections of the Tamanuki ward], on an auspicious day in April 2022.

Appendix 1: Tables

Table 7 Placement of drums other than *hiradaiko* in relation
to the levels inside the float.

	Shimedaiko	Ōtsuzumi	Kotsuzumi
Bottom level	Nagao: all floats		Nagao: all floats Ōashi
Middle level	Fuki-Ichiba Ichihara Higashi-Ōdaka Ōashi	Nagao	
Upper level	Kaminoma Kosugaya	Ichihara Kaminoma Kosugaya Ōashi Ōtani Sakai	Ichihara Kaminoma Kosugaya Ōtani

Note: The middle level is used for *shimedaiko, ōtsuzumi,* and/or flute(s). The
bottom level below it may be utilized for *shimedaiko.* The *ōtsuzumi* and *kotsuzumi*
can be placed on the upper level, which may also in some cases be used for other
instruments (Kaminoma, Ōtani, Sakai).

Table 8 Seating with *tsuzumi* drums in the rear part of floats in the Chita Peninsula.

Ōtsuzumi	Kotsuzumi	Fue
Fuki: Honwakakai 2	Fuki: Honwakakai 1	Fuki: Honwakakai 1–2
Fuki: Fuki-Ichiba 1	Fuki: Fuki-Ichiba 1	Fuki: Fuki-Ichiba 1–3
Futto: Hirata 1		Futto: Hirata 1
Futto: Ōike 1		Futto: Ōike 2
Futto: Uemura 1		Futto: Uemura 1–2
	Nagao: Age 3	
	Nagao: Banba 3	
	Nagao: Ichiba 3	
	Nagao: Komukae 3	
	Nagao: Shitamo 3	
	Nagao: Tamanuki 3	
	Nishinokuchi: *Raijinsha* 1–2	Nishinokuchi: *Raijinsha* 1–2
	Nishinokuchi: *Saihōsha* 1–2	Nishinokuchi: *Saihōsha* 1–2
	Ōashi 3	
	Yokosuka: Daimon 2	
	Yokosuka: Honmachi 2	
	Yokosuka: Kitamachi 2	
	Yokosuka: Kōtsū, *Entsūsha* 2	
	Yokosuka: Kōtsū, *Hachikōsha* 2[a]	

Note: The table lists neighbourhoods with ensembles that have at least one type of *tsuzumi* seated in the rear. In all these cases the exact seating and number of instruments varies in some places. For instance, in Fuki: *Honwakakai* there are five instrumentalists that may be in the rear, but normally only three sit there at a time. A common combination is 2 *ōtsuzumi* and 1 *fue*. The information given here is what appears to be the most stable and common in each place.

---

a The information about Yokosuka: Kōtsū with *Entsūsha* and *Hachikōsha* is based on *Owari Yokosuka matsuri: Kōtsūgumi, Entsūsha* [Owari Yokosuka festival in Yokosuka city: the float Entsūsha of the neighbourhood Kōtsūgumi] and *Owari Yokosuka matsuri: Kōtsūgumi, Hachikōsha* [Owari Yokosuka festival in

Table 9 *Sanbasō* performances in the Chita Peninsula and neighbouring Hekinan in Mikawa.

Area / District	Neighbourhood	Float	Dance	Karakuri	Puppet
Agui					
Daigone	Daigone	Hachimansha dashi			X
Miyazu	Miyazukitagumi	Miyazu kitagumi dashi			X
	Miyazuminamigumi	Miyazu nansha dashi			X
Yokomatsu	Yokomatsu	Yokosha yamaguruma			
Chita					
Okada	Nakagumi	Amaguruma			X
	Okugumi	Kazaguruma			X
	Satogumi	Higuruma			X
Handa					
Itayama	Hon-Itayamagumi	Honkosha			X
	Koitagumi	Asahiguruma			X
Kamezaki	Higashigumi	Miyamotoguruma			X
Kamihanda	Minamigumi	Irimiyamaru	X		
	Kitagumi	Sumiyoshimaru	X		
Kyōwa	Sunagogumi	Hakusansha			X
Narawa	Higashigumi	Asahiguruma			X
Nishinarawa	Nishigumi	Keishinguruma			X
Okkawa	Asaiyama	Miyamotoguruma			X
Shimohanda	Kitagumi	Karakoguruma			X
Yanabe	Giretsugumi	Hachimansha			X
Yanabe Shinden	Okugumi	Asahiguruma			X
	Hiraigumi	Shinmeiguruma			X

Table 9 (continued)

Area / District	Neighbourhood	Float	Dance	Karakuri	Puppet
Mihama					
Futto	Ōikegumi	Sannōsha	X		
Kōwa	Nakagumi	Shiofukisha		X	
Ōbu					
Yokone	Ishimarugumi	Ishimarusha	X		
	Nakagumi	Nakasha	X		
	Minamigumi	Minamisha	X		
Taketoyo					
Nagao	Age	Miyamotosha			X
	Ichiba	Jingūsha	X		
Tokoname					
Kosugaya		Hakusansha		X	
Ōtani	Hamajō	Hōraisha			X
	Okujō	Tōōsha			X
Tokoname-chiku	Okujō	Tokoishiguruma			X
Tōkai					
Yokosuka	Daimongumi	Daimongumi dashi		X	
Hekinan (Mikawa)					
Hekinan	Ōhamanaka-ku	Nakanokirisha			X
	Tsurugasaki-ku	Tamaguruma			X

Table 10 Comparison of *kagura* and *dashibayashi* tunes.

	KAGURA	DASHIBAYASHI					
	Atsuta	Atsuta	Nagao Komukae	Handa Kamezaki	Handa Kamihanda	Ōtani	Kaminoma
Bonden	○		○				
Okamesan	○		○				
Tōka ebisu	○	○	○				
Sagariba	○	○	○		○	○	○
Shinguruma	[○]	○	○			○	○
Yaguruma	○	○	○		○	○	
Gionbayashi		○			○		
Shagiri			○	○	○	○	
Yukagura			○	○	○	○	
Obaba			○			○	
Jūroku			#	○		○	○
Shinbayashi					○	○	○
Hayakagura					○	○	
Kyōgen					○	○	
Manuke					○	○	
Hayabune						○	○
Seme						○	○

Note: *Kagura* is subdivided into *Atsuta kagura* (Kasadera) and *Miyaryū kagura* (Kamezaki). Only tunes in these repertoires that are also found in Komukae are included in the table. The *dashibayashi* music section is subdivided into Nagao (Komukae), Handa (Kamezaki, Kamihanda), Ōtani, and Kaminoma. Tunes that exist in at least two of these areas are listed. The tunes in the Komukae repertoire that occur in the other localities as well are listed in bold in a central column. Square brackets mean that *Shinguruma* in Kamezaki is a different tune compared to the others. The sign # marks that the tune *Jūroku* is used in Nagao by the neighbourhoods Banba and Ichiba but is called *Shinpō* in Komukae and Tamanuki.

Sources: *Taketoyo-chō Komukae-ku: Matsuribayashi 1–4* [Taketoyo town, Komukae ward: festival music 1–4] 1987–1990; *Komukae-ku Hōōsha: matsuribayashi* [The float Hōōsha of the Komukae ward: festival music] (Internet reference); *Atsuta kagura to Miyaryū kagura* [Atsuta kagura and Miyaryū kagura] (AV reference); *Handa-shi shi: sairei minzoku hen* [Handbook of Handa city: festival and folklore] 1984, pp. 217–230; *Tokoname-shi shi: bunkazai hen* [Handbook of Tokoname city: cultural assets] 1983, pp. 560–573; Hayakawa 2003a, pp. 65–66 (Kaminoma); oral information in Ōtani 27 March 2016.

Appendix 2: Fieldwork list

The main source material consists of video recordings, photographs, and fieldnotes from fieldwork in the listed locations. Dates are rendered in eight digits, denoting the year, month, and day of recording, in that order.

A = Assembly of float, M = Music rehearsal

CHITA PENINSULA
Agui-chō
Daigone 2003–04–20
Hagi 2004–04–11, 2006–04–09
Miyazu 2003–04–20, 2006–04–16
Yokomatsu 2015–04–27, 2017–04–23

Chita-shi
Hinaga (*omanto*, horse festival) 2012–04–08
Kitakasuya 2012–04–08, 2018–04–08
Okada 2006–04–16, 2016–04–16/17, 2017–04–16

Handa-shi
Handa dashimatsuri 2017–10–07
Itayama 2000–04–15, 2001–04–15, 2003–04–12, 2015–04–15,
    2017–04–15/16
Kamezaki 2015–05–08, 2017–05–04
    Higashigumi 2016–11–06A
Kamihanda 2001–04–07, 2003–04–13, 2004–04–03P, 2004–04–09,
    2016–04–10
    Sanbasō 2004–04–02/03M
Kyōwa 2001–04–15, 2004–04–10, 2012–04–15, 2016–04–10,
    2017–04–15
Narawa 2001–04–15, 2006–04–15, 2012–04–15, 2016–04–10,
    2018–04–15, 2019–04–13
Nishinarawa 2000–04–15, 2003–04–15, 2012–04–15, 2017–04–15/16
Okkawa 2002–03–23/24, 2017–03–19

Shimohanda 2000–04–15, 2003–04–19/20, 2014–04–19, 2016–04–22, 2018–04–22
Yanabe 2001–04–14, 2012–04–14, 2017–04–08
Yanabe Shinden 2001–04–14, 2004–04–10

Mihama-chō
Futto 2004–04–03, 2005–04–02, 2017–04–01/02, 2018–04–01
    Ōikegumi 2002–03–24M
Kaminoma 2002–03–30/31, 2016–03–26/27, 2017–03–26, 2018–03–25, 2019–03–31
Kitagata 2017–04–01
Kōwa 2004–04–04, 2017–04–02
    Uemura 2002–03–18M, 2004–04–04
Noma 2017–04–01
Okuda 2013–03–31, 2017–03–25
Tokishi 2017–04–02

Minamichita-chō
Gōdo 1999–10–24
Morozaki 2014–10–11
Toyohama, *Tai matsuri* 1995–07–15, 1997–07–21
Utsumi 2010–04–04, 2017–04–02
    Highashibata 2002–03–29M
Yamami 1999–10–24

Ōbu-shi
Chikasaki (*omanto*, horse festival) 2017–10–08
Kitasaki 2014–10–12, 2017–10–08, 2019–10–13/14
Yokone 2014–10–12

Taketoyo-chō
Fuki
    Fuki–Ichiba 2004–04–03, 2005–04–02, 2016–04–02, 2019–04–06/07
    Honwakakai 2004–04–03, 2005–04–02, 2016–04–02, 2019–04–07
    Ichihara 2004–04–04, 2016–04–02
Higashi-Ōdaka 2004–04–04, 2016–04–02, 2017–04–01/02, 2018–03–31/04–01
Nagao harumatsuri 1992–04–11/12, 2001–04–14/15, 1993-01-01 (*isami*), 2003–04–12, 2004–04–10, 2006–04–09, 2007–04–13/14, 2012–04–14, 2014–04–12, 2016–04–08/09, 2017–04–08/09, 2018–04–13/15
    Age 2018–04–08M, 2019–04–14
    Komukae 1992–04–07M, 2016–04–04/05M
    Shitamo 1992–04–07M
    Tamanuki 2016–03–24/25M, 2019–04–13

Ōashi Jaguruma matsuri 1994–07–23, 1995–07–22/23, 1997–07–19M,
    2001–07–21, 2002–07–20/21, 2003–07–19/20, 2005–07–16
Taketoyo Fureai dashimatsuri 2014–10–12, 2019–10–14

Tōkai-shi
Ōta 2015–10–04, 2016–10–01
Yokosuka 2015–09–26/27

Tokoname-shi
Koba 2018–04–18
Kosugaya 2004–04–03, 2010–04–04, 2013–04–07, 2016–04–02/03,
    2018–04–01, 2019–04–07
Nishinokuchi 2003–04–19M, 2016–04–16, 2017–04–30
Ogura 2002–04–27/28, 2016–04–16, 2017–04–23
Ōno 2002–04–27/28, 2017–04–29/30
Ōtani 2002–03–30, 2016–04–02, 2018–03–31
Sakai 2002–03–30, 2017–03–25/26, 2018–03–24
Taya 2001–04–07
Tokoname town 2001–04–14, 2014–04–13, 2017–04–08
    Ichiba 2002–03–27M
    Matsuribayashi concert 2002–03–17
    Tokoname dashimatsuri 2019–10–13
Yata 2006–04–09

OWARI (EXCEPT CHITA PENINSULA)
Inuyama
Inuyama matsuri 2001–04–08

Iwakura
Iwakura dashi natsumatsuri 1997–07–19

Nagoya
Arimatsu 2017–10–01
Hira 2017–10–15
Honji 2016–10–02
Kawahara jinja 1990–07–04
Nagoya jinja 2002–07–16
Nagoya matsuri 2014–10–19, 2015–10–18, 2016–10–16
Narumi Omotekata 2015–10–18, 2016–10–16
Narumi Urakata 2015–10–11, 2016–10–09
Toda 2014–10–05, 2015–10–04
Ushidate 1997–07–27

Tsushima
Tsushima akimatsuri 2014–10–05, 2017–09–29
Tsushima Tennō matsuri 1999–07–25
Kamori 2017–09–29

MIKAWA
Chiryū
Aimatsuri 2017–04–29
Dashibunraku show 2010–07–04
Nishimachi 2017–04–29A

Gamagōri
Miya matsuri 2016–10–15

Hekinan
Ōhamanaka-ku 2017–10–07/08
Tsurugasaki-ku 2017–10–07

Kariya
Ogakie 2018–10–21, 2019–04–14

Miyoshi 2019–10–20

Toyota
Koromo matsuri 2014–10–18
Hirai 2015–10–04/05, 2019–10–06
Shiga 2015–10–25, 2016–10–23

Toyokawa
Goyu 2003–07–27
Kō 2003–07–27

OUTSIDE AICHI
Kyoto
Gion matsuri 1995–07–16/17
Kyoto 1200th celebration congratulatory float parade 1992–07–24

Takayama
Harumatsuri 1992–04–15

Appendix 3: List of Japanese words

akimatsuri	autumn festival
Asahiryū	a school of *kagura* music
Atsuta kagura	*kagura* originated in Atsuta jingū, Nagoya
bonden / bonten	two spires in the back of the roof of a festival float
bugaku	court music and dance
bunkazai hogohō	Law on the protection of cultural properties
bunraku	puppet theatre, cf. *ningyō-jōruri*
butsudansha	'Buddhist altar *dashi*'; pre-*state Shintō* style, often colourful
changiri	another name for *chappa*
chappa	cymbals
chigo	sacred child of *Gion matsuri*
chiku	district, administrative unit smaller than *shi*
chintorobune	a type of boat festival float, cf. *danjiri*
chō	city
chōnaikai	neighbourhood, see *kumi*
chūdaiko	middle size barrel drum, cf. *ōdaiko*
chūdan or *chūdan no ita*	middle level or board, a 'shelf' inside the float in its front part
chūkan	middle size *nōkan*
dadaiko	another name for *ōdaiko*
daidai kagura	*hōnō* or 'honorific' *kagura*
daimyō	feudal lord
dan	a scene in drama
danjiri	festival float, boat festival float
dashi	festival float
dashibayashi	float ensemble; musical ensemble seated inside a float, cf. *hayashi*

dashibunraku	*ningyō-jōruri* performed on and in front of a float
dashigura	storing house for floats, cf. *sayagura*
dashimatsuri	festival with floats; often synonymous with modern city float-festivals
debayashi	ensemble in *kabuki*
dengaku	medieval field rituals with music
detoi	square wooden tube for ropes that control a *karakuri-ningyō*
don	onomatopoetic word for large drum, like *hiradaiko*
donden / donten	turning a float 360 degrees or more
dōchūgaku	another word for *michiyuki*
dōnaga	another name for *ōdaiko*
dōyama	first storey of a festival float
Edo period	the period 1603–1868, also called *Tokugawa period*
Enbukyoku	dance tune in *Sanbasō* performance
fue	flute, generic term
furedaiko	message drum, warning drum
furyū	ornamental
futsū kagura	general *kagura*, cf. *isami*
gagaku	court music
gaku/-daiko, /-ko	drum, sometimes referring to *hiradaiko*
gakunin	*gagaku* musicians
geza ongaku	off-stage music in *kabuki*
gohei	a symbol of *kami*, zigzag-shaped strips of folded paper suspended atop an upright wand
goningumi	administrative unit of five households
goten manzai	parlour entertainment by *manzai*
hanaguruma	'flower car', a kind of float
handozuna	'safety-rope' that protects the float from falling over
hangiri	suspended flat drum, cf. *hiradaiko*
happi	short jacket used at festivals
harumatsuri	spring festival
hayashi / -bayashi	musical ensemble and the music they play (in compounds: *-bayashi*)
hayashi yatai	float in the form of a wagon with a roof and open sides
Heisei period	the period 1989–2019

hikiyama	festival float, see *dashi*
hikizome	first pulling of a float on the day before the festival eve, cf. *tameshibiki, zenyasai*
hiradaiko	suspended flat drum; sometimes referring to *shimedaiko*
hiragana	Japanese alphabet mainly used for Japanese words (as opposed to loanwords)
hirazuridaiko	another name for *hiradaiko*
hoko	festival float in *Gion matsuri*, Kyoto
honmatsuri	festival day, main day of a festival
hōnō	offering
Hōyeki era	1751–1764
hōnōgaku	offertory or honouring music
hōrōgei	term for the art of itinerant performers
hosobue	another name for *shinobue*
hozonkai	preserving association
hyōshigi	wooden clappers
inari	deity of rice, prosperity, fertility, and foxes
isami	courageous, protective, or gratitude music; a kind of *kagura* music
isamibayashi	cf. *isami*
isamidaiko	cf. *isami*
Isewan taifū	the Ise Bay typhoon that hit the Chita Peninsula in 1959
ishidoriguruma	three-wheeled wagon with *ōdaiko* in the back
iwaikomi	celebrating a person with music, cf. *hōnōgaku*
jichikai	neighbourhood, cf. *kumi*
jingū	*Shintō* shrine connected to the Imperial House, cf. *jinja*
jinja	general *Shintō* shrine, cf. *jingū*
jōruri	recitation accompanied by the *shamisen* lute in puppet performance, cf. *Ningyō-jōruri*
kabuki	classical music drama
kadozuke	'door-to-door entertainment' by *manzai*
kagura	performance addressed to *kami*, cf. *futsū kagura, mikagura, miyakagura, satokagura*
kagurabue	side-blown flute, cf. *kusabue*
kaguraden	stage for *kagura* at a shrine
kagurasuzu	see *suzu*
kami	*Shintō* deity
kamishibai	paper theatre
kane	gong

kanji	Chinese character used in writing for Chinese loanwords
kankaradaiko	barrel drum played with two long sticks
karako	'China child' type of *karakuri-ningyō*
karakuri	puppet on a float; strictly: mechanical doll, also *karakuri-ningyō*
karakuri-ningyō	puppet on a float; strictly: mechanical doll, also *karakuri*
karasutobi	*Sanbasō* jumping like a crow
katakana	Japanese alphabet mainly used for loanwords
keigo	respectful performing arts at a shrine
kobachi	another name for *shimedaiko*
kodaiko	another name for *shimedaiko*
kodomo Sanbasō	children *Sanbasō*
kodomobayashi	children ensemble
kokyū	vertically held fiddle
koshagiri	small *shagiribue*
kotobuki Sanbasō	auspicious *Sanbasō* performance
kotsuzumi	small hourglass drum, cf. *tsuzumi*
kozuke	another name for *shimedaiko*
kōminkan	neighbourhood community house
ku	ward, administrative unit
kuchishōga	see *shōga*
kumi / -gumi	neighbourhood, administrative unit usually smaller than *ku* (in compounds: *-gumi*)
kuromisu ongaku	another name for *geza ongaku*
kuruma	festival float cf. *dashi*
kusabue	side-blown flute, cf. *kagurabue*
kyōgen	comic plays at *nō* performances
machi	town
maedana	the central front opening of a float
maedana-ningyō	puppet for performance in the central front opening of a float
manzai	type of entertainer, traditionally often itinerant
matsuri	festival (Japanese term, cf. *wago*), cf. *sairei*
matsuribayashi	festival music ensemble, cf. *dashibayashi*
Meiji period	the period 1868–1912
michibiki	another word for *michiyuki*
michiyuki	parading a festival float; music for parading
mikagura	court *kagura*, cf. *kagura*
Mikawa manzai	*manzai* from Mikawa, Aichi prefecture
miko	shrine maiden performing dances at shrines
mikomai	shrine maiden dance

mikoshi	carried festival palanquin
minyō	folksong
minzoku geinō	folk performing arts
mitsubyōshi / mitsuboshi	*three strokes rhythm*
miso	soybean paste
miyakagura	shrine *kagura*, cf. *kagura*
miyaryū kagura	another name for *Atsuta kagura*
momi no dan	*Sanbasō* waving sleeves and stamping
mukei minzoku bunkazai	intangible folk cultural properties
mura	village
Nakasendo	an unrealized railway project planned to connect Tokyo and Kyoto
natsumatsuri	summer festival
ni-kai	second 'floor' inside a float
ningyō-jōruri	puppet performance accompanied by *jōruri* recitation, cf. *bunraku, jōruri*
nō	classical music and dance drama
nōbue,	cf. *nōkan*
nōgaku	includes both *nō* and *kyōgen* plays
nō hayashi	musical ensemble in *nō*
nōkan	side-blown flute used in *nō* drama
norito	*Shintō* priest's invocation
o-	respectful prefix: *okuruma, ohayashi* etc.
ōdaiko	large barrel drum; sometimes also referring to *hiradaiko*
ōdo	can mean *ōtsuzumi*; sometimes referring to *hiradaiko, ōdaiko*, or *shimedaiko*
oizuna	'safety rope' that protects the float from falling over
ōkawa	another name for *ōtsuzumi*
okedaiko	two-headed laced cylindrical drum
Okina	*nō* play and lead character in that play together with *Sanbasō*
okuridaiko	a kind of drumming in Higashi-Ōdaka
okuruma	festival float, cf. *dashi*
omatsuri hōan	the 'festival law' from 1992
orei isami	thanking the deity, cf. *isami*
ōsaiya ōsaiya	phrase chanted at *Sanbasō* performance
otoshikomi	transition from one tune to another, 'medley'
ōtsuzumi	hourglass drum, larger than *kotsuzumi*
Owaridaiko	a drumming style in Owari in which the drummer twirls a drumstick
Owari manzai	*manzai* from Owari, Aichi prefecture

reisai	annual festival, cf. *matsuri, sairei*
Reiwa period	started in 2019
roppō (no fue)	side-blown flute, cf. *kagurabue*
saibara	a song genre
Saimeryū	a school of *Atsura kagura* music
sairei	'religious festival', cf. *matsuri*
sairei iinchō	festival general
saizō	*manzai* character holding a *kotsuzumi*
sakaki	an evergreen used in shrine rituals
sake	rice wine [often written *saké*]
Sanbasō	a character in *nō* that became a puppet used at festivals
Sanbasōbayashi	instrumental ensemble and the music accompanying *Sanbasō* performance; also name of a tune
san-kai	third 'floor' inside a float
sankyoku manzai	*manzai* with drums and *shamisen*
satokagura	village *kagura* or local *kagura*, cf. *kagura*
sayagura	storing house for festival floats, cf. *dashigura*
senbedaiko	another name for *hiradaiko*
shagiri	turning a float 90 degrees; sometimes synonymous with *donden*
shagiribue	another name for *nōkan*
shamisen /- jamisen	three-stringed long-necked lute
shi	township
shigaku / shingaku	the day before the festival day, 'festival eve', cf. *zenyasai*
Shiki Sanbasō	ceremonial *Sanbasō* performance
shimedaiko	flat laced drum
shinobue	side-blown flute common in *dashibayashi*, cf. *yokobue*
Shintō	collective name for indigenous practices of religious ritual
shirabe	*shimedaiko*; the laces of *kotsuzumi*
shishimai	lion dance
shitadashi Sanbasō	puppet scene of *Sanbasō* sticking out its tongue
shite	lead character in *nō*
shōga	vocalizing melodies or drum patterns as a mnemonic technique
shōgun	military leader
shōji	sliding doors
shōkonsai	memorial of Japan's 1905 victory over Russia
sore	collective exclamation when pulling a float

state Shintō	a reform intended to separate Buddhism and *Shintō* practices
surigane	gong; also cymbals cf. *chappa*
suzu	'bell-tree', also *kagurasuzu*
suzu no dan	*Sanbasō* dancing with the *suzu*
taiko / -daiko	generic term for drum (in compounds: *-daiko*)
Taishō period	the period 1912–1926
tama	jade, the first part of the *kumi* name Tamanuki
tameshibiki	practice pulling of a float at the beginning of a festival, cf. *hikizome*
tayū	*manzai* character holding a fan
tek-kon-pan	onomatopoeia for *three strokes rhythm*, cf. *mitsubyōshi*
Tōkaidō line	railway connecting Tokyo and Kobe
Tōkaidō road	route connecting Tokyo and Kyoto in the *Edo period*
Tokugawa period	the period 1603–1868, also called *Edo period*
torii	gate of a shrine
toshi sairei	city float-festival
tsuke / tsukeita	wooden board played with two clappers
tsukedaiko	suspended flat drum, cf. *hiradaiko*
tsure	secondary character in *nō*
tsuzumi	hourglass shaped drum, commonly *kotsuzumi*; cf. also *ōtsuzumi*
utai	singing in *nō* style
utaibayashi	vocal piece, cf. *hayashi*
utaibue	another name for *shinobue*
uwayama	upper storey of a festival float
uwayama-ningyō	puppet for performance on the top of a float
wago	Japanese word as opposed to Sino-Japanese
wakamono-gumi	young men's organization
wasshoi	collective exclamation when pulling a float, like 'heave-ho!'
yakata	miniature house (for a mask of a lion's head) mounted on a wagon
Yakata (-type dashi)	a type of float in Higashiura
yama	festival float, cf. *dashi*
yamaboko	festival float in *Gion matsuri*, Kyoto
yamaguruma	another name for float, cf. *dashi*
Yamato kotoba	see *wago*

yatai	festival float, cf. *dashi*
Yata manzai	*manzai* from Yata, Tokoname
yoimatsuri	the day before the festival day, 'festival eve', cf. *zenyasai, honmatsuri*
yoiyama	festival eve, cf. *zenyasai*; the day before the festival day
yokobue	side-blown flute common in *dashibayashi*, cf. *shinobue*
yomiya	festival eve, cf. *zenyasai*; the day before the festival day
yukata	light summer kimono
zaifuri-ningyō	'commander puppet' (often a *karako*) that turns its head and waves its arms as the float is moved along
zenyasai	the day before the festival day, 'festival eve', cf. *yoimatsuri, honmatsuri*

References

A. Unpublished references

Kairan: Tamanuki san kumin no minasama e [Circular: to the residents in the three sections of the Tamanuki ward] 回覧：玉貫三区民の皆様へ 2022. Tamanuki-ku dashi unkō ni kansuru onegai [A request concerning the dashi pulling by the Tamanuki ward] 玉貫区山車運行に関するお願い. Reiwa 4, 4-gatsu kichijitsu [On an auspicious day of April, Reiwa 4] 令和 4 年 4 月吉日 [6 sheets leaflet].

Okkawa-mura sairei emaki [Okkawa village festival scroll] 乙川村祭禮絵巻 1755. Handa Shiritsu Hakubutsukan [English name]. Handa Municipal Museum 半田市立博物館.

Shashin de miru Kamezaki shiohimatsuri: Yunesuko mukei bunka isan kōho kinen [*Kamezaki shiohimatsuri* in pictures: in commemoration of the candidacy for UNESCO Intangible cultural heritage] 写真でみる亀崎潮干祭り： ユネスコ無形文化遺産候補記念 2017. Handa shiritsu hakubutsukan: Kikakuten [Handa Municipal Museum: Special Exhibition] 半田市立博物館 企画展.

Taketoyo-chō Komukae-ku: Matsuribayashi 1–4 [Taketoyo town, Komukae ward: festival music 1–4]. 武豊町小迎区： 祭り囃子 1987–1990. Aoki Yoshinobu and Sugisaki Shōji (eds) 作成者、青木義信、杉崎昭二 [Unpublished notations].

B. Published references

Agui-chō shi: shiryō hen 8, Minzoku [Handbook of Agui town: reference material 8, Folklore] 阿久比町誌： 資料編八（民俗）. Agui, Agui-chōshi Hensan Iinkai [The Committee for Documentation of Agui] 1995.

Aichi dashi zukan [Picture-book of the festival floats in Aichi] あいち山車図鑑 [2nd edition] 2017. Aichi Dashimatsuri Nippon Ichi Kyōgikai hen [Edited by] the Aichi Dashi Matsuri Nippon Ichi Council あいち山車まつり日本一協議会編. [Nagoya].

Aichi dashimatsuri zukan [Picture book of the float-festivals in Aichi] あいち山車まつり図鑑 2020. Aichi Dashimatsuri Nippon Ichi Kyōgikai hen

[Edited by] the Aichi Dashi Matsuri Nippon Ichi Council あいち山車まつ
り日本一協議会編. [Nagoya].

Akaike, Noriaki 1976. 'Festival and neighborhood association: a case
study of the Kamimachi neighborhood in Chichibu'. *Japanese Journal of
Religious Studies* 3: 2–3, 127–174.

Alaszewska, Jane 2012. 'Promoting and preserving the Chichibu night
festival: the impact of cultural policy on the transmission of Japanese
folk performing arts'. In Keith Howard (ed.): *Music as Intangible
cultural heritage: policy, ideology, and practice in the preservation of
East Asian traditions*. SOAS Musicology Series. Farnham/Burlington:
Ashgate, pp. 197–212.

Allen, Michael 1996. *The cult of Kumari: virgin worship in Nepal*.
Kathmandu: Mandala Book Point.

Anderson, Mary 1977. *The festivals of Nepal*. Calcutta: Rupe & Co.

Andersson, Tommy D. and Getz, Donald 2009. 'Tourism as a mixed
industry: differences between private, public and not-for-profit festivals'.
Tourism Management 30: 6, 847–856.

Andō, Reiji 安藤礼二 2022. 'Sinpan kaisetsu Shukusai no ronri 新版解
説・祝祭の論理' [Comment to the new edition: the logic of festivals].
In Yanagita Kunio 柳田国男: *Nihon no matsuri* [Japanese festivals]
日本の祭. [New edition, 22nd printing]. Kadokawa sofia bunko. Tokyo:
Kadokawa, pp. 257–262.

Arai, Ken 1996. 'New religions'. In Tamaru Noriyoshi [田丸徳善] and
David Reid (eds): *Religion in Japanese culture: where living tradi-
tions meet a changing world*. Tokyo/New York/London: Kodansha
International, pp. 97–111.

'Araya no dashi' chōsa hōkokusho [The festival wagon in Araya ward:
an investigation report] 「新屋の山車」調査報告書 1988. [Edited by]
Miyoshi-chōritsu Rekishi minzoku shiryōkan [Museum of history and
folklore in Miyoshi town] 三好町立歴史民族資料館編集.

Arisawa, Shino 2012. 'Dichotomies between "classical" and "folk" in the
intangible cultural properties of Japan'. In Keith Howard (ed.): *Music as
Intangible cultural heritage: policy, ideology, and practice in the preservation of East Asian traditions*. SOAS Musicology Series. Farnham/
Burlington: Ashgate, pp. 181–195.

Ashkenazi, Michael 1993. *Matsuri: festivals of a Japanese town*. Honolulu:
University of Hawai'i Press.

Asuke-chō no matsuri to dashi [Festivals and wagons of Asuke town]
足助町の祭りと山車 1998. 72 pp. [Edited by] Asuke shiryōkan [Asuke
Museum] 足助資料館編.

Avenburg, Karen 2012. Interpellation and performance: the construction of identities through musical experience in the Virgen del Rosario
Fiesta in Iruya, Argentina. *Latin American Perspectives*, March 2012,
39: 2, 134–149. Arts, culture, and politics: part 1: Art, activism, and
performance.

Averill, Gage 1994. 'Anraje to Angaje: carnival politics and music in Haiti'. *Ethnomusicology* 38: 2, 217–247.

Bauer, Helen and Carlquist, Sherwin 1974 [1965]. *Japanese festivals.* Rutland, Vermont/Tokyo: Tuttle.

Becker, Judith 1968. 'Percussive patterns in the music of mainland Southeast Asia'. *Ethnomusicology* 12: 2, 173–191.

Bilby, Kenneth 2010. 'Surviving secularization: masking the spirit in the Jankunu (John Canoe) festivals of the Caribbean'. *New West Indian Guide* 84: 3–4, 179–223.

Bloomer, Kristin C. 2017. *Possessed by the Virgin: Hinduism, Roman Catholicism, and Marian possession in South India.* https://doi.org/10.1093/oso/9780190615093.001.0001 (accessed 21 February 2025).

Bishū Nagao Komukaegumi Hōōsha: sōken hyakugojisshūnen kinenshi [The festival float Hōōsha of the neighbourhood Komukae, Nagao district, Owari province: memorial magazine for the 150th anniversary of its construction] 尾州長尾小迎組鳳凰車: 創建百五十周年記念誌 2013. [Aichi, Taketoyo 愛知、武豊].

Bocking, Brian 1995. *A popular dictionary of Shintō.* Richmond: Curzon Press.

Brandon, James R. 1978. 'Form in kabuki acting'. In William Malm (ed.): *Studies in kabuki: its acting, music, and historical context.* Honolulu: University of Hawai'i Press, pp. 63–132.

Brandon, James R. and Leiter, Samuel L. (eds) 2002. *Kabuki plays on stage. Vol. 3: Darkness and desire, 1804–1864.* Honolulu: University of Hawai'i Press.

Breen, John 2020, 'Sannō matsuri: fabricating festivals in modern Japan'. *Journal of Religion in Japan* 9, 78–117.

Brucher, Katherine 2013. 'Crossing the longest bridge: Portuguese bands in the diaspora'. *The World of Music* 2: 2, 99–117.

Castelo-Branco, Salwa El-Shawan 2000. 'Portugal'. In Timothy Rice et al. (eds): *The Garland encyclopedia of world music. Vol. 8: Europe.* London: Routledge, pp. 576–587.

Chiryū matsuri, Chiryu festival 知立まつり 1990. [Edited by] Museum of History and Folklore in Chiryū city 知立市歴史民俗資料館編. Chiryu 知立市. 16 pp. (Text also in English 英文併記).

Cowdery, James R. 1984. 'A fresh look at the concept of tune family'. *Ethnomusicology* 28: 3, 495–504.

Cudny, Waldemar 2014. 'The phenomenon of festivals: their origins, evolution and classification'. *Anthropos* 109: 2, 640–656.

Dale, Peter N. 1990/1986. *The myth of Japanese uniqueness.* London: Routledge and Nissan Institute for Japanese Studies.

DaMatta, Roberto 1991 [1979]. *Carnivals, rogues, and heroes: an interpretation of the Brazilian dilemma.* Notre Dame, Indiana: University of Notre Dame Press.

Dashi to karakuriningyō: Iwakura-shi shitei yūkei minzoku bunkazai [Floats and mechanical puppets: the city-designated tangible cultural property of Iwakura city] n.d. Iwakura-shi kyōiku iinkai [The Iwakura City Board of Education] [No pagination]. [Brochure]

Davis, Martha Ellen 1972. 'The social organization of a musical event: the Fiesta de Cruz in San Juan, Puerto Rico'. *Ethnomusicology* 16: 1, 38–62.

Den, Makoto デン真 2017. *Nihon man'naka dashimatsuri. Dashi matsuri of the central Japan: Miryoku afureru Aichi to Chūbu Nihon no dashimatsuri, karakuri-ningyō* [The fascinating float-festivals and mechanical puppets of Aichi and the central Japan] 日本真ん中山車祭り: 魅力あふれる愛知と中部日本の山車まつり・からくり人形. Den Makoto shashinshū [Den Makoto's photography book] デン真写真集. Nagoya: Chūnichi shinbunsha 名古屋、中日出版社.

Downing, Sonja Lynn 2010. 'Agency, leadership, and gender negotiation in Balinese girls' gamelans'. *Ethnomusicology* 54: 1, 54–80.

Edelson, Loren 2009. *Danjuro's girls: women on the kabuki stage.* New York: Palgrave Macmillan 2009.

Ellefson, Dylan C. 2011. 'In place over time: a spatial approach to popular culture and identity formation through the Danjiri festival of Kishiwada City, 1745–1928'. Diss. University of Southern California.

Endō, Jun 2003 [1998]. 'The early modern period: in search of a Shinto identity'. In Inoue Nobutaka (ed.): *Shinto: a short history.* London/New York: Routledge Curzon, pp. 108–158.

Endō, Yuki 遠藤由起 2020. 'Ronbun: Gion matsuri to ekibyō. 2019-nen shingata korona uirusu kansen kakudai e no taiō o chūshin ni 論文: 祇園祭と疫病: 2019 年新型コロナウィルス感染拡大への対応を中心に'. [English title:] Japanese Gion festival and epidemic: responses to infection of coronavirus disease 2019. *Nihon Daigaku Daigakuin Sōgō Shakai Jōhō Kenkyūka Kiyō.* Nihon University, Graduate School of Social and Cultural Studies. 日本大学大学院総合社会情報研究科紀要. Vol. 21, pp. 189–200. https://gssc.dld.nihon-u.ac.jp/wp-content/uploads/journal/pdf21/21-189-200-Endo.pdf (accessed 2 April 2022). [Japanese text with English summary].

Fahm, AbdulGafar Olawale 2015. 'Ijebu Ode's Ojude Oba festival: Cultural and spiritual significance'. *Sage Open* January–March 2015, 1–11. https://journals.sagepub.com/home/sgo (accessed 23 October 2022).

Falassi, Alessandro 1987. *Time out of time: essays on the festival.* Albuquerque, New Mexico: University of New Mexico Press.

Fitzgerald, Timothy 1997. 'A critique of "religion" as a cross-cultural category'. *Method & Theory in the Study of Religion* 9: 2, 91–110.

Frost, Nicola 2016. 'Anthropology and festivals: festival ecologies'. *Ethnos* 81: 4, 569–583.

Fujie, Linda 1983. 'Effects of urbanization on matsuri-bayashi in Tokyo'. *Yearbook for Traditional Music* 15, 38–44.

—— 1986a. 'Matsuri-bayashi of Tokyo: the role of supporting organizations in traditional music'. Columbia University. PhD thesis. Proquest Dissertations and Theses, UMI 8623522.

—— 1986b. 'The process of oral transmission in Japanese folk performing arts: the teaching of *matsuri-bayashi* in Tokyo'. In Tokumaru Yoshihiko and Yamaguti Osamu (eds): *The oral and the literate in music*. Tokyo: Academia Music, pp. 231–238.

Fujita, Takanori 2008. 'Nō and kyōgen: music from the medieval theatre'. In Alison McQueen Tokita and David W. Hughes (eds): *The Ashgate research companion to Japanese music*. SOAS Musicology Series. Farnham/Burlington: Ashgate, pp. 127–144.

Fukaya, Yoshihiro 深谷佳弘 (ed.) 1996. *Saihōsha no chōchin to ohayashi* [The lanterns and the ensemble music of the dashi Saihōsha] 西寶車の提燈とお囃子. [Published by] Tokoname-shi Nishinokuchi-ku Saihōkai [The Association of the Festival Float Saihōsha, Nishinokuchi ward, Tokoname city] 常滑市西之口区西寶会. [Tokoname 常滑].

Fukutake, Tadashi 1967. *Japanese rural society*. Ithaca/New York: Cornell University Press.

Garfias, Robert 1965. 'The sacred mi-kagura ritual of the Japanese court'. Los Angeles: University of California: *Selected Reports in Ethnomusicology* 1: 2, 149–178.

Gerow, Aaron 2005. 'Nation, citizenship and cinema'. In Jennifer Robertson (ed.): *A companion to the anthropology of Japan*. Malden: Blackwell Publishing.

Groemer, Gerald 2002. 'Japanese folk music'. In Robert C. Provine et al. (eds): *The Garland encyclopedia of world music. Vol. 7: East Asia, China, Japan, and Korea*. London: Routledge, pp. 599–606.

Gunji, Masakatsu 郡司正勝 1971. *Nihon no hōrōgei...* [Wanderers' performing arts in Japan...]. 日本の放浪芸.... [Appendix pamphlet to Ozawa, Shōichi; Ogawa, Yōzō and Ichikawa, Katsumori (eds) 1971.]

—— 1973. 放浪芸能の系譜 Hōrōgeinō no keifu [Lineage of wanderers' performing arts]. In *Kokubungaku kaishaku to kanshō* 国文学解釈と鑑賞 1973: 1.

Gyokushinsha: dashi kenzō 70-shūnen kinenshi [The festival float *Gyokushinsha*: memorial magazine for the 70th anniversary of its construction] 玉神車：　山車建造七十周年記念誌　2018. [Publisher] Tamanuki Dashi Hozonkai [Tamanuki Festival Float Preservation Society] 発行元：玉貫山車保存会. [Aichi, Taketoyo 愛知、武豊].

Halperin, Ehud 2016. 'Palanquins of the gods: Indigenous theologies, ritual practice, and complex agency in the Western Indian Himalayas'. *Religions of South Asia* 10: 3, 300–323. https://doi.org/10.1558/rosa.31666 (accessed 22 September 2022).

Hamachiyo, Sayumi 濱千代早由美 2000. 'Toshisairei no seisei to denshō: Ise to iu toshishakai o ikiru tame no "tsunagari"' [The development and continuation of city float-festivals: a 'link' to life in a large city community like Ise] 都市祭礼の生成と伝承：伊勢という都市社会を生きるための「つながり」. In *Shukusai no 100-nen: Seikatsugaku dai 24 satsu* 祝祭の 100 年 [A hundred years of festivals: Lifology 24] 祝祭の 100 年：生活学第 24 冊. Nihon Seikatsu Gakkai [Japan Society of Lifology] 日本生活学会. Tokyo: Domesu Shuppan 東京、ドメス出版, pp. 42–60.

Handa dashimatsuri gaidobukku: oideya Handa, Chita-ji no sora ni Handa ga moeru [Handa Float-festival guidebook: welcome to Handa, a fiery city under the sky of the Chita Peninsula] 半田山車祭りガイドブック： おいでやはんだ、知多路の空にはんだが燃える 1995. Handa-shi and Handa-shi Kankōkyōkai [Published by: Handa-city Tourism Association] 半田市観光協会. Handa: Seishindō 半田、誠進堂.

Handa-shi shi: sairei minzoku hen [Handbook of Handa city: festival and folklore] 半田市誌：祭礼民俗篇. 1984. [Published by] Handa-shi, Aichi-ken 愛知県半田市. *Shinto: a history.* https://doi.org/10.1093/acpr of:oso/9780190621711.001.0001 (accessed 21 July 2023).

Hardacre, Helen 1989. *Shintō and the state, 1868–1988.* Princeton, New Jersey: Princeton University Press.

—— 2016. *Shinto: a history.* New York: Oxford University Press. https:// doi.org/10.1093/acprof:oso/9780190621711.001.0001 (accessed 21 July 2023).

Harich-Schneider, Eta 1973. *A history of Japanese music.* London: Oxford University Press.

Harnish, David 1997. 'Music, myth, and liturgy at the Lingsar temple festival in Lombok, Indonesia'. *Yearbook for Traditional Music* 29, pp. 80–106.

Hashimoto, Hiroyuki 1998. 'Re-creating and re-imagining folk performing arts in contemporary Japan'. *Journal of Folklore Research* 35: 1, Special issue: International rites, 35–46.

—— 2003. 'Between preservation and tourism: folk performing arts in contemporary Japan'. *Asian Folklore Studies* 62, 225–236.

Havens, Norman 1988. Translator's postscript: Matsuri in Japanese religious life. In Inoue Nobutaka (ed.): *Matsuri: Festival and rite in Japanese life.* Kokugakuin University, Tokyo, Institute for Japanese Culture and Classics: Contemporary Papers on Japanese Religion No. 1, 147–155.

Hayashi, Kenzō 林謙三 1992. *Kaisetsu* [Commentary] 解説. [Commentary to] *Gionbayashi.* [Gion festival music] 祇園囃子. Tokyo: King Records KICH 104. CD.

Häussermann, Hartmut and Siebel, Walter 1993. Die Politik der Festivalisierung und die Festivalisierung der Politik. *Leviathan* 13, 3–31.

Hayakawa, Masao 早川政夫 1984. *Tōkai-shi no matsuribayashi* [Festival music in Tōkai city] 東海市の祭ばやし. Tōkai 東海.

—— 2003a. *Aichi-ken no dashibayashi* [Festival-float ensembles in Aichi prefecture] 愛知県の山車囃子. Tōkai 東海.

—— 2003b. *Chūbu Nihon no dashibayashi* [Festival-float ensembles in Central Japan] 中部日本の山車囃子. Tōkai 東海.

Higuchi, Hiromi 樋口博美 2012. 'Gion matsuri no yamaboko sairei o meguru matsuri-en to shite no shakai kankei: matsuri o sasaeru hitobito' 祇園祭の山鉾祭礼をめぐる祭縁としての社会関係： 祭を支える人々. [English title:] Social relations brought by festivals (*matsuri-en*): observation in people involved with ritual (*yamaboko junko*) of Gion festival. *Senshū daigaku ningenkagaku ronshū: Shakaigakuhen.* [English title:] Bulletin of Senshu University school of human sciences. *Sociology* 専修大学人間科学論集社会学篇 2: 2, 113–125. https://core. ac.uk/download/pdf/71787429.pdf (accessed 2 April 2022).

Hikawa, Kōhei 日川好平 2011. *Saigo no manzaishi: Owari manzai iemoto godaime Chōfuku dayū Kitagawa Kōtarō* [The last manzai performer: the head family of Owari manzai, the fifth leading performer, Chōfuku dayū, i.e. Kitagawa Kōtarō] 最後の万蔵師： 尾張万蔵家元、五代目長福大夫、北川幸太郎. Nagoya: Fūbaisha 名古屋、風媒社.

Hiraoka, Akitoshi 平岡昭利 (ed.) 2008. *Chizu de yomitoku Nihon no chiiki henbō* 地図で読み解く日本の地域変貌. [English title:] Geographical changes in regions of Japan. Ōtsu: Kaiseisha 大津、海青社.

Hobsbawm, Eric 1983. 'Introduction: inventing traditions'. In Eric Hobsbawm and Terence Ranger (eds): *The invention of tradition.* Cambridge: Cambridge University Press, pp. 1–14.

Horii, Mitsutoshi 2021. *'Religion' and 'secular' categories in sociology: decolonizing the modern myth.* Cham: Palgrave Macmillan.

Hughes, David W. 1984a. 'Hayashi'. In Stanley Sadie (ed.): *The New Grove dictionary of musical instruments 2 G to O.* London: Macmillan Press, 208.

—— 1984b. 'Ōtsuzumi'. In Stanley Sadie (ed.): *The New Grove dictionary of musical instruments 2 G to O.* London, Macmillan Press, 976.

—— 1984c. 'Tsuzumi'. In Stanley Sadie (ed.): *The New Grove dictionary of musical instruments 3 P to Z.* London: Macmillan Press, pp. 662–663.

—— 2008. *Traditional folk song in Modern Japan.* Folkestone: Global Oriental.

Ido, Shinji 井戸慎二 2006. 'Kuchishōga: ibunka kan de kyōyūsareru kyōyō kyōiku' [An analysis of oral mnemonics: the intercultural sharing of liberal arts education] 口唱歌の分析： 異文化間で共有される教養教育. *Tōhoku daigaku kōtōkyōiku suishin sentā kiyō* [CAHE (the Centre for the Advancement of Higher Education) Journal of Higher Education] 東北大学高等教育開発推進センター紀要 1, pp. 181–189.

Iga, Takatoki 伊賀高時 (ed.) 1994. *Chita no dashimatsuri* [The float-festivals of Chita] 知多の山車まつり. Nagoya: Sōmusha 名古屋、創夢社.

Inokuchi, Shōji 井之口章次 1988(?). 'Mikoshi [palanquin]' in *Nihon daihyakka zensho (Nipponika)*. [English title:] Encyclopedia Nipponica. 「神輿」日本大百科全書 (ニッポニカ). Tokyo: Shōgakukan 東京、小学館.

https://kotobank.jp/word/%E7%A5%9E%E8%BC%BF-138437 (accessed 19 August 2022).

Inoue, Nobutaka 2003. 'The modern age: Shinto confronts modernity'. In Inoue Nobutaka (ed.): *Shinto: a short history*. London/New York: Routledge Curzon, pp. 159–197.

Iwakura no dashi [Festival floats in Iwakura] 1991. Hakkōsha: Iwakura-shi kyōiku iinkai [Published by The Iwakura City Board of Education].

Iizuka, Erito 飯塚恵理人 1999. *Shodai Fujita Seibē no geitō: Nagoya nōgakudō tokubetsu ten 'Fujita-ke denrai meihin ten' tenran shiryō kara* [The founder of the *nōgaku* art tradition of the Fujita school, Fujita Seibē and his art:...]. 初代藤田清兵衛の芸統： 名古屋能楽堂特別展 『藤田家伝来名品展』展観資料から. In Sugiyama kokubungaku 椙山国 文学 1999. 23, 111–130. https://core.ac.uk/download/230632361.pdf (accessed 23 November 2023).

Janse, Helga 2019. *Changes in gender roles within Intangible cultural heritage: a survey of gender roles and gender restrictions within the yama hoko yatai float-festivals in Japan*. MDPI Academic Open Access Publishing. https://mdpi-res.com/d_attachment/heritage/heritage-02-001 26/article_deploy/heritage-02-00126.pdf (accessed 11 July 2021).

Jingūsha sairei no ayumi: Ichiba-ku [History of the Jingūsha float-festival: Ichiba ward] 神宮車祭礼のあゆみ： 市場区 2007. Jingūsha Hozonkai [Jingūsha Float Preservation Society] 神宮車保存会. [Aichi, Taketoyo 愛知,武豊].

Jensen, Marius B. 1989. 'Japan in the early nineteenth century'. In *The Cambridge history of Japan* vol. V. New York: Cambridge University Press, pp. 50–115.

Jones, Stephen 1995. *Folk music of China: Living instrumental traditions*. Oxford: Clarendon Press.

—— 2002. 'Ensembles: Northern Chinese'. In Robert C. Provine et al. (eds): *The Garland encyclopedia of world music. Vol. 7: East Asia: China, Japan, and Korea*. London: Routledge, pp. 199–204.

—— 2007. *Ritual and music of north China: shawm bands in Shanxi*. London: Routledge.

Kagura ga musubu chiiki ya sedai [Areas and generations connected by kagura] in *Asahi shinbun (yūkan)* [The Asahi Evening Edition)] 「神楽 が結ぶ地域や世代」。朝日新聞(夕刊). 12 March 2010, 6. http://atsutak agura.com/shinbun/asahi.htm (accessed 4 August 2021).

Kaimi, Hidehisa 皆見秀久 2017. Aichi-ken no dashimatsuri netto wāku [Network of float-festivals in Aichi prefecture] 愛知県山車まつりネッ トワーク. In *Bunka isan no sekai* [English title:] The world of cultural heritage 文化遺産の世界. Vol. 28 [Hajimeni はじめに, Foreword]. https://www.isan-no-sekai.jp/feature/20-17-01-06, updated 27 January 2017 (accessed 14 February 2022).

Kamezaki Shiohimatsuri shashinshū: Shōwa no kioku, Heisei no fukko, sono saki e. 亀崎潮干祭写真集：昭和の記憶、平成の復古、その先へ [Kamezaki Shiohimatsuri in pictures: memory of Shōwa era, vitalization of Heisei era, and onwards] 2019. *Yunesuko mukei bunka isan tōroku kinen* ユネスコ無形文化遺産登録記念. [English title:] Kamezaki Shiohi-matsuri: UNESCO Intangible cultural heritage. Kamezaki Shiohi Matsuri Hozonkai, Daisankai hen [Edited by Kamezaki Shiohi Festival Preservation Society] 亀崎潮干祭保存会・代参会編. [Handa 半].

Kárpáti, János 2000. 'Music of the lion dance in Japanese tradition'. *Studia Musicologica Academiae Scientiarum Hungaricae* 41: 1–3, 107–117.

——2008. 'Typology of musical structures in the Japanese Shintō ritual kagura'. *Asian Music* 39: 2, 152–166.

Kawahashi, Noriko 2008/2005. 'Folk religion and its contemporary issues'. In Jennifer Robertson (ed.): *A companion to the anthropology of Japan.* Malden: Blackwell Publishing, pp. 452–466.

Kawano, Satsuki 2005. *Ritual practice in modern Japan: ordering place, people, and action.* Honolulu: University of Hawai'i Press.

Keller, Marcello Sorce et al. 2000. 'Spain'. In Timothy Rice et al. (eds): *The Garland encyclopedia of world music. Vol. 8: Europe.* London: Routledge, pp. 588–603.

Kitagawa, Yūchi 北川宥智 2013. *Tokug-awa Muneharu: 'Edo' o koeta senkenryoku* [Lord Tokugawa Muneharu, his foreseeability exceeded the capital city Edo (Tokyo)] 徳川宗春：「江戸」を超えた先見力. Nagoya: Fūbaisha 名古屋、風媒社.

Kitō, Hideaki 鬼頭秀明 2021. 'Chitahantō no sairei: kōenroku'. [Festivals of Chita Peninsula: a lecture record] 知多半島の祭礼：講演録. In *Chitahantō no rekisi to genzai* 知多半島の歴史と現在. No. 25. [English title:] Chita Peninsula, its history and present, pp. 119–129.

Klien, Susanne 2020. 'Demographic change in contemporary rural Japan and its impact on ritual practices'. *Journal of Religion in Japan* 9, 248–276.

Kōhō Taketoyo [Public relations brochure Taketoyo] 広報たけとよ. No. 1062 (1 March 2019). https://www.town.taketoyo.lg.jp/chousei/10 01548/1002651/1003535/1002663/index.html.

Komparu, Kunio 1983. *The noh theater: principles and perspectives.* New York: Weatherhill/Tankosha.

Konishi, Jin'ichi 1984. *A history of Japanese literature. Vol. 1: The archaic and ancient ages.* Translated by Aileen Gatten and Nicholas Teele. Edited by Earl Miner. Princeton, New Jersey: Princeton University Press.

Kōno, Kazuo 河野和夫 2015. *Kariya no daimyō gyōretsu to dashimatsuri* [The feudal lord procession and the float-festival in Kariya] 刈谷の大名行列と山車祭. Nagoya: Fūbaisha.

Koromo matsuri to dashi [The Koromo festival and floats] 挙母祭りと山車 1981. Koromo Matsuri Dashi Enkaku Chōsa Iinkai hen [Edited by the Investigative Committee of Koromo Festival Float

History Survey] 挙母祭り山車沿革調査委員会編. Toyota-shi bunkazai sōsho [Toyota-city Cultural Propertiy Series. 4] 豊田市文化財叢書: 第 4. [Toyota 豊田].

Koyano, Atsushi 小谷野敦 2020. *Kaguki ni joyū ga ita jidai* [When female actors were present in *kabuki*] 歌舞伎に女優がいた時代. Paperback Shinsho. Tokyo: Chūō kōron shinsha 東京、中央公論新社.

Kuligowski, Waldemar 2016. 'Festivalizing tradition: A fieldworker's notes from the Guča Trumpet Festival (Serbia) and the Carnival of Santa Cruz de Tenerife (Spain)'. *Lietuvos Etnologua: socialinės antropologijos ir etnologijos studijosm* 16: 25, 35–54.

Kurata, Yoshihiro 倉田喜弘 1997. *Hayashi – shitte okitaikoto* [Ensemble music, the things you should know about] 囃子 – 知っておきたいこと. [Commentary to] *Nihon no matsuri: matsuribayashi hen* [Japanese festivals: a compilation of festival ensembles] 日本の祭り: 祭囃子編. Tokyo: King Record Co. Ltd. KICH 2046. CD booklet.

Kuroda, Takashi and Yokoi, Makoto 黒田剛司・横井誠 2013. *Tsushima no dashimatsuri: rekishi to sairei bunka* [The float-festival in Tsushima: history and festival culture] 津島の山車祭: 歴史と祭礼文化. Tsushima: Taisei shoten 津島: 泰聖書店.

Lameiro, Paulo 1997. 'Práticas musicais nas festas religiosas do concelho de Leiria: O lugar privilegiado das Bandas Filarmónicas'. In Cascais, Câmara Municipal: *Actas dos 2°s Cursos Internacionais de Verão de Cascais (17a22 Julho)*, pp. 1–14.

Lancashire, Terence A. 2011. *An introduction to Japanese folk performing arts*. SOAS Musicology Series. Farnham/Burlington: Ashgate.

Law, Jane Marie 1997. *Puppets of nostalgia: the life, death and rebirth of the Japanese Awaji ningyō tradition*. Princeton, New Jersey: Princeton University Press.

Leiter, Samuel L. 1997. *New Kabuki encyclopedia: a revised adaptation of Kabuki jiten*. Westport, Connecticut: Greenwood Press.

—— 2006. *Historical dictionary of Japanese traditional theatre*. Lanham, Maryland/Oxford: The Scarecrow Press.

Levy, Marion Jr. 1966. *Modernization and the structure of societies: a setting for international affairs, Vol. 1–2*. Princeton New Jersey: Princeton University Press.

Littleton, C. Scott 1986. 'The organization and management of a Tokyo Shintō shrine festival'. *Ethnology* 25: 3, 195–202.

Lord, Albert 1960. *The singer of tales*. Cambridge, Mass.: Harvard University Press.

Lundström, Håkan 2010. *I will send my song: Kammu vocal genres in the singing of Kam Raw*. Copenhagen: NIAS Press.

Mair, Judith (ed.) 2018. *The Routledge handbook of festivals*. Routledge.

Malm, William P. 1959. *Japanese music and musical instruments*. Rutland, Vermont/Tokyo: Tuttle.

—— 1963. *Nagauta: the heart of Kabuki music*. Rutland, Vermont/Tokyo: Tuttle.

—— 1975. 'Shoden: a study in Tokyo festival music. When is a variation an improvisation?' *Yearbook of the International Folk Music Council, Vol. 7.* Urbana: Cambridge University Press, pp. 44–66.

McLaren, Sally 2001. 'Women dance in defiance of Gion taboo: "discovery" brings clash of opinion'. *The Japan Times* 18 July 2001, p. 3.

McPherson, Sean H. 2007. 'A tradition of change: a history of Chita dashimatsuri 1600–2005'. Computer printout. Diss. UCLA. PhD thesis. Proquest Dissertations and Theses, UMI 3306250.

—— 2012. 'National agendas and local realities: festive material and ritual culture, nationalism, and modernity in the Chita region of Japan'. *Cross-Currents. East Asian History and Culture Review, E-Journal* 3 (June 2012). https://escholarship.org/content/qt4j51v506/qt4j51v506_noSp lash_7f4a5254b3c1bd64f1c0859ee01878fb.pdf?t=qbps2n (accessed 6 August 2023).

Miyanishi, Naoko 宮西ナオ子 2005. Josei nōgakushi to 2-tsu no kabe – Nōgaku Kyōkai to Nihon Nōgakukai nyūkai 女性能楽師と２つの壁 – 能楽協会と日本能楽会入会. [English title:] A study of two barriers against female noh professionals. *Nihon Daigaku Daigakuin Sōgō Shakai Jōhō Kenkyūka Kiyō.* [English title:] Nihon University, Graduate School of Social and Cultural Studies. 日本大学大学院総合社会情報研究科紀要. 6, pp. 86–97 (2005).

'Miyoshishimo no dashi' chōsa hōkokusho [The festival wagon in Miyoshishimo ward: an investigation report] ＜三好下の山車＞ 調査報告書 1986. [Edited by] Miyoshi-chōritsu Rekishi minzoku shiryōkan [Museum of history and folklore in Miyoshi town] 三好町立歴史民族資料館編集.

Molinié, Antoinette 2013. 'Les deux corps de la Reine et ses substituts: la souveraineté d'une Vierge andalouse'. *Archives de sciences sociales des religions* 58, pp. 161, 269–291.

Moisala, Pirkko 2000. 'Nepal'. In Timothy Rice et al. (eds): *The Garland encyclopedia of world music. Vol. 5: Europe.* London: Routledge, pp. 696–708.

Mori, Mizue 2003. 'Ancient and classical Japan: the dawn of Shinto'. In Inoue Nobutaka (ed.): *Shinto: a short history.* London/New York: Routledge Curzon 2003/1998, pp. 12–62.

Nagoya jōka no dashi gyōji chōsa hōkokusho: *Nagoya no dashi gyōji sōgō chōsa* [Survey report of festival float events in the castle town Nagoya: a comprehensive survey of Nagoya festival float events] 名古屋城下の山車行事調査報告書: 名古屋の山車行事総合調査 2018. Nagoya-shi kyōiku iinkai henshū [Edited by The Nagoya City Board of Education] 名古屋市教育委員会編集.

Nakahashi, Toshio 中橋俊夫 (ed.) 2011. *Waga machi waga dashi* [My town my dashi, festival float] わが町わが山車. Nagoya: Chūnichi shin-bunsha 名古屋、中日新聞社.

Nettl, Bruno 1983. *The study of ethnomusicology: twenty-nine issues and concepts*. Urbana/Chicago: University of Illinois Press.

Nihon minzoku jiten [Japanese folklore encyclopedia] 日本民俗事典 1975. [Edited by] Ōtsuka minzoku gakkai 編纂者 大塚民俗学会. Tokyo: Kōbundō 東京、弘文堂.

Nihon zenshi: Japan kuronikku: Japan Chronik 1991. 日本全史：ジャパン・クロニックJapan Chronik. Tokyo: Kōdansha.

Nishikawa, Takeo and Sazanami, Yasuhisa 西川丈雄、漣泰寿 2011. *The Nagahama hikiyama festival and its transmission*. Nagahama Hikiyama Cultural Association, Session 5, 5 February 2011. [no pagination]. https://www.irci.jp/wp_files/wp-content/uploads/2018/01/session5.pdf (accessed 3 May 2015).

Nketia, J. H. Kwabena 1974. *The music of Africa*. New York/London: W. W. Norton & Company.

Norbeck, Edward 1971. 'Associations and democracy in Japan.' In R. P. Dore (ed.): *Aspects of social change in modern Japan*. Princeton: Princeton University Press, pp. 185–200.

Ōbu-shi bunkazai chōsa hōkokusho 1: Ōbu-shi shitei yūkei minzoku bunkazai Fujii jinja, Yamano jinja sairei dashi 1 [Report on the investigation of Ōbu city folk cultural properties. 1: The city-designated tangible cultural property: Fujii shrine, Yamano shrine festival floats 1] 大府市文化財調査報告書第一集： 大府市指定有形民俗文化財藤井神社・山之神社祭礼山車 1. 1996.

Okuyama, Keiko 2002. 'Theatrical genres: hayasi'. In Robert C. Provine et al. (eds): *The Garland encyclopedia of world music. Vol. 7: East Asia, China, Japan, and Korea*. London: Routledge, pp. 683–685.

Omigbule, Morufu Bukola 2017. 'Rethinking African indigenous ritual festivals, interrogating the concept of African ritual drama'. *African Studies Quarterly* 17: 3, 71–88.

Ono, Sokyo 1991 [1962]. *Shinto: the kami way*. Rutland, Vermont/Tokyo: Tuttle.

Orikuchi, Shinobu 1975. *Orikuchi Shinobu zenshū*. Dai 2-kan. [The complete works of Orikuchi Shinobu. Vol. 2]. Kodai kenkyū (Minzokugaku hen 1). Chūkō Bunko. Tokyo, Chūō kōronsha.

Ōtani kushi: wasurenai Ōtani ima, mukashi [The Ōtani ward: remember Ōtani now and past] 大谷区誌： 忘れない大谷今・昔 2017. Tokoname 常滑.

Owari-manzai [尾張万歳]: *an important intangible folk cultural asset* 1997. [An English attached sheet to] Furusato no kaori tsutaeru Owari manzai: Jūyō mukei minzoku bunkazai [Owari manzai, carrying a fragrance of our hometown] ふるさとの香り伝える尾張万歳： 重要無形民俗文化財. Chita-shi Kyōiku Iinkai [Chita city board of education] 知多市教育委員会. Chita 知多. Brochure 英文シート.

Ozawa, Shōichi 小沢昭一 1974. *Nihon no hōrōgei* [Wanderers' performing arts in Japan] 日本の放浪芸. Tokyo: Banchō shobō 東京: 番長書房.

Ozawa, Shōichi, Ogawa, Yōzō, and Ichikawa, Katsumori (eds) 小沢昭一、小川洋三、市川捷護（編集）1971. *Dokyumento Nihon no hōrōgei: michi no gei, machi no gei* [Document of wanderers' performing arts in Japan: road and street performance] ドキュメント日本の放浪芸：道の芸・町の芸. Tokyo: Victor Company of Japan 東京、ビクター. 7 LPs.

Ozawa Shōichi ga maneita Nihon no hōrōgei [Wanderers' performing arts in Japan invited by Ozawa Shōichi] 小沢昭一が招いた日本の放浪芸 1974. [Presentation programme] Tokyo: Shinjuku Kinokuniya Hall, 27 June–1 July 1974 東京、新宿紀伊國屋ホール. Pamphlet パンフレット.

Paden, William E. 1994 [1988]. *Religious worlds: the comparative study of religion*. Boston: Beacon Press.

Peacock, James L. 1968. *Rites of modernization: symbolic and social aspects of Indonesian proletarian drama*. Chicago: University of Chicago Press.

Pinto, Tiago de Oliveira 1994. 'The Pernambuco carnival and its formal organisations: music as expression of hierarchies and power in Brazil'. *Yearbook for Traditional Music* 26, 20–38.

Plutschow, Herbert 1996. *Matsuri: the festivals of Japan*. Richmond: Curzon Press, Japan Library.

Porcu, Elisabetta 2020. 'Gion matsuri in Kyoto: a multilayered religious phenomenon'. *Journal of Religion in Japan* 9, 37–77.

—— 2022. 'The Gion matsuri in Kyoto and glocalization'. *Religions* 13: 689, 1–13. https://doi.org/10.3390/rel13080689 (accessed 5 August 2023).

Reader, Ian 1991. *Religion in contemporary Japan*. Basingstoke: Macmillan.

—— 2016. 'Problematic conceptions and critical developments: the construction and relevance of "religion" and religious studies in Japan'. *Journal of the Irish Society for the Academic Study of Religion* 3, 198–218.

Reily, Suzel Ana 1994. 'Musical performance at a Brazilian festival'. *British Journal of Ethnomusicology* 3, 1–34.

Roy, Christian 2005. *Traditional festivals: a multicultural encyclopedia, Vol. 1–2*. Santa Barbara, Calif.

Saitō, Kiyotaka and Saitō, Setoko 齋藤清隆、齋藤せと子 2006. *Taketoyo Taga jinja no ayumi* [A history of Taketoyo Taga shrine] 武豊多賀神社の 歩み. [Aichi, Taketoyo 愛知、武豊]. [No pagination ページ付けなし].

—— 2008. Tamanuki [The Tamanuki ward] 玉貫. [Aichi, Taketoyo 愛知、武豊].

Sakai no ayumi to matsuri [History and festival of Sakai] 坂井の歩みと祭り 2005. Sakai no ayumi to matsuri henshū iinkai henshū [Edited by the Editorial Board for the History and Festival of Sakai] 坂井の歩みと祭り編集委員会編集. Tokoname 常滑.

Schnell, Scott 1999. *The rousing drum: ritual and practice in a Japanese community*. Honolulu: University of Hawai'i Press.

Senda, Yasuko 千田靖子 1997. *Karakuri-ningyō no hōko: Aichi no matsuri o tazunete* [The treasure chamber of mechanical puppets: visiting the festivals in Aichi] からくり人形の宝庫: 愛知の祭りを訪ねて. Aichi sensho 愛知選書 2. [3rd edition]. Nagoya: Chūnichi Shuppansha 名古屋: 中日出版社.

—— 2006. *Zusetsu. Karakuri-ningyō no sekai* [The world of mechanical puppets. Illustrated] 図説からくり人形の世界. 2nd printing [1st printing 2005]. Tokyo: Hōseidaigaku Shuppankyoku [Hosei University Press] 東京: 法政大学出版局.

Shimada, Takashi 島田崇志 2006. *Shashin de miru Gion matsuri no subete* 写真で見る祇園祭のすべて. [English title:] Kyoto Gion festival photo collection. Kyoto: Mitsumura Suiko Shoin 京都、光村推古書院.

Shinshū Nagoya-shi shi 2001 [A history of the city of Nagoya. New edition]. *Vol. 9: Minzoku hen* [Folklore edition]. [Edited by Shinshu Nagoya City History Editorial Committee].

Shoham, Hizky 2011. 'Rethinking tradition: from ontological reality to assigned temporal meaning'. *European Journal of Sociology* 52: 2, 313–340.

Siuda-Ambroziak, Renata and Mariano, Fabiene Passamani 2021. 'Contemporary transformations in the Brazilian popular Catholic festivals: the case of the Holy Divine Spirit Festival (Festa do Divino)'. *International Journal of Latin American Religions* 5: 224–245. https://doi.org/10.1007/s41603-021-00150-6 (accessed 20 September 2022).

Sonoda, Minoru 1975. 'The traditional festival in urban society'. *Japanese Journal of Religious Studies* 2: 2–3, 103–136.

Suzuki, Seiko 鈴木聖子 2023. *Sukuwareru koe, katarareru gei: Ozawa Shōichi to 'Dokyumento Nihon no hōrōgei'* [A multitude of voices, a myriad of arts: Ozawa Shōichi and 'Document of wanderers' performing arts in Japan]. [2. pr./刷 (2023)]. 掬われる声、語られる芸: 小沢昭一と 【『ドキュメント日本の放浪芸』】. Tokyo, Shunjūsha 東京、春秋社.

Suzumura, Yusuke 鈴村裕輔 2013. Players, performances and existence of women's noh: focusing on the articles run in the Japanese general newspapers. Hosei university research center for international Japanese studies: *Kokusai Nihongaku ronsō*. [English title:] Journal of International Japanese Studies. 国際日本学論叢. 10, pp. 41–52.

Tajima, Mami 1983. 'The fate of Nagoya's mechanical festival floats'. *Asian Folklore Studies* 42: 2, 181–208.

Takahashi, Masao 高橋正雄 1975. 'Manzai'. In *Nihon minzoku jiten*, pp. 678–679.

Takamura, Shōichi 高村正一 1982. 'Atsuta daidai kagura …'. In Ikeda Chōzaburō (ed): *Atsuta fudoki [The provincial description of Atsuta]* Vol. 8, 36–80.

Takayama matsuri no yatai 高山祭の屋台. [English title:] The floats of Takayama Festival 1991. [Commented by] Kuwatani Masamichi 桑谷正道 解説.

Taketoyo-chō shi: honbun-hen [Handbook of Taketoyo town: main text] 武豊町誌: 本文編. 1984. Taketoyo: Taketoyo-chō Shi

Hensan Iinkai [The Committee for Documentation of Taketoyo] 武豊町誌編さん委員会.

Taketoyo-chō shi: shiryō-hen 2 [Handbook of Taketoyo: reference material 2] 武豊町誌：資料編二. 1983. Taketoyo: Taketoyo-chō Shi Hensan Iinkai [The Committee for Documentation of Taketoyo] 武豊町誌編さん委員会.

Tatematsu, Hiroshi 立松宏 1994. 'Chita no dashibunka' [The cultural tradition of festival float of Chita Peninsula] 知多の山車文化. In Iga (ed.): *Chita no dashimatsuri* [The float-festivals of Chita] 知多の山車まつり, pp. 24–27.

Teeuwen, Mark 2023. *Kyoto's Gion festival: a social history.* London: Bloomsbury Publishing.

Teeuwen, Mark and Breen, John 2003. 'Translators' introduction'. In Inoue Nobutaka (ed.): *Shinto: a short history.* London/New York: Routledge Curzon 2003/1998, pp. ix–xii.

Thornbury, Barbara E. 1994. 'The cultural properties protection law and Japan's performing arts,' *Asian Folklore Studies* 53: 2, 211–225.

—— 1997. *The folk performing arts: traditional culture in contemporary Japan.* Albany, New York: State University of New York Press.

Tingey, Carol 1994. *Auspicious music in a changing society: the damāi musicians of Nepal.* London: School of Oriental and African Studies, University of London.

—— 1995. 'The pancai bājā: reflections of social change in traditional Nepalese music'. In *Kasilash* (Kathmandu) 17, pp. 1–2, 11–22.

Tokoname-shi shi: bunkazai hen [Handbook of Tokoname city: cultural assets] 常滑市誌：文化財編. 1983. Tokoname-shi Shi Hensan Iinkai [The Committee for Documentation of Tokoname] 常滑市誌編さん委員会. Tokoname 常滑.

Urita, Michiko 瓜田理子 2015. 'Punitive scholarship: postwar interpretations of Shinto and Ise jingū'. Symposium: peace by other means, part 4. *Common Knowledge* 21: 3, 484–509. https://www.researchgate.net/publication/282287786_Punitive_scholarship_Postwar_interpretations_of_Shinto_and_Ise_Jingu (accessed 24 May 2021).

Vlastos, Stephen 1998. 'Tradition: past/present culture and modern Japanese history'. In Stephen Vlastos (ed.): *Mirror of modernity: invented traditions of modern Japan.* Berkeley: University of California Press, pp. 1–16.

Williams, E. Leslie 2000. 'A unity of pattern in the kami tradition: orienting "Shinto" within a context of pre-modern and contemporary ritual practice'. *Journal of ritual studies* 14: 2, 34–47.

Wolf, Richard 2000. 'Music and seasonal and life-cycle rituals'. In Arnold, Alison (ed.): *The Garland encyclopedia of world music. Vol. 5: South Asia: The Indian subcontinent.* London: Routledge, pp. 599–606.

—— 2006. *The black cow's footprint: time, space, and music in the lives of the Kotas of South India.* Urbana/Chicago: University of Illinois Press.

Yanagita, Kunio 柳田国男 1993 [1985]. 'The evolution of Japanese festivals: from matsuri to sairei', introduction and translation by Stephen Nussbaum. In Koschmann, J. Victor et al. (eds): *International perspectives on Yanagata Kunio and Japanese folklore studies*, Ithaca/New York: Cornell University, East Asia Program [3rd edition], pp. 167–202 [English translation of Yanagita 1942: 35–65, *Matsuri kara sairei e*].

—— 2022 [1942]. *Nihon no matsuri* [Japanese festivals] 日本の祭. [New edition, 22nd printing]. Kadokawa sofia bunko 角川ソフィア文庫. Tokyo: Kadokawa. See Andō, Reiji 安藤礼二 2022.

Yokone Fujii jinja: sairei dashi, Sanbasō [Fujii shrine in Yokone, Ōbu city: festival floats, *Sanbasō* dances] 横根藤井神社: 祭礼山車・三番叟 [2007]. [Ōbu 大府]. [Brochure].

Yoneyama, Toshinao 米山俊直 1986. *Toshi to matsuri no jinruigaku* [Anthropology of cities and festivals] 都市と祭りの人類学. Tokyo: Kawade shobō 東京、河出書房.

—— 2000. 'Toshisairei to chiikishakai no kasseika: Handa-shi no dashimatsuri o rei to shite' [Activation of city festivals and local communities: the example of the float-festival of Handa city] 都市祭礼と地域社会の活性化: 半田市の山車まつりを例として. In *Shukusai no 100-nen: Seikatsugaku dai 24 satsu* [A hundred years of festivals: Lifology 24] 祝祭の 100 年: 生活学第 24 冊. Nihon Seikatsu Gakkai [Japan Society of Lifology] 日本生活学会. Tokyo: Domesu Shuppan 東京、ドメス出版, pp. 24–41.

Zhao Xiaohuan 2021. 'Form follows function in community rituals in North China: temples and temple festivals in Jiacun Village'. *Religions* 12, 1105. https://doi.org/10.3390/rel12121105 (accessed 3 March 2025).

C. Internet references

Aichi dashi zukan [Picture book of the festival floats in Aichi] あいち山車図鑑 2017 [2nd edition, Web version]. https://www.pref.aichi.jp/soshiki/bunkazai/0000089212.html, updated 22 Janury 2021 (accessed 4 August 2021).

Aichi no dashimatsuri: Aichi-ken no dashimatsuri pōtarusaito あいちの山車まつり: 愛知県の山車まつりポータルサイト 2018. https://www.dashi-aichi.jp/. [English title:] Float-festivals in Aichi, portal website for float-festivals in Aichi prefecture. [Subtitle] Aichi, the greatest place for festival floats in Japan 山車日本一あいち. Copyright: Aichi Dashi Matsuri Nippon Ichi Council あいち山車まつり日本一協議会. https://www.dashi-aichi.jp/en/ (accessed 24 August 2021).

Aichi-ken shōgai gakushū jōhō sisutemu: Manabi-netto Aichi [Aichi prefecture lifelong learning information system: Learning-net Aichi] 愛知県生涯学習情報システム: 学びネットあいち. https://www.manabi.pref.aichi.jp/contents/19100005/0/top.html (accessed 19 June 2021).

→ *Owari Nishibiwajima matsuri: Yoritomo-sha no matsuribayashi* 尾張西枇杷島まつり：頼朝車の祭囃子 [The Nishibiwajima festival in the Owari province: the music of the festival float, *Yoritomo-sha*] 2018. https://www.manabi.pref.aichi.jp/movie/19100005/h30kiyosu06.mp4 (accessed 19 June 2021).

Amagoi matsuri, junran gōkana kabuki gyōretsu: Heisei 29-nen 8-gatsu 20-nichi [The Amagoi praying for rain festival, with a splendid kabuki procession, 2017–08–20] 雨乞いまつり、絢爛豪華な歌舞伎行列： 平成29 年 8 月 20 日. [Toyokawa 豊川]. https://www.youtube.com/watch?v=DFTGW5d_xZY (accessed 8 November 2017).

Anjo City Museum of History. https://ansyobunka.jp/

→ *Mikawa manzai*. https://ansyobunka.jp/rekihaku/collection/manzai/co-manzai.html (accessed 22 November 2024).

Arimatsu dashimatsuri: mukei minzoku bunkazai [The Arimatsu float-festival: an Intangible folk cultural property] 有松山車まつり：無形民俗文化財. http://www.arimatsunomachi.com/dashimatsuri.html (accessed 23 July 2021).

Atsuta kagura to Miyaryū kagura [*Atsuta kagura* and *Miyaryū kagura*] 熱田神楽と宮流神楽. Created by Kanō Yoshio. http://atsutakagura.com/, updated 1 September 2019 (accessed 14 November 2022).

→ *Daidai kagura* 太太神楽. http://www.atsutakagura.com/daidai/daidaitop.htm (accessed 12 December 2021).

→ *Atsuta kagura: kanren no sekihi* [Stone monuments related to Atsuta kagura] 熱田神楽：関連の石碑. http://atsutakagura.com/shiryou/sekihi.htm (accessed 26 May 2021).

→ *Atsuta kagura, Miyaryū kagura no rekishi: Atsuta, Kasaderakei* [A history of Atsuta kagura and Miyaryū kagura: Atsuta and Kasadera lineages] 熱田神楽・宮流神楽の歴史（熱田・笠寺系）. http://atsutakagura.com/rekishi/rekishitop.htm(accessed 1 August 2023).

→ *Idota no Ōyamaguruma* (Tsugata jinja *sairei*) [Floats of Idota district, Nagoya, Ōyamaguruma (Tsugata shrine festival)] 井戸田の大山車（津賀田神社祭礼. http://atsutakagura.com/shiryou/ooyama.htm (accessed 26 May 2021).

→ *Miyaryū kagura no bunrui* [Classification of Miyaryū kagura] 宮流神楽の分類. http://atsutakagura.com/rekishi/bunrui.htm (accessed 22 January 2023).

→ *Miyaryū kagura no taiko no uchikata* [How to play the drum in Miyaryū kagura] 宮流神楽の太鼓の打ち方. http://www.atsutakagura.com/taiko_kaisetsu/taiko_uchikata.htm (accessed 14 November 2022).

→ *Miyaryū kagura to ohayashi* [Miyaryū kagura and festival music] 宮流神楽とお囃子. http://www.atsutakagura.com/index_e.html, updated 6 June 2013 (accessed 23 July 2021).

→ *Kyoku no shōsaina kaisetsu* [Atsuta kagura pieces] → *Shinguruma omote (Arimatsu, Hayame)* [Shinguruma omote (Arimatsu, Hayame)] 新車表

(有松・早目). http://www.atsutakagura.com/kaisetsu/K15shinguruma. htm (accessed 6 July 2017).

→ *Sound source of Atsuta kagura (Miyaryu kagura)* [English text]. http:// www.atsutakagura.com/ongen/ongentop_e.htm, updated 6 June 2013 (accessed 21 January 2023).

→ *Tsugata jinja: dashi, ohayashi no yurai* [Tsugata jinja: the origin of the festival float and float music] 津賀田神社： 山車・お囃子の由来. http://atsutakagura.com/shiryou/tsugata.htm, updated/更新 6 June 2013 (accessed 21 January 2023).

Bishū Handa: dashi emaki [Owari province Handa: festival-float picture scroll] 尾州半田山車絵巻 2017. [By] Dai 8-kai Handa Matsuri Jikkōiinkai [The Committee of the 8th Handa Float-festival] 第八回 はんだ山車まつり実行委員会. [Editorial supervising by] Handa Dashimatsuri Hozonkai [Handa Float-festival Preservation Society] 半田山車祭り保存会監修. https://www.youtube.com/watch?v=coOa-RkQkQA (accessed 8 November 2021).

Chiryū matsuri: Shigaku 4–5 [Chiryū festival: the 1st day of the festival 4–5] 知立まつり： 試楽(しんがく), 4–5. https://www.youtube.com/watch? v=XDJyGHrq4uM; https://www.youtube.com/watch?v=aCkaMl2mGSc (accessed November 2016).

Chiryū no dashibunraku to karakuri: UNESCO mukei bunka isan tōroku kinen tokubetsu jōen. 12 November [A special performance of Chiryū festival float, puppet theatre and mechanical puppets, in commemoration of the registration as UNESCO Intangible cultural heritage] 知立の山車文楽とからくり： ユネスコ無形文化遺産登録記念特別上演 2017. https:// www.youtube.com/watch?v=KzjuTgYz6xQ (accessed 3 September 2021).

Cultural heritage online. Agency for Cultural Affairs, Government of Japan. https://bunka.nii.ac.jp/

→ *Owari manzai.* https://bunka.nii.ac.jp/heritages/detail/136964 (accessed 22 November 2024).

Gion festival, Saki-matsuri: twenty-three floats gorgeously parade through ancient capital's streets. The Kyoto Shimbun: 17 July 2016. https://e. kyoto-np/news/20160717/2163.html (accessed 9 November 2022).

Handa Dashimatsuri Hozonkai [Handa Float-festival Preservation Society] 半田山車祭り保存会. https://dashimatsuri.jp/.

→ *Dashibayashi* [Festival float music] 山車囃子. https://dashimatsuri.jp/ miryoku/hayashi (accessed 16 March 2022).

→ *Handa dashimatsuri* [Handa float-festival] はんだ山車まつり. https:// dashimatsuri.jp/dashimatsuri (accessed 16 April 2022).

→ *Handa Dashimatsuri Hozonkai towa* [About the Float-festival Preservation Society] 半田山車祭り保存会. https://dashimatsuri.jp/hozonkai (accessed 28 December 2022).

Handa-shi: Handa no dashi tenji [Handa city: Handa float exhibition] 半田市： 半田の山車展示. https://www.city.handa.lg.jp/hkbutsu/bunka/ gejutsu/hakubutsukan/h25-1kyogikai.html (accessed 15 May 2022).

Heisei Onnaboko Sayanekai web [Heisei female festival float association web]. 平成女鉾清音会 Web. https://onnaboko.com/sample-page-2 (accessed 27 January 2022).

Hida Furukawa matsuri: Sanbasoutai [Hida Furukawa festival: the festival float Sanbasōtai]. 飛騨古川祭: 三番曳台 2019. https://furukawa-fes. com/yatai/sanbasoutai/ (accessed 25 November 2022).

Iconography of kagura performance at Ise 1. Copyright: Akiko Hirai [平井暁子]. https://www.akikohirai.com/post/iconography-of-kagura-performance-at-Ise, updated 14 December 2021 (accessed 19 March 2022).

Invitation to Kabuki: Guidance for Japanese traditional performing arts Kabuki 2019. Japan Arts Council. https://www2.ntj.jac.go.jp/unesco/ kabuki/en/ (accessed 22 February 2023).

Iwau gei kara no hajimari [Originating from a blessing art]. The Japan Arts Council's Culture Digital Library. https://www2.ntj.jac.go.jp/ dglib/contents/learn/edc20/rekishi/manzai/index1.html (accessed 24 November 2024).

Kabuki A to Z: the Japan Arts Council's Culture Digital Library. 2018. https:// www2.ntj.jac.go.jp/dglib/modules/kabuki_dic_en/letter.php?init=01 (accessed 22 February 2023).

Kanō, Yoshio 狩野良雄 → *Atsuta kagura to Miyaryū kagura* [*Atsuta kagura* and *Miyaryū kagura*].

Kiyosu-shi kankō kyōkai: Eikijūjitsu Kiyo supotto 清須市観光協会: 英気充実きよスポット. In English: Kiyosu city tourism association: Full of energy Kiyo spot. https://kiyosu-kanko.org/nishibimatsuri/ (accessed 15 October 2022).

→ *Owari Nishibiwajima matsuri* 尾張西枇杷島まつり [The Nishibiwajima festival in the Owari province].

Nagoya castle: special historic site: the zenith of early modern castle design and construction. https://www.nagoyajo.city.nagoya.jp/en/ (accessed 2 August 2023).

Network 2010: Nagoya 100km ken'nai no jōhō hasshin nettowāku [Network for information transmission within 100 km of Nagoya] 名古屋 100km 圏内の情報発信ネットワーク → *Ōashi Jaguruma matsuri, Aichi-ken, Taketoyo-chō.* 大足蛇車まつり 愛知県武豊町. http://network 2010.org/article/324, updated 23 March 2021 (accessed 25 August 2022).

Nōgaku yōgo jiten 能楽用語事典 [English version 英語版]. https://db2. the-noh.com/jdic/2021/06/post_544.html (updated 更新日 9 June 2021).

→ *Noh Terminology: Fujitaryū.* https://db2.the-noh.com/edic/2021/06/ fujitaryu.html. (Accessed 24 November 2023).

Nomi Shinmeigū taisai... [Nomi Shinmeigū shrine's Grand festival, Okazaki] 能見神明宮大祭... 2022. https://www.youtube.com/watch?v= 1c1pWgrFZtA, 8 May 2022 (accessed 19 December 2022).

Ōi natsumatsuri: Minamichita-chō... [Ōi summer festival, Minamichita town] 大井夏祭り: 南知多町... 2022. 1–3.

→ 1) https://www.youtube.com/watch?v=2BjOsYlnlAQ

→ 2) https://www.youtube.com/watch?v=YRTrV6RGvsg

→ 3) https://www.youtube.com/watch?v=vCGAZDC9f5c (accessed 25 January 2023).

Ōmori Tennōsai [Omori Tennō festival] 大森天王祭 2014. [Nagoya-shi, Nagoya city 名古屋市]. https://www.youtube.com/watch?v=cOt8 Grxgs2I (accessed 5 May 2022).

Owari manzai: an important intangible cultural asset. Owarimanzai Preservation Association and Chita Board of Education. https://www.owarimanzai.jp/en/ (accessed 24 November 2024).

Owari Nishibiwajima matsuri a. 尾張西枇杷島まつり [The Nishibiwajima festival in the Owari province]. In *Kiyosu-shi kankō kyōkai: Eikijūjitsu Kiyo supotto* 清須市観光協会: 英気充実きよスポット. In English: Kiyosu city tourism association: Full of energy Kiyo spot. https://kiyosu-kanko.org/nishibimatsuri/ (accessed 15 October 2022).

Owari Nishibiwajima matsuri b: Tonya-machi Yoritomosha.... 尾張西枇杷島まつり: 問屋町頼朝車... [The Nishibiwajima festival in the Owari province...] 2022. https://www.youtube.com/watch?v=WL5tFl4QOBs (accessed 15 October 2022).

Owari no dashimatsuri [Float-festivals of the Owari province] 尾張の山車まつり. http://dashi-matsuri.com/, updated 8 December 2023 (accessed 14 December 2023).

→ *Chita no dashikan A: Handa-shi Okkawa matsuri, Nishiyama Kaguraguruma* [Festival float museum of Chita: the festival float Kaguraguruma of the neighbourhood Nishiyama, Okkawa district, Handa city] 知多の山車館: 半田市乙川祭り、西山神楽車. https://dashi-matsuri.com/dashikan/chita/okkawa/ok_kagu.htm, updated 10 February 2010 (accessed 5 May 2022).

→ *Chita no dashikan B: Kōwa Tenjinmatsuri, Nakagumi* [Festival float museum of Chita: the festival float of the neighbourhood Nakagumi, Tenjinmatsuri, Kōwa district, Mihama town] 知多の山車館: 河和天神祭中組. https://dashi-matsuri.com/dashikan/chita/kowa/nak.htm, updated 31 July 2005 (accessed 1 June 2022).

→ *Chita no dashikan C: Mihama-chō, Futto Hirata-chiku* [Festival float museum of Chita: the festival float of the Hirata ward, Mihama town] 知多の山車館: 美浜町・布土～平田地区. https://dashi-matsuri.com/dashikan/chita/futo/hirata.htm (accessed 30 May 2022).

→ *Chōshū zakki: Kamezaki Nakagirigumi Rikijinsha, dashi chōkoku shūfuku fukugen* [Miscellaneous notes on Owari: Rikijinsha, the festival float of Nakagiri neighbourhood, Kamezaki district [Handa], restoration of the sculptures] 張州雑記: [半田] 亀崎中切「力神車」出車彫刻修復復元. https://dashi-matsuri.com/main/topics/tp2010/111005.htm, updated 10 September 2020 (accessed 3 September 2021).

→ *Mikawa no dashikan: Hirai-chō Hachimansha sairei* [Festival float museum of Mikawa: the festival of Hachimansha shrine in Hirai town,

Toyota] 三河の山車館: 平井町八幡社祭礼. https://dashi-matsuri.com/dashikan/mikawa/hirai/index.htm, updated 12 April 2000 (accessed 4 October 2015).

→ *Mikawa no dashikan: Shiga jinja sairei* [Festival float museum of Mikawa: the festival of Shiga shrine in Shiga town, Toyota] 三河の山車館: 志賀町志賀神社祭礼. https://dashi-matsuri.com/dashikan/mikawa/siga/index.htm, updated 12 April 2000 (accessed 4 October 2015).

→ *Ōmori Tennōsai: Nagoya-shi Moriyama-ku* [Ōmori Tennō festival in Moriyama-ward, Nagoya city] 大森天王祭: 名古屋市守山区. https://dashi-matsuri.com/dashikan/owari/oomori/, updated 14 January 2010 (accessed 7 August 2011).

→ *Owari Chita chihō no dashimatsuri, Tokoname matsuri no tokushusei ni tsuite* [Dashimatsuri in the Chita area, Owari province, about special aspects of the Tokoname matsuri] 尾張の山車まつり: 尾張知多地方の山車祭, 常滑祭の特殊性について. https://dashi-matsuri.com/dashikan/chita/tokoname/kaihou.htm (accessed 1 March 2023). (By Kataoka, Hikaru 片岡光, pen name: Saikichi 祭吉. Originally published by Kōgakkan University, Ise city, in *Shintō gakkai kaihō* [Bulletin of the Shintō society], 17 (1995): 9–10, based on the unpublished graduation thesis 'Chita hantō ni okeru dashimatsuri no kenkyū: tokuni Tokoname matsuri o chūshin ni' [A study of *dashimatsuri*, float-festivals, in Chita Peninsula: with a focus on the Tokoname festival], Kōgakkan University 1994.)

Owari Yokosuka matsuri: Kōtsūgumi, Entsūsha [Owari Yokosuka festival in Yokosuka city: the float Entsūsha of the neighbourhood Kōtsūgumi] 尾張横須賀まつり…公通組、圓通車. https://www.youtube.com/watch?v=kU8wUqNj3yw 2018 (accessed 29 September 2022).

Owari Yokosuka matsuri: Kōtsūgumi, Hachikōsha [Owari Yokosuka festival in Yokosuka city: the float *Hachikōsha* of the neighbourhood Kōtsūgumi] 尾張横須賀まつり…公通組、八公車. https://www.youtube.com/watch?v=10k1CitVycM 2019 (accessed 29 September 2022). 東海市.

Sawarabayashi: Tokushū [A feature article on Sawarabayashi, Chiba] 特集佐原囃子 [千葉]. *Kōhō Katori. Web-ban* 広報かとり Web 版 [Public relations brochure Katori. Web-version 1 October 2014]. 205: 2–3. https://www.city.katori.lg.jp/government/koho/koho_web/koho_web_h26/20141001.files/katori141001-2-3.pdf (accessed 24 February 2020).

Shitamo Hachimansha kurabu: Bishū Nagao Shitamogumi [The festival-float *Hachimansha* club of the neighbourhood Shitamo, Nagao district (Taketoyo, Owari province)] 下門八幡車クラブ: 尾州長尾下門組. [English title:] Shitamo Hachimansha club. http://www.shitamo.com/, updated 17 March 2020.

→ *Hayashi* [Festival music] 囃子. http://www.shitamo.com/hayashi/hayashi.html (accessed 21 February 2022).

Tahara no matsuri [The festival of Tahara city] [田原祭り]田原のまつり. 1983. https://www.youtube.com/watch?v=52tGSLQEkHM (accessed 12 December 2016).

Takeo jinja: Nagaojō atochi, Tsukiyominomori [Takeo shrine: the site of the Nagao castle, Tsukuyominomori] 武雄神社：長尾城跡地・月詠. https://takeojinja.jp/, copyright 2014.

→ *Takeo jinja: Takeo jinja ni tsuite, reisai* [Takeo shrine: about Takeo shrine: annual festival] 武雄神社について、例祭 2014. https://takeojinja.jp/about.php (accessed 25 July 2021).

→ [外国語参考資料] [Takeo jinja 武雄神社 2014]. English version: *Information about Jinja and Takeo Jinja: annual festival.* https://takeojinja.jp/greeting.php (accessed 25 July 2021).

Taketoyo chiebukuro: Taketoyo chimeikō hoi [Taketoyo wisdoms: supplemental information on place names in Taketoyo town] 武豊知恵袋：武豊地名考補遺. Taketoyo-chō kankōkyōkai, Taketoyo Tourism Association 武豊町観光協会. http://taketoyo.info/chiebukuro/40.php (accessed 27 July 2021).

Taketoyo town 武豊町 (2022). *Taketoyosen no rekishi: kaitsū made no michinori* [A history of the Taketoyo line: the road to its opening] 武豊線の歴史：開通までの道のり. https://www.town.taketoyo.lg.jp/chousei/1001538/1001551/1002275/1002358.html, updated 21 October 2022 (accessed 21 December 2023).

Tokoname dashi zukan [Encyclopedia of float-festivals, Tokoname city] 常滑山車図鑑. http://www.city.tokoname.aichi.jp/kurashi/gakko/1002943/1003040/1003042/index.html, updated 2 November 2022 (accessed 2 November 2022).

Uki-e Ise daijingū ryōsho daidai mi-kagura no zu (Perspective picture of a most solemn kagura performance held at the two shrines in the Grand Shrine of Ise). 浮絵伊勢大神宮両所太々御神楽之図. https://www.britishmuseum.org/collection/object/A_1941-1010-0-2 (accessed 23 November 2020).

D. Audiovisual references

Some of these recordings are available at local libraries. Others are in the possession of the respective neighbourhoods.
S = Contains the tune *Shagiri.*
H = Contains the tune *Hayakagura.*

Handa-shi Sumiyoshi-ku Kitagumi matsuribayashi [The festival music of the neighbourhood Kita, Sumiyoshi ward, Handa city] 半田市住吉区北組祭り囃子 2003. Rokuon. Recorded 12 April 1955. CD. *S, H.*

Kamezaki shiohimatsuri: matsuribayashi to Miyaryū kagura [Kamezaki shiohi festival: festival music and Miyaryū kagura] 亀崎潮干祭：祭り囃子と宮流神楽 2003. Seisaku chosaku, Kagurakai [Production rights: The Kamezaki Kagura Association] 制作・著作：亀崎神楽会. 2 CDs [with booklet 解説書]. *S.*

Kamihanda Minamigumi Fukujinsha dashibayashi [Festival-float music the float Fukujinguruma of the neighbourhood Minami, Kamihanda] 上半田南組福神車山車囃子 1997. Kamihanda Minamigumi Fukujinkai [Association of the Float Fukujinguruma of the Neighbourhood Minami, Kamihanda] 上半田南組福神会. [Handa 半田]. CD. *S, H.*

Kariya no matsuri: Taga jinja Isami bayashi hoka [A festival in Kariya: Isami festival music of Taga shrine] 苅屋の祭り：多賀神社勇み囃子他 2003. Shūroku, Kariya Isami bayashi iinkai hoka. 収録、苅屋勇み囃子委員会ほか [Recorded by the Committee for Kariya Isami Festival Music and others]. [Tokoname 常滑]. CD [with a sheet of music titles 曲名シート].

Komukae-ku Hōōsha: matsuribayashi [The float Hōōsha of the Komukae ward: festival music] 小迎区鳳凰車祭り囃子 1959. 壱−弐 [1−2]. Shōwa 34-nen 4-gatsu rokuon ban [Recorded in April 1959] 昭和 34 年 4 月 10 日録音版. Komukae-ku Hōōsha Matsuribayashi Hozonkai [Komukae Ward Festival Music Preservation Society] 小迎区祭囃子保存会. 2 CDs. *S.*

Matsuribayashi: Kyōwasha Nishigumi [Festival music: festival float Kyōwasha, the neighbourhood of Nishigumi (Narawa, Handa)] 祭囃子：協和車西組 [半田市、成岩]. [Performed by] Kyōwasha Hayashikata [The Hayashi ensemble of the festival float Kyōwasha] 協和車囃子方. CD. *S, H.*

Matsuribayashi: Tokoname-chiku, Ichibagumi [Festival music: Tokoname district, the neighbourhood Ichiba] 祭囃子：常滑地区市場組 1998. 壱−弐 [1−2]. 2 CDs [with booklet 解説書]. *S, H.*

Mihama dashimatsuri: Mihama chōsei 60-shūnen kinen jigyō [Mihama float-festival: a commemorative project for the 60th anniversary of municipal organization] みはま山車まつり：美浜町制 60 周年記念事業. 1−2. 2015. Seisaku: Chitahantō Kēburu Netto Wāku [Produced by: Try and Create CCNC] 制作：知多半島ケーブルネットワーク. 2DVDs.

Nagao-bu harumatsuri [Taketoyo]: Sanbasō, Mikomai tokubetsuhen [The spring festival of Nagao district, Taketoyo: special edition of Sanbasō and Miko dances] [武豊] 長尾部春祭り：三番叟・巫女舞特別編 2015. Seisaku chosaku, Ichiba-ku sairei-bu [Production rights: Festival Committee, Ichiba ward] 制作・著作、市場区祭礼部. DVD.

Nagao-bu harumatsuri [Taketoyo]: hikikomi, hikidashi sōshūhen [The spring festival of Nagao district, Taketoyo: an omnibus edition of offering the festival float at the shrine] [武豊] 長尾部春祭り：曳き込み・曳き出し総集編 2015. Seisaku, Nagao-bu jimukyoku [Produced by Bureau of the Nagao district] 制作：長尾部事務局. DVD.

Ōno Jūō: matsuribayashi [Festival music of Jūō ward in Ōno town, Tokoname city] 大野十王：祭りばやし [n.d.]. (Tokoname City Library collection 常滑市立図書館蔵). Cassette tape. *S, H.*

Otaga kōin ni yoru ohayashi [Festival music played by Taketoyo Taga shrine parishoners] お多賀講員によるお囃子 [武豊多賀神社] 2006. Fukugen, seisaku: Restored and produced from the 1965 recording by Saitō Kiyotaka 昭和 40 年収録テープの復元・制作：齋藤清隆. CD.

Sakai no matsuri Matsuo jinja hōnō (*dashibayashi, kagurabayashi*) [Sakai's float-festival: Matsuo shrine offering (festival-float music and Shintō music)] 坂井の祭・松尾神社奉納：山車ばやし 1973. Sakai Saiten Gyōji Hozonkai en [Played by: Sakai Festival Events Preservation Society] 坂井祭典行事保存会演. Kaisetsu [Commented by: Takemoto Genji] 解説 竹本源次. Tokoname 常滑. Cassette tape.

Serakusha: Matsuribayashi [Serakusha Festival Music, Tokoname-city, Segi ward] 世楽車：祭囃子 [常滑市瀬木区] 2002. CD [with booklet]. S, H.

Shinmeisha Kitajō matsuribayashi [The festival music of the float Shinmeisha of the neighbourhood Kitajō, Tokoname] 神明車北条祭り囃子 1991. I–II. Tokoname-shi Shitei Mukei Minzoku Bunkazai [a Tokoname City-designated Intangible folk cultural property] 常滑市指定無形民俗文化財. Kitajō Hayashi Hozonkai [Kitajō Festival Music Preservation Society] 北条囃子保存会. Tokoname 常滑. 2 CDs [with booklet]. S, H.

Tagajinja taisai uchiage [Taketoyo Taga shrine's Grand festival, wrap-up party]: Shōwa 41-nen 3-gatsu [March in 1966] 多賀神社大祭うちあげ：昭和 41 年3 月 2006. Fukugen, seisaku [Restored and produced by:] Saitō Kiyotaka 復元・制作：齋藤清隆. [Aichi, Taketoyo 愛知、武豊]. CD.

Tagakō kagura [Kagura of the Taga shrine parish] 多賀講神楽. No. 1. [Recorded 1965 in Tamanuki, Taketoyo. Transferred to CD from an open-reel tape by Saitō Kiyotaka, n.d.] [オープンリール収録：1965 、武豊玉貫、CD 版コピー：齋藤清隆、制作年不明]. CD. S.

Tamanuki no matsuribayashi: keigo [Festival music of Tamanuki ward: *keigo* music] 玉貫の祭囃子：敬語 1998. Ensōsha Hayashikata ichidō [Players: all the members of the festival music ensemble] 演奏者：囃子方一同. Heisei 10-nen, 6-gatsu kichijitsu [Recorded on an auspicious day of June, Heisei 10] 平成 10 年 6 月吉日収録. CD. S.

Tamanuki no matsuribayashi [Festival music of Tamanuki ward] 玉貫の祭囃子 2018. Heisei 30, 11-gatsu shūroku [recorded Heisei 30, November] 2018（平成 30），11 月収録. CD [with a sheet of music titles 曲名シート]. S.

Tokoname dashi matsuri: Tokoname shisei 60-shūnen kyōsan jigyō [Tokoname float-festival: a cooperative project for the 60th anniversary of municipal organization] とこなめ山車まつり：常滑市 60 周年協賛事業.

Warau kado niwa fuku kitaru [Fortune comes in by a merry gate: welcome to Itayama *manzai*] 笑う門には福来る 2008. Vol. 1. Handa Itayama Manzai Hozonkai [Handa Itayama Manzai Preservation Society] 半田板山万歳保存会. DVD.

Index of Japanese festivals

Numbers in italics refer to pages with illustrations.
n = footnote, t = table
* = historical, no longer active festival
Festival names are mainly taken from *Aichi dashimatsuri zukan*, published in 2020.

Index of tunes

General index

festival law 209, 214
festival music
  borrowing of tunes 210–211
  demography and 207
  ensembles 219–221
  functions of 217–218
  gender and 207, 227
  recruitment to 203, *204*, 205
  research on 231–232
  sanctity of 222–225
  styles of 219–221
  see also dashibayashi music
festivalization 197, 228–231
Fiesta de Cruz (Puerto Rico) 228
fireworks 48, *49*
Fitzgerald, Timothy 7n14
float festival, definition of 7
flute *see fue*
folia do Divino (Brazil) 221
folk performing arts 24
fue 59
  chūkan 59
  hosobue 59
  koshagiri 59
  kagurabue 59
  kusabue 59, 110n9
  nōbue 167
  nōkan 59
  roppō 59
  shagiribue 59
  shinobue 59
  utaibue 59
  yokobue 59
Fujie, Linda 7n13, 10–11, 73,
  179n48, 197, 209n50,
  211n57, 221n23
Fujita, Rokurobyōe 184, 188n39
Fujita, Seibē Shigemasa 184–185
Fujita, Takanori 131n19
Fujitaryū 184–185
Fukaya, Yoshihiro 84n4, 188n39,
  207n42
Fukumoto, Takahisa 134n30,
  136n34, 159n18
Fukutake, Tadashi 187n28

furedaiko 46–47, *61*, 226
furyū 24, 223
futsū kagura 68, 189 *see also*
  kagura

gagaku 126, 153, 182
gaku 60 *see also hiradaiko*
gakudaiko 101 *see also hiradaiko*
gakuko 60 *see also hiradaiko*
gakunin 181
Garfias, Robert 182n7
Gerow, Aaron 212n59
Getz, Donald 229
geza ongaku 63, 64n2, 128, 234
Gion Shōja 20
Gionbayashi 178
gohei 36
gong 63, 79, 83, 87, 89, 95, 102,
  105, 113, *114*, 179, 218, 231
  see also kane
goningumi 19–20
Gozu Tennō 20, 30n1
glocalization 216
Groemer, Gerald 79n1, 224n37
Gunji, Masakatsu 126n8

Hachimangū (shrine, Hirai,
  Toyota) 110
Hachimansha (shrine)
  Fuki 49, 50, 51
  Miyoshi 238
  Nagao 186
  Wakamiya, Nagoya 93n1, 183
Halperin, Ehud 10n31, 216n3,
  222n24–26
handozuna 27
hangiri see hiradaiko
happi 36, 97, 171, 204, 207
Hardacre, Helen 7n14, 27n27,
  67n11, 198, 200n20, 206,
  208n44, 208n46, 214, 216n7
Harich-Schneider, Eta 181n2,
  181n4
Harnish, David 10n35, 218, 223,
  232n65

EU authorised representative for GPSR:
Easy Access System Europe, Mustamäe tee 50,
10621 Tallinn, Estonia
gpsr.requests@easproject.com